Honor's Disguise

KRISTEN HEITZMANN

◆◆◆◆◆◆◆◆◆◆◆◆◆◆◆◆◆◆◆◆◆◆◆◆

Honor's Disguise

BETHANY HOUSE PUBLISHERS
MINNEAPOLIS, MINNESOTA 55438

Hei

Honor's Disguise
Copyright © 1999
Kristen Heitzmann

Cover illustration by Joe Nordstrom
Cover design by Dan Thornberg

Unless otherwise identified, Scripture quotations are from the King James Version
of the Bible.

Scripture quotations identified NASB are taken from the NEW AMERICAN
STANDARD BIBLE®, Copyright © 1960, 1962, 1963, 1968, 1971, 1972, 1973,
1975, 1977, 1995 by the Lockman Foundation. Used by permission.

Published by Bethany House Publishers
A Ministry of Bethany Fellowship International
11400 Hampshire Avenue South
Minneapolis, Minnesota 55438
www.bethanyhouse.com

Printed in the United States of America by
Bethany Press International, Minneapolis, Minnesota 55438

Library of Congress Cataloging-in-Publication Data

Heitzmann, Kristen.
  Honor's disguise / by Kristen Heitzmann.
    p. cm. — (Rocky Mountain legacy ; 4)
    ISBN 0-7642-2203-1
I. Title. I. Series: Heitzmann, Kristen. Rocky Mountain legacy ; 4.
PS3558.E468   H65   1999
813'.54—dc21   99-6537
                                                                              CIP

To Jessica,
my daughter, my joy, my inspiration

She opens her mouth in wisdom,
And the teaching of kindness is on her tongue.

PROVERBS 31:26 NASB

Rocky Mountain Legacy

◆◆◆◆◆◆◆◆◆◆◆◆◆◆◆

Honor's Pledge

Honor's Price

Honor's Quest

Honor's Disguise

KRISTEN HEITZMANN was raised on five acres of ponderosa pine at the base of the Rocky Mountains in Colorado, where she still lives with her husband and four children. A music minister and artist, Kristen delights in sharing the traditions of our heritage, both through one-on-one interaction and now through her bestselling series, ROCKY MOUNTAIN LEGACY.

One

The slanting light of the bright November morning glinted off the polished silver fork in Cole Jasper's work-worn hand. With its flowered handle and tapered tines, it looked too fine and dainty for the job of taking food from the plate to his mouth. As out of place in his hand as he felt in the room.

Cole glanced around the long cherrywood table at Matt and Will and Curtis. They shoveled in the stringed beef and hot cakes as though they were eating Charlie's grub in the bunkhouse. Weren't they even aware of the fine china, the lace cloth . . . Abbie at the end of the table? It nearly took his appetite.

Abbie glanced up, her quick, eager eyes taking in his hesitation. Her thick brown curls were pulled back with combs, but they framed her face and slender neck and hung long down her back. Too clearly he recalled the feel of that hair, his fingers threaded through.

"Aren't you hungry, Cole?"

"Yeah, I'm hungry, a'right."

"Do you want something different?"

"Nope. This is fine." Too fine. He'd never get used to eating in here, in the fine dining room of the big house. He'd take a chaw of jerked beef on horseback over all this fancy—

"You wants eggs, Mistuh Jazzper?"

He picked up his fork again and eyed Pearl in all her

9

mahogany girth. "No, ma'am. This here's just fine."

Cole caught Abbie's smile before she masked it. So she was amused, was she? He took a bite of the stringed beef. It was fork-tender and seasoned just right. He dug in, careful to keep the gravy from his mustache. It wouldn't hurt for the others to learn some manners, too.

Now that he was running this ranch again, he'd slap them in line so fast. . . . Take Will's rubbing his mouth on his sleeve, and Matt eating a bite from his knife. No one might care when they ate around the fire, but there were young'uns at the table.

Cole glanced at four-year-old Elliot working his knife awkwardly through his hot cakes. The boy set down the knife, switched the fork to the other hand, and took his bite. There now. Even the little one knew how to do it right.

Beside Elliot, Jenny had hardly taken her dark eyes from him. Her little pointy face was too grave for her seven years, and he felt as though she were sucking him in. Why or how he didn't know, just that her clutch on his heart nearly staggered him. But he saw a wariness, too, as though she thought he might up and disappear any moment. Maybe now he'd have a chance to convince her otherwise.

Cole swigged his coffee. It was strong and black as he liked it, without being bitter. That was an accomplishment only female hands seemed to master. Good coffee or not, he might feel more at ease if Pearl and James joined them at the table. But having them hover about, filling his plate and cup and dern near wiping his mouth, was powerful uncomfortable.

He caught Abbie smiling again and realized he must be wearing a scowl the size of Texas. He tossed his napkin in his plate, stood, and eyed the men. "Y'all know your jobs for the day. Hit the range as soon as you're through." Which might be a week from Sunday the way they were slopping down. He started for the door.

"May I be excused?" Elliot chimed behind him, and Cole kicked himself.

"You may." There was a laugh in Abbie's voice that he did not appreciate.

"Mister Cole?"

Cole stopped at the doorway. "Just Cole."

"Have you made my animals yet, Cole?"

"Nope." He squatted down. "What animal would you like me to start with?"

"Can you make my pony?"

Cole rubbed his mustache. "I reckon I can." The boy's blue eyes fairly shone. Who'd have thought his little carvings would cause such a look?

"Can you make it today?"

"I'll see about that. I got a heap of work to do for your ma."

"She won't mind." He shook his head confidently.

Cole glanced back at Abbie's indulgent face. He reckoned Elliot was right at that. She'd no doubt grant the boy's every wish, within her means. He ruffled Elliot's small, dark head and went out.

The air was brisk and the breeze rattled the drying leaves. He stood on the porch beneath the soaring portico supported by tall white pillars. He breathed the air and felt the faint sunshine on his face. He looked south across the yard of the Lucky Star ranch to the buff-colored range and beyond to where the mountains wound around from the west in a hazy blue.

A man could get used to the sight. Especially if he'd spent years sweating and worrying over the place. No matter that the ranch was Abbie's, not his. He'd been branding the cattle, mending the fences, irrigating the land, and riding herd with its cowhands long enough to put down roots he never expected.

Even during the four years after Abbie ran him off, the Lucky Star was his first concern. With the promise he'd made to her late husband to look after her and the children, it couldn't have been any other way. And he'd done it in the only way he could, by secretly sending money to her headman.

How Abbie had bucked when she found out! Maybe it still stung her, but they'd reached a tentative peace. At least he hoped so. He heard her skirts swish as she joined him on the porch. Her blue eyes held more than a little mischief, and he knew she'd seen his discomfort.

He frowned. "That bad, eh?"

"You'll get used to it." Abbie smiled, showing even, white teeth between the soft lips he avoided thinking on.

"No, I won't. I nearly coldcocked Matt when he blew his nose in the napkin."

She laughed, and it sounded so good he grinned back. How long had it been since she'd laughed like that? Something about her seemed different this morning, as though ... a storm cloud had been lifted.

She almost looked like a girl again, as she had when he first saw her the day she came looking for Montgomery Farrel ... the man she loved and married. She wasn't a girl now but young yet, younger than her grieving made her seem. At twenty-six—even more than before—she made a man stand up and take notice. The hard part was keeping it to himself.

"You mind if I take an hour an' carve Elliot a critter or two?"

"I'd consider it a supreme favor. Those animals have been a point of contention between the children since Elliot was old enough to notice."

"That right?" Cole felt the need of a grin but fought it off.

Abbie put a hand on his arm, and he felt it clear through to his soul. "I appreciate your staying." Her lashes drooped over her eyes, and they seemed to deepen and draw him in till he felt like a mouse in the gaze of a bull snake. If she opened up he'd hop right in, death or no.

He cleared his throat. "That's a'right, Abbie. No thanks required."

Abbie looked up into Cole Jasper's sage green eyes, high cheekbones, and rugged jaw. His peaked brows drew down to the crease above the bridge of his nose as he tried to shrug off her gratitude. She couldn't express how thankful she was that he was there, not just to run the ranch, but . . . but what?

She wasn't ready to admit there might be more, wasn't willing to recall what she'd felt in his arms, feelings that went beyond comfort. She'd bared her grief, the desperate pain of losing Monte. She'd opened the pit of fear and sorrow that had kept her bound these last four years.

Cole had been shaken by her tears. She'd sensed his helpless distress. But he'd reacted as a man, and his lips had wakened emotions she thought never to feel again. More than that, her heart had reached out and met his waiting. He'd made her want and hope and need. He'd almost made her believe.

But since that kiss, he'd kept back, careful not to offend—so careful she wondered if that moment of passion had been as foreign to him as to her since losing her husband, her love. Yet here he was, solid and capable and willing to work for next to nothing. Was it only his promise to Monte that kept him?

Cole had loved her once; Abbie knew that. But out on the prairie when she'd shamelessly clung to him, he'd been the one to step back. She was thankful for that—and so many other things. More grateful than words could say. But she felt the need to try.

"I wonder if you know how much it—" She halted as a rider came up the drive at a gallop.

Cole looked up and frowned, then slipped Abbie's hand from his arm and walked down the stairs, stopping squarely in the yard. His slightly bowlegged stance was wary, but he made no other move.

Abbie looked from Cole to the rider, whose broad leather chaps flapped as he swung down from the horse. In two strides, he reached Cole and swung a fist to his face. Cole sprawled in the dirt. Abbie gasped, but she knew Cole could take him. She'd seen him fight two men his size and send them running. She waited for him to spring up and show the man what for.

Cole gained his knees before the man kicked his ribs and punched his jaw. Cole's head snapped back, but he didn't raise a hand. Why didn't he defend himself? The man kicked him again, hard in the ribs, pulled him up by the shirt and—

"Stop!" Abbie rushed down the stairs, ready to scream for help if needed, though the men had reached the range by now and only James would hear.

Cole staggered up. "Stay out of it, Abbie." He thrust her aside.

The stranger punched him squarely in the mouth.

She pressed in between them. "Who are you? What is this?"

The man shoved her away and hurled himself at Cole. Cole sprawled with the man on top and took a punch to the cheekbone.

Abbie tugged at the man's collar as he dragged Cole up, arm raised to strike again. She reached into her pocket, took out the pistol, and cocked it next to his head. "Don't think I won't use it."

The man froze, but she felt his rage still and hoped he wouldn't call her bluff. His breath came thickly as he knelt, undecided. Her own pulse throbbed in her ears while her finger hugged the trigger. Slowly he released Cole's shirtfront. Cole collapsed, rubbing the blood from his lip with the back of his hand.

The man kept his eyes on Cole, and she saw his large hands shaking with each labored breath. His voice came low and gravelly. "This ain't the end of it. You'll pay for Auralee if it's the last thing I do." He picked up his hat and lurched to his feet.

Abbie held her breath, half expecting him to charge again. But he mounted, then dug his spurs and galloped from the yard.

Abbie dropped to her knees beside Cole. She was shaking worse than he. "Come into the house and I'll take care of—"

"I'll take care of myself." He held his ribs as he stood and spat blood.

Her anger kindled. "Oh yes, I saw that. Why didn't you fight back? You could have taken him."

"It ain't your business." He picked up his hat from the dust and limped to the pump. It squealed as he filled his hands and doused his face. The icy water dripped from his sun-streaked hair and dark blond mustache. He turned away.

"Cole!"

He kept walking for the bunkhouse.

An ache started in Abbie's chest. Something was wrong. Very wrong. She followed him to the bunkhouse and watched as he rolled his belongings tightly into a blanket from the bunk.

Surely he wasn't leaving. He'd as much as promised to stay on. She could see the swelling beneath one eye and across his jaw. He winced and grunted when he bent, and his breath came in shallow gasps as he tied the roll.

"Cole, who was that man?"

He buckled his gun belt on his hip and checked the loads in the Colt .44 revolver. "My brother."

"Your . . ." Now Abbie realized the resemblance. The hair had been darker but the eyes just as green, the same rough-hewn features, the lean, lanky build. "What's going on? Why would your brother . . ."

Cole holstered the gun and reached for his sheepskin coat. She saw the pain in his eyes from the motion. "Where are you going? You can't ride like this."

He laid the coat beside the bedroll. "I gotta work this out with Sam."

"Not if you can't even—"

He caught her into his arms and kissed her hard enough to split open his lip.

Abbie's heart beat her ribs. She tasted his blood and clung to him. "Please, Cole . . ."

"Don't." His arms tightened, and he searched again for her mouth, softly, then desperately.

Abbie felt a matching need, but he pushed her back at the sound of horses in the yard. He limped to the door and pulled it open. Over his shoulder she saw two men with rifles. Cole stepped out as they dismounted, and Abbie tried to see past him through the narrow doorway.

The older of the two men took a paper from his vest. "Cole Jasper, you're wanted for the murder of Auralee Dubois."

Abbie's breath caught in her throat, but before she could move, the man swung his rifle butt into Cole's belly. The heavy-set one smacked the back of Cole's head with a length of iron pipe. She cried out as Cole crumpled.

The gray-haired man thrust up his hand to her with a look that froze her blood. "It says here dead'r alive. Dead's easier, but if you don't interfere, we might give 'im a chance."

Anger surged through Abbie. "Who are you? You're not lawmen."

"No, ma'am."

"Bounty hunters?" She watched as the second man roughly bound Cole's wrists.

Cole groaned. Abbie's heart wrenched. She was shaking all over as they pulled off his boots to find a knife, then unbuckled his gun belt and hauled him to his feet. He staggered, and the second man crammed his hat onto his head.

"You're making a mistake. Cole's been here with me. He can't possibly be involved. . . ."

They hoisted him to the back of a third horse they had in tow and tied his wrists to the pommel. "How long's he been with you?"

"The last two months, straight through."

"It's taken us near four to track 'im down. He's wanted down in El Paso for the murder of a harlot."

Abbie's breath left her chest. "That's not possible." Her voice came thin and pale.

"That's fer the law to decide. We're haulin' him back to Texas to stand trial . . . if he makes it there." The man swung astride his piebald mare.

She tried to catch Cole's eye, but he was dazed. He winced when the horse jolted to a trot, pulled by the reins in the other man's hand. They headed south, but not toward town. She stared after them. *Dear God . . .* She looked down at Cole's black leather boots lying in the dirt. She picked them up and held them to her chest. *Oh, dear God . . .*

Two

Grant. The thought came to Abbie with sudden clarity. Her brother would know the law. He would help her, help Cole. Her chest squeezed as she ran to the stable, still clutching Cole's boots.

The men were out on the range and hadn't heard a thing. What if they had? What if they'd come running? Would the bounty men have shot Cole then and there? Abbie shuddered. She could get Will and Matt now, but she hesitated to do so. She had to think this through.

She saddled Zephyr, every step taking longer for the shaking of her hands. *Why now, Lord? Why must trouble come just as I started to trust, just as I started to hope?* But for once the trouble wasn't hers. It was Cole's.

Cole Jasper. Cowboy, trail boss, foreman. He'd been a friend to her and Monte both. He'd been a hard and loyal worker, and more than that, he'd been honest and outspoken enough to set her straight when she'd needed it most.

He'd been with Monte when he died, and though he hadn't been responsible for his death, she'd blamed Cole in her heart. She knew the truth of it now, and every accusation she'd flung at him stuck in her throat. He'd done his best to save her husband from the crazed bull that gored him, but that wasn't God's will. Abbie felt a cold shiver.

Though she believed in God's sovereignty, she still feared

19

His will. Sometimes it just hurt too much. But now was not the time to brood. Cole was in trouble, and his trouble was hers. Abbie mounted and rode for town.

Every mile seemed to take twice as long as usual. Her thoughts rushed and surged and circled back on themselves. *Grant will know. Grant will tell me what to do.* Her brother was not in his office, so Abbie rode to his yellow frame house and banged the door.

He pulled it open. "For heaven's sake, Abbie, Marcy's upstairs with a headache." He caught her as she staggered against him, and his brow furrowed. "What is it?"

"They've taken Cole."

"Who? What are you talking about?"

"Bounty hunters."

"What?" Grant took her by the shoulders and his brown eyes searched over her. "Come in here and sit down. You'd better start at the beginning."

She let him take her into the parlor. She hoped Marcy would stay where she was. It was bad enough with four-year-old Emily Elizabeth staring out from behind the curtains. Abbie sat down where he placed her.

"All right, tell me." His voice was gentle, but insistent.

She tried to gather her thoughts, but words came faster. "A man rode in this morning, Cole's brother, and they fought. No ... Cole didn't fight, he just let his brother beat him. Sam, that's Cole's brother, said something about making him pay for Auralee. I broke them up, and Sam rode off."

Abbie pushed the hair from her eyes. "Cole meant to go after him, to work it out, he said. But before he could leave, they came."

"The bounty hunters?"

She nodded. "They knocked him unconscious, and—" Her voice broke. "Can they just take him like that? Without proof, without..." She spread her hands and saw they trembled.

"They said he's wanted for murder in El Paso. They said dead or alive and dead's easier."

Grant's face was grave. "Did they have a warrant or . . ."

"A poster. I think it was a poster."

"Did you get a look at it?"

She shook her head. "Not clearly."

Grant sat back. His jet buttons glimmered on his vest, and his sleeves were linked crisply at his wrists. "I'm sorry, Abbie. Assuming the poster is valid for Cole's arrest, he's fair game."

"Arrest for what?" Marcy stood at the landing to the stairs, wrapped in a blue silk gown tied high on her bulging waist.

Abbie dropped her face into her hands. The last one she wanted in on this was Marcy. "Is there nothing we can do?"

Grant released a slow breath. "Technically, until he's in the hands of the law, anyone has rights to him."

Abbie shuddered.

"If these men have been sent by Texas authorities to track him down and bring him back, then their claim has weight. But if they're working off a poster, they may just be out for the reward money, in which case . . ."

"Is anyone going to tell me what's going on?" Marcy flounced into the room.

Abbie shook her head. "But you know as well as I do that Cole can't be guilty of murder."

"Murder!" Marcy sank to a chair.

Abbie was too distraught to heed her. "There's obviously some mistake, but those men were . . . brutal. I'm afraid for Cole. I don't trust them. Why didn't they turn him in to Sheriff Davis? Why haul him to Texas when they could collect the money here and be done with it?"

"There's some validity to your question, but . . ."

"It's because they'll get the money for him dead, even if he had nothing to do with this . . . Auralee."

Grant's frown deepened.

"What is it?" Abbie's voice was scarcely above a whisper.

"I don't think that's very likely—not if his brother also mentioned her name. Cole must be involved somehow."

Abbie closed her eyes.

Marcy huffed. "I always said . . ."

Abbie flew from her chair and stopped with a finger just short of Marcy's smug face. "Marcy, if you say one thing against Cole, I'll slap you silly."

Marcy shrank back, ashen, but two spots of color rose up on her cheeks. "Grant, are you going to let her speak to me like that?" Her whine set Abbie's teeth on edge.

Grant turned. "Perhaps it would be best if you went back to bed, dear. You don't want to tax yourself in your condition."

"*Well.*" Marcy pressed her hand to her belly. "It's clear where your loyalties lie." She tossed her blond curls and stalked upstairs.

"I'll pay for that one." Grant smiled grimly. "Now, then. Abbie, I'm afraid your hands are tied."

Abbie winced, remembering Cole's wrists roped to the saddle.

"Unless you think you can take him physically from the men who found him, he's their booty, so to speak. If Cole goes along peaceably and doesn't try to escape, he should make it safely enough to trial. Did he give you any indication that he was on the run?"

"Of course not. He was as stunned as I was. He knows nothing about this, you can be sure."

"Can I?"

"What do you mean?"

"First off, he gave no argument to his brother's accusations . . . or did I miss something?"

"No. He didn't."

"He let his brother beat him. That's the behavior of a guilty man. Second, Cole's first thought was to pack up and leave.

That sounds like a man on the run."

"But—"

"I'm only saying how it looks. Maybe when he learned his brother was on to him, he guessed others would follow. Cole may have suspected his brother would lead them to him."

A low wail started in Abbie's throat. *No. It isn't possible.* But she thought of the way he'd held her when she'd begged him to stay. There was desperation in his grasp. "I can't believe it."

"I'm not saying it's so."

She looked up at Grant with tears stinging her eyes. "I'm afraid for him."

Grant reached over and held her hand. "I know. But you're going to have to let the law handle it."

The law. But Cole wasn't in the hands of the law. He was in the grip of two merciless men driven by greed. Abbie stood. "Thank you, Grant. I'm sorry about Marcy."

"I'll make up to her. She always comes around." He smiled, then squeezed her arm. "Are you all right?"

Abbie nodded, but she wasn't all right. She owed Cole more than she wanted to think. It weighed on her like lead. Honor? Did she at last know how Monte felt, bowed down by a debt of honor? Cole had risked his life for her more than once. He had met her needs again and again. She could not abandon him now.

Abbie went outside and unfastened Zephyr's reins. But what could she possibly do? The helplessness overwhelmed her. She was one woman. Where could she turn? The sky was clouding over with cold, gray clouds and the air smelled of snow. Cole had no coat, no boots, and he was in no condition to ride.

She felt desolate. For the first time this morning she'd been able to breathe as though something hard around her heart had cracked open. Watching Cole's discomfort at the breakfast table had amused her, but she appreciated his concern even more. For all his rough edges, Cole cared about things. He wanted them right.

It was not possible that he was involved in some lurid murder of . . . Grant's arguments were powerful, but he didn't know Cole as she did. Did she? Did she know anything about him, really?

What had he done before he signed on with Monte? Where had he been for the last four years? Abbie thought when she had told him to leave he'd take a position with one of the nearby ranches, but he'd gone away. To Texas?

What had he said? *It was too hard keeping track of her from . . . El Paso.* Was he in El Paso four months ago? Abbie's heart pounded. Could he have taken the cattle drive to Kansas with her, knowing he was hunted? Was it just another way to keep moving, to hide himself?

She felt his arms around her as he'd held her on the plain. *We got to sort things out.* Did he know then he was in trouble? Zephyr stamped, and Abbie clutched the reins. What she really ached to know would not be stilled. Who was Auralee Dubois?

The emotion attached to that thought frightened her. She hadn't felt such . . . jealous anger since Monte married Sharlyn. What was wrong with her? What was it to her if Cole . . . Abbie dropped her forehead to Zephyr's neck. Even if he knew this . . . woman, Cole could not have hurt her. It wasn't in his nature. Abbie knew that to her core.

She swung astride and heeled the mare. Zephyr bolted away, and Abbie scarcely cared where she ran. Confusion swirled inside—anger that he was in this trouble along with a burning need to help him. Somehow she must help. Somehow. She passed through stands of scrub oak and headed up the rocky slopes. Yes, the mountains. She had always gone to the mountains to think, to pray, to find answers.

Oh, Lord, what can I do? Did you bring Cole back only for this? How can I leave him in the hands of men who think nothing of his life? She shuddered, hearing again the thud of the pipe on Cole's skull. *"Dead is easier."* She had no doubt the men would kill him if it suited them.

Zephyr lunged upward through the pines, and Abbie governed her thoughts. Where could she turn? Whom could she trust? Pa? He would agree with Grant, and Grant thought Cole was guilty.

Sheriff Davis? He would consider justice was already being served. Her men? Matt and Will could not be spared from the ranch again so soon after the last drive, and Curtis was too weak from the ravages of typhoid.

Oh, Lord, Cole showed me what a mockery I made of your grace. Help me now to follow where you lead. Show me what to do.

Zephyr had slowed to a walk, her breath expelled in white huffs. The craggy mountainside was steep and cold. They had left the sun behind, and fog swirled through the pines. Higher up there would be snow, but here in the foothills it was no more than gray breath that masked what lay ahead. Zephyr's ears perked and stood up. Abbie straightened in the saddle. What was it? What did the mist hold?

Suddenly Abbie sensed that she was not alone. She listened intently. No sound of movement, but a chill ran up her spine like so many spiders' icy feet. Then from the mist came a man. Buckskin pants and woolen coat, quiver and bow, black hair twined with feathers and fur. She breathed with deep expectancy.

He looked like he had the first time she'd seen him, only now there were fine strands of silver in the black of his hair. Then he'd ridden a paint mustang instead of leading the horse Monte had given him some years before. That was the day he'd been hunted for a crime he didn't commit, hunted as Cole was now. He had found her in his need, and now he came in hers.

Had God conjured him from the mist? Abbie waited until

he stopped beside Zephyr's head, then swung down and stood before him. "Gray Wolf."

"Wise One rides with fear."

Had God put an urging on Gray Wolf's heart to find her here? Was he connected in a way that God understood, but she could not? She felt a stillness inside and realized her fear and confusion had fled. Here was one who could help. Gray Wolf must certainly be God's answer to her plea.

"I must find a man who's been taken captive. Will you ride with me?" Until that moment Abbie hadn't considered actually going after Cole herself. Somehow it had been impressed on her heart, and she spoke it without knowing. But the stillness remained.

He looked at her steadily. His broad face, angular cheekbones, hawklike nose, and straight down-sloped mouth revealed nothing. Then he inclined his head slightly. "Gray Wolf will ride."

Her relief was immediate, followed closely by a stabbing ache at the thought of leaving the children again.

◆◆◆◆◆◆

Samuel Jasper held his hand in the icy flow of the mountain stream. Nowhere in Texas did water run so clear and cold. The edges were ice, but the center of the creek ran swiftly, and it was there he soaked his damaged hand. Cole had always possessed a hard head and bony jaw.

He grimaced as he clenched the hand and drew it from the water. He'd ridden a long way to give Cole that beating. He wasn't nearly satisfied when that woman pulled the gun and made her threats. Would she have shot him? Maybe. Cole seemed to have a mesmerizing way with the ladies these days. He certainly had with Auralee.

Sam's blood boiled. Dern him! He splashed the water angrily, then rubbed his wet hands over his face. He hadn't gotten the answers he'd come for. Did Cole do it? Was it possible his little brother was guilty of what they said? He groaned with dark memories, memories that had tainted him. How badly did they still burn Cole?

He stared at the rocky bottom of the creek. His breath formed a cloudy mist above the running water. He knew Cole could kill. Did he kill Auralee? Sam's heart withered inside him. *Oh, Auralee. Why? Why did you choose him to throw your heart away on?* He staggered back to the bank and sank to the dry, frozen earth.

Tears froze on his cheeks as he fought the grief and fury. "Why!" He gripped his head between his hands. His anger wasn't half spent. He wanted to bloody Cole until . . . Images filled his mind, visions of Cole's young back slashed with bleeding welts, his face and arms blue and swollen.

Sam groaned and looked at his hands. He'd taken after his pa in size. Cole hadn't grown so tall, holding up at six foot one, while he had the extra four inches his pa bragged on. Sam felt the throbbing in his hand.

He looked at the fingers, splayed, then fisted them. He'd raised his hand to Cole before, when it was due him, when he'd stepped too far over the line. He'd taken him down when Cole was strong enough to clean his whistle, though he never had.

But Sam had never before taken after him with such murderous rage—one he wasn't sure he could stop. He sagged against the pine trunk, its sappy roughness supporting his limp weight. He closed his eyes and felt the furrow deepen between his brows.

Cole would come to him. He knew it. Whatever that woman might try to say or do, Cole would come to settle it. They had blood between them.

Three

Cole's head swam, and he realized he was cold. Where in the blazes was his blanket, and what was he doing on the ground? He raised his head and pain shot through like fire. He stifled a groan. Why couldn't he think? His head felt like tar, thick and heavy.

He tried to raise a hand to feel the lump at the base of his skull, only to realize his arms were tied at the wrist. Memories rushed in, and with them every ache and bruise in his body. He was so cold his joints were stiff, and he noticed the ground was covered with a thick white hoarfrost that stood up like needles before his face.

Cole looked up without moving his head. Every blade of grass, every branch of sage and juniper was outlined in white. The sun was pale through the milky sky, but well up. He risked raising his head and saw the men lying near the embers of their fire. He was near enough the fire himself that it kept him alive, but little more.

He must be lying where they had dumped him from the horse. Cole had a vague recollection of the pain that had shot through his ribs when he hit the ground. He tried to move his legs, but they were tied at the ankles, his heavy stockings crusted with frost. He dropped his head back to the ground. At least the cussed wags could have given him a blanket.

Cole looked up at the sky again, tried to get his bearings.

His eyes went in and out of focus. His head throbbed. He was in no condition to think, much less move. He closed his eyes. If the bounty hunters meant to waste good daylight, he'd take advantage of their sloth.

A kick in the ribs brought him around, and he clenched his teeth against the pain. Rough hands yanked him up to sit. With his frozen fingers, he could hardly hold the tin cup shoved his way, but the coffee thawed his innards. His lips were cracked and bruised and it hurt to breathe, but he wasn't dead yet. Not that he held much hope of that continuing for long.

He needed a smoke. He felt his pocket for papers and tobacco. They were there, but with his hands tied and stiff with cold, he'd never get it rolled. He looked across the fire at the two men. Something stirred in the back of his mind, but it was like a blue-tailed fly flitting in and out of his muddled thoughts.

One man squatted beside the fire. His duster was more black than tan, but his boots were snakeskin. Where would a man like that get snakeskin boots? He pulled out a thin cigar, and Cole watched him smoke it. He reckoned the fella knew he wanted a smoke, but no offer was made. Cole felt every draw somewhere deep in his chest, but he kept the need from his face.

"You thinkin' on that night?" The man's voice was thin and grating, too small for his bulk.

"What night?"

"Ninth of August. The night you killed Auralee Dubois."

The man put the emphasis on *Du*. Where had he heard that before? *August ninth.* Cole's head swam. Why couldn't he think? He turned and examined the other man.

He was older, maybe sixty. Again that fleeting unease of something trying to get through. The man opened a can of peaches and held it out. Cole had to stick his hands nearly into the fire to get it. If he held them there long enough he could burn off the rope. Only by then his hands would be crisped like Mr. Farrel's.

The thought brought Cole up short, and he realized he'd been trying real hard not to think of the Farrels, one in particular. Sheez, what must Abbie think? And what on earth happened to Auralee? He couldn't drag up a memory of her in trouble, leastwise none beyond her own making.

He brought the can up and poured the peaches into his mouth the best he could. He needed to remember, but his mind was confused. There was something about Sam. Did he dream Samuel came after him? The bruises on his face and body told him that was real enough.

Paying him back for Auralee. Well, he'd expected as much. The rift had been spreading between them long enough. Only . . . Cole squinched his eyes and tried to force the memory. He'd thought his leaving town would put an end to it.

Cole winced when the younger, dark-haired man sliced the rope that held his legs and yanked him to his feet with a cheap six-shooter to his head. "Git on your horse."

"You suppose I might take care of nature first?"

The man gave a curt nod. "Right there in clear sight."

When he was done, Cole gripped the pommel and pulled himself painfully up. "Don't suppose you gentlemen have a blanket I could make use of."

The older man untied the woolen blanket from behind Cole's saddle and threw it over his shoulders. By maneuvering his legs, Cole tucked it around to cover his feet and stuck them in the stirrups. There. At least he might go to the noose with all his toes.

The horse's hooves crunched on the frost until the sun broke out and turned it soft. Everything was so dazzling white it made his eyes water. The frost dropped with soft plops from the twisted branches of the piñon pines and the yuccas stood like upended icicles. Abbie would like this scenery. He frowned.

With all the long miles ahead in the saddle, the last thing he wanted was to start thinking on her, the look of her eyes with them lashes, the feel of her hand on his arm. . . . Funny how clear that was, when so much else was like mud. He could have sworn she'd taken down her wall. If Sam hadn't come when he did . . .

Samuel Jasper. Where in tarnation was his older brother? Did he lead these fellas onto him like Judas to the Lord? Though he hadn't thought on it for years, he pictured that scene his ma had described to him. It had both terrified and fascinated him to think a trusted friend could turn on a good man like that. But it was no kiss that marked Sam's betrayal.

Cole moved his jaw side to side. He was lucky to have his teeth. A couple felt loose in the sockets, but he figured he'd keep them. For all his lanky arms, Sam's wallop wasn't so bad. Still, this wasn't the first time his brother had thrashed him, nor the first time he'd deserved it.

What happened to Auralee? He'd thought Sam's fury was jealous rage. He understood that. By the time he had realized what she meant to Sam, she'd sunk her hooks, and no amount of wiggling could shake her free. But that didn't account for this other business. Not murder. Not by a long shot.

He tried to unravel his thoughts. He could conjure up a clear enough picture of the vixen. She was alive and fuming when he'd seen her last . . . wasn't she? The dull ache at the bottom of his skull spread upward, and he stopped trying to remember. It would come in its own time. Meanwhile he had only to stay alive.

♦♦♦♦♦♦♦

Abbie ducked her face to the cold, biting wind. The morning's frost lingered, the sun swallowed by sullen clouds that hung heavy through the fourth day of riding. Gray Wolf was like a shadow ahead in the dimming light.

Beside her, Will led the two packhorses and Whitesock. Abbie felt a surge of comfort that Will had insisted on coming. Matt and Curtis could handle the ranch, but he'd go after Cole.

Will's claim was as good as her own. Cole had looked after him better than she suspected, and Will was adamant. He wasn't wild about a Comanche guide, but he kept his head and bolstered her. He was the one who thought to bring a spare horse for Cole if they found him—when they found him.

Abbie insisted it be Whitesock, as Cole had developed a fondness for the gelding after losing Scotch. The chestnut was fresh, its one white sock stepping out eagerly, Monte's Winchester .44 rifle resting easily in its scabbard against the horse's side.

She stared at the empty saddle and tried to imagine Cole filling it. *He will*, she told herself again and again. They would get to him in time, and somehow they would get him away.

Gray Wolf kept to himself. Sometimes he galloped out of sight. The first time he did, she feared that he'd left them. But he appeared again without a word, and they angled to the east. At times she could pick up the tracks he followed, though on the frozen stubble it was harder than any tracking she'd done. The horses' hooves chipped the dirt like marble, leaving only the slightest mark to be seen.

They had come across rope discarded at a campsite. The fire was cold, but she had lifted the rope and held it to her chest. It had likely bound Cole, and that meant he lived still. If he were dead, the men might have him tied, but they would have no need to cut the restraints.

Abbie watched Gray Wolf riding straight-backed on the roan gelding Monte had parted with. The horse was lean, she noted, but not ill treated, though Gray Wolf had slit its ears in the Comanche manner. He bent and studied the ground, then leaped forward on the horse and rode in a wide loop to the right.

When he came back, they went on as before, as they'd been for days. She looked up at the first swirling pellets of corn snow. The wind was cruel and her spirits sank. She had hoped to overtake them before now, but they must be pushing hard, as well. Her urgency was now shot with dread. Would they be too late?

Will rode in close. "Thought for a minute he'd lost the trail. I can't see for the life of me what he's finding to follow."

She nodded. "We can't do better than an Indian guide. Gray Wolf knows what he's about."

"Let's hope we don't find he's led us off to some Comanche war chief."

Abbie smiled. "Is that why you came? To protect me from Comanche war chiefs?"

Will flushed. "Partly. Mostly cuz Cole needs help."

"Well, Gray Wolf rides alone. Too many of his people have been killed or taken off to reservation lands assigned them by the government. He chooses his solitary path over either alternative."

"I still don't get how you found him and—"

"I didn't find him. He found me. It's always that way."

"I don't like the sound of that."

Abbie pushed the hair from her forehead. "Don't worry, Will. Gray Wolf is a godsend. How would we do this without him?"

Will shook his head. "I don't know. But I never thought I'd be trusting my way to a redskin."

Will's attitude didn't surprise her. Gray Wolf *was* something of an enigma. Comanches were not native to Colorado, though they hunted there at times—especially if fires or war sent them north. But in other areas, their reputation for brutality was well deserved.

She knew Gray Wolf could be as violent and bloodthirsty as any man. She'd seen him kill, seen him glory in it. With the outlaw Buck Hollister's scalp on his belt, he'd gloated and crowed, his face smeared with other men's blood.

But she'd accepted his hand fresh from the kill, and he'd brought her home to safety. What was it Cole had said? She must have some powerful medicine over the brave. Maybe, but she didn't know what.

She didn't fear him. That had earned her the title "Wise One." She recalled his first words to her, *"Wise One, not afraid."* And she'd been stunned that he spoke her tongue, though in a way, they'd communicated better without words.

They understood each other, shared a love for freedom and for the land. No, she didn't fear Gray Wolf, though she couldn't come close to understanding him, not in his complexity. Nor did she tell Will her belief that God had sent him. Not even Will's simple faith could be stretched that far.

Like many, Will likely doubted Indians had a soul. But how else to explain Gray Wolf's appearance, his answer to her need, just like the first time she'd prayed and Gray Wolf came to her rescue. He was open to the moving of God's spirit, and she firmly believed God used whomever He chose.

◆◆◆◆◆◆◆

Sam slouched in the threadbare chair in a room at the Rocky Bluffs Hotel, the plain hotel whose purpose was to room travelers, not the folks who meant to gamble and wench. He had no intention of either. As far as he was concerned, if he never saw the inside of a bawdy house or gaming room again, that would suit him fine.

He ran his hand over his beard-roughened cheeks. The road to sin was paved with good intentions . . . and a whole hell full of heartache. Knowing Cole might agree didn't assuage the situation. Knowing he hadn't yet sought him out both irked and confused Sam. That woman must have a greater hold on Cole than he imagined.

He'd give him three more days, one solid week, and if he hadn't come by then, he'd drag Cole out from behind her skirts and thrash him before the woman's eyes. Then he'd get his answers. Then he'd know. His heart told him it couldn't be Cole. An eyewitness said it was. Cole would tell him which was true. Sam prayed he could let his brother live if Cole confessed.

Four

The warmth of the crackling fire sank into her back as Nora Flynn sat beside the hearth in the spacious kitchen of the adobe mission house. Across from her, Davy McConnel crouched on the three-legged stool, his hulking shoulders bent forward. He'd only just settled there but already looked uncomfortable enough to pick up his hat and take his leave.

"What is it on your mind, then?" Nora sounded more snappish than she meant, but she had a good idea what filled his mind, and the day was too cold and stormy to tussle inside where the warmth ought to bring laughter and merriment. At least that was how it used to be. "Spit it out, will ye?"

"I'm workin' up to it." His eyes were like two robin's eggs sunk into nests of lashes in his blunt, freckled face.

Nora liked his freckles. They matched her own in number, though hers were more tawny to match her copper hair. She liked him all right, though it irked her to think so. Hadn't she tried every way imaginable to shake him loose? Worse than the potato blight, the way he hung on.

"Well, work it up, then, for I haven't all day to sit waitin'."

"That's sort of what I mean to say, too." He drew a long breath. "Nora, it's like this. I've talked myself out, askin' you this way and that way to be my wife. I've come today with an ultimatum. Either you agree to a Christmas wedding, or I'll consider that your final no."

37

Nora suddenly felt as heavy as the iron kettle hanging over the fire. Here he was offering to leave her be, and she had no doubt he meant it. Four years was a long time to expect a man to keep calling, not that she'd expected it. Davy called by his own wanting, not by any needing of hers.

So why was her heart a lump of lead in her chest? She pressed her hands together, desperate for a fitting remark, one to let him know it was nothing to her if he finally took her at her word. Abbie would have one ready to her lips. Abbie would know what to say. Hadn't she turned down all of nine suitors in the last four years?

"Davy . . ." It stuck in her throat. Could it be that she didn't want to turn him down?

He kept his big hands on his knees, his blacksmith's hands. He wasn't a farmer as her Jaime had been. He hadn't the quick wit or fiery temper. He hadn't the fine dark Irish looks or the lilting Irish in his voice. Davy had his American ways, his frontier speech, his muleheaded, plodding stubbornness.

But she'd worn him out. She'd used up his patience, and now he waited for her answer. "Davy, I . . ." She stared down at his brogans. How many times had he muddied her floor with the heavy work shoes, coming through any weather to do a chore, bring a gift, or sit here at the fire?

How many backbreaking hours had he spent seeing to her needs, to all their needs: her sister Glenna and Glenna's husband, Alan; Mary and Nolan Donnelly; her smaller sister, Maggie, who lived with her and Father Padriac O'Brien. He'd helped them all, her brother Doyle and Kyle Donnelly included. They all liked and accepted him. Did she?

Like, yes, but *love*? How could she? How not? How many times had he teased and cajoled and asked her to consider him? But never had he worn the frank, serious face with which he now brought his ultimatum. This was the last he'd say on the matter, and it was up to her.

Nora brought her eyes to meet his. He waited with the same fortitude that had kept him courting her four years with little reward but a sharp tongue. She tried to respond and felt herself gasping. His eyes softened. She'd never told him about Jaime. But somehow she suspected he knew. Maybe one of the others . . .

She pictured Jaime burning with the fires of freedom, throwing his life energy into the fight, the cause, the land and country that gave so little in return. She saw him raise a stick to the red-coated soldier who gave the order for their cottage to be pulled down on the heads of her mother and grand-mother within. She saw his back stripped of flesh by the lash until no part remained. She saw the life leave his body, clutched in her arms though he never knew she held him.

Nora trembled. Her voice came thinly. "It's a fearsome thing to love again."

"Aye." He said it with the soft inflection of the Isle-born.

Her heart swelled inside. Tears stung her eyes, and she suddenly sat straight up. "What'll I tell Abbie?"

Davy's brows raised, and he spread his hands. "It's what you'll tell me, I'm waitin' for."

"Yes, you fool man, of course yes. I already said it."

He furrowed his brow, but she pushed his shoulder roughly. "I said I'd do it, now, didn't I? If it's a Christmas wedding you're wantin', then let's be about it."

His smile broke broadly across his face. "Are you sure?"

"No, let me think awhile yet."

Davy jumped up from his stool and caught her up with him. "Not a moment more, Nora, or you'll talk yourself out of it. I know you will."

"Then perhaps you'll be wantin' to kiss me."

He stood dumbfounded, and she felt a pang. Jaime had never been so reluctant or shy. But Davy took her in his arms and brought his mouth to hers warmly. "I love you, Nora."

"I know it."

"And maybe there's a bit of love in you for me, too."

"Aye, maybe."

"You won't be sorry."

"I'm sorry already the way you keep runnin' on." But she said it with a smile and planted a kiss square on his mouth. He pressed his hands into her back and returned it.

"And in me own kitchen, no less."

They both spun at Father Paddy's words. But he was wearing a grin nearly as broad as Davy's.

"I'm marrying the girl, Father."

"And that you will, laddie." Father Paddy laughed. "If it's my blessing you're after, you have it and more. The very saints are smilin' on you both."

Nora felt her cheeks burning. Was Jaime one of those saints? Now she clearly understood what Abbie had said, feeling her late husband so close sometimes that she gauged what she did by what he would think. Nora raised her eyes to the ceiling.

Will you forgive me, Jaime? It's a terrible lonesome life without home and family.

But what would Abbie say? They'd shared their lot and their hearts a long while, now. Would she feel betrayed? Nora looked back at Davy and sighed. It had to be. He'd given her an ultimatum, and she'd answered as she knew she would. Abbie would have to understand.

◆◆◆◆◆◆◆

Cole coughed, sending fire to his chest above and between the racking pain in his ribs. He shifted in the saddle and tried to control the shakes that seized him. The single blanket did little to cut the cold as he rode in the failing light. But he guessed some of this chill was his own.

They'd been riding six days as near as he could figure it, if his first waking had been the morning following his capture. He suspected so by their location now, high up Raton Pass. They were heading due south, and once they left the mountains behind, the cold of the upper altitudes would give way.

He coughed again. Even if he could roll his tobacco, the cough would keep him from smoking it. And the cravings were growing less frequent. Likely due to the burning in his chest. His tongue was thick with thirst, though the little food they fed him was more than he wanted.

A wave of heat rushed over Cole, but he kept the blanket in place. It would be chills again soon enough. If he could just clear his head, he might figure a way out of this. He studied the man riding ahead of him. That niggling familiarity would not go away.

And the one riding behind with the packhorses. Something in his voice and the tilt of his head . . .

The man caught up from behind. "Crete, you see that?"

Crete. Cole grasped the detail and tangled with it. Why did that name resonate . . .

"See what?"

"I seen somethin' in the rocks behind us."

Crete looked back over his shoulder, drew his gun from the holster, then swung around.

"You expectin' company, Jasper?"

Not likely in this life. Cole held his peace, though a cough was fighting its way up his throat.

"Maybe that brother o' yourn?"

He doubted Sam would raise a finger in his defense. Not anymore. Cole pressed his elbows to his ribs and coughed. It felt as though his lungs were tearing out. Maybe it was time to give up the tobacco for good.

"Whatcha think, Crete?"

Crete. It was there, but he couldn't dredge it out. What was it . . .

"A'right, Finn. You stick on Jasper like a burr. I'll have a look."

Crete Marlowe and Jackson Finn. Cole's breath made a slow escape from his lips. And here he was, weak as a cub.

Cole hung his head and fought the exhaustion. Whatever it was in the rocks gave him his first chance at them separately. Not that he'd call it a chance with his hands tied and the fever making him sick as a dog. But he'd worked the rope loose on the pommel, though it still bit his wrists. He just ... might ... work it ... off. ...

He stopped trying when Finn looked his way, then pulled again when the man looked back at Crete heading into the rocks and pines behind. Cole reckoned four or five minutes for Crete to reach the top and have a look at the back side. And if Finn called out, he'd tear back down like a hellcat or shoot from where he was. But Cole had to try.

He guarded his strength until he had the rope free of the pommel, then looked up beneath his lowered hat and gauged the distance between his horse and Finn's. He'd have one try at Finn in the saddle. If he made the leap and caught him clean with his fists at the temple ...

Crete was nearly up. Cole gathered himself, drew a breath, but the cough broke loose from his throat, burning, hacking. When Finn's eyes fixed on him, he slumped.

"Here." Finn unscrewed the cap of his canteen and brought his mount one step nearer.

Cole lunged, smashed his fists into Finn's face, and fell hard with him to the ground. Finn rolled and hollered, but Cole brought his fists up under Finn's jaw and heard the teeth smack together. He scrambled for the gun at Finn's hip, but Finn kicked with his knee, and Cole took it in the chin.

His head snapped back, but his fingers reached the pistol butt. Finn smashed his cheekbone with a fist, and Cole lost his hold of the gun. As he raised his hands to strike Finn's head, he heard the whiz of a bullet, felt it hit, then heard the report just as pain exploded in his left shoulder.

He staggered up, but Crete was on him, diving from the horse. Cole went down under his weight. A burst of light filled his head, and he spat blood, then lay gasping and wheezing. Crete held a gun to his chest. The way Cole felt at that moment, he'd welcome a bullet to end it.

Crete gripped the shirt at his throat and dragged his head up. "If I didn't want so bad to see you swing, I'd blast your heart an' leave you lie."

Cole drew a slow, wheezing breath. He didn't doubt it for a minute.

Abbie's heart pounded in her chest as the echo died away. Gray Wolf had ordered them not to move as he crept alone through the dusky light into the pile of boulders and piñon pines. But with the gunshot, her fear rose up like a living thing. *Please, God. Please.*

She wanted to bolt up into the rocks where the echo died, but she was held back by the force of Gray Wolf's command. Had they seen him? Had they shot at him? One shot only? They would have kept shooting at an Indian in the rocks.

Cole? She couldn't bear to think that Cole was shot. It could have been anything, a squirrel, a rabbit, a misfire. She stared up into the mounds of moss-covered rocks on the sharp incline, where the pass narrowed before dropping steeply down. She could see nothing of Gray Wolf, hear nothing of his movements.

Her heart beat painfully. God had sent Gray Wolf, and she must trust him. Abbie stared at the spot where he had disappeared into the rocks, knife in hand. She felt Will beside her, as tense as she. "Pray, Will."

He nodded.

She bit her lip. The silence seemed ominous, heavy. Where

was Gray Wolf? Why didn't he . . . She caught her breath when his head appeared over the boulder to the left of the cut. He crept back with more speed and stealth than she thought possible. She left her crouch and ran to him.

He held up a hand. "Your friend is shot."

Her chest lurched, and Will caught her arm as images flooded her mind, blood-crusted, gunshot bodies, cold, pale flesh. *Cole shot.* The gun's echo sounded again in her head. They were too late. Too late. *Why, God, why?*

Abbie forced her voice to come. "How badly is he shot? Did he move?" She steeled herself for the answer.

"He lives."

Her legs felt weak. "Tonight . . ." She cleared her throat. "We must take him tonight." This was the best country for it. The land before the pass had been too open and desolate. "Are they moving on now?"

Gray Wolf shook his head.

"I want to see."

He looked back at the towering rocks, then started walking. In the near darkness, she followed, crouching where he crouched, stepping where he stepped, making scarcely more noise than he. Below them, the camp lay in the open some small distance from the ridge. The men were not fools. They had a fire lit, and she could make out the silhouettes of one . . . two . . . Her heart leaped to her throat. Where was Cole?

One of the men leaned over the fire, and she caught the glint of a knife. He stepped back and kicked a bundle on the ground. It moved. *Dear God. Cole.* She felt a tremor inside at the sight of him helpless. Cole, who had always managed everything, who had faced down a stampeding herd, who had seemed strong and indestructible. She didn't want to think of him as vulnerable. It struck terror in her soul.

The shorter man blocked her view a moment, then hunched down and gripped Cole where he lay. She saw a flash from the knife in the other's hand, then Cole screamed. Her chest constricted as he bit off the scream and thrashed against the man's hold. They were digging out the bullet.

He hollered again, a string of words that raised the hair on her head, then fell silent, and she guessed he'd lost consciousness. She wet her lips, realizing her mouth had gone dry. How long they sat there in the darkness, she couldn't tell. Gray Wolf was silent.

They watched the men eat, heard snatches of voices but no words. One rolled out his blankets and lay down. The other sat huddled with a rifle across his knees. If Cole wakened at all, he made no move. Her heart sank.

She couldn't tell from what part of him they'd dug the bullet. They wouldn't have bothered if he was gutshot. But any gunshot wound, not to mention his other injuries, would take its toll. What if he were too weak to ride?

Oh, Lord, help me. This looks impossible, but I know all things are possible with you.

Gray Wolf motioned, and they crept back down as quietly as they'd gone up. Abbie answered Will's questioning look with a nod. "He's alive. They dug the bullet out." She kept her voice steady. "We have to get him away, but we can't kill the men. Whatever we do will be held over Cole."

She heard Will's shallow breath. He was afraid, but then, which of them wasn't? Except maybe Gray Wolf. Had she thought to this point? Yes, but had she considered the difficulty and danger of taking an injured prisoner from two armed bounty hunters?

She wouldn't let fear stop her. "We can do it. We have the will and the courage. All we need is a plan." *And a miracle.*

Five

Through his stupor, Cole heard the coyote howl. It struck him strange somehow, like he should know something he couldn't grasp. He wanted to slip back into the daze that covered the pain. But the sound kept niggling, and with a rush he knew. It was no coyote call, it was a Comanche, a sound he'd heard all too often and one that haunted his dreams.

Maybe he was dreaming now. Maybe he was slipping into a place where the mind wandered. He cracked his eyes only enough to see Finn sitting with the Henry rifle across his knees. Blood encrusted the place where his fists had connected with Finn's nose, and he looked sore and cross and ornery.

The horses stirred, and Finn looked up. He stared into the darkness, then stood and walked slowly toward the rope that tethered them, rifle poised in his hands. He must suspect coyotes were troubling the camp. He wouldn't know the difference. Cole saw the shadow move before Finn did. It looked like a Comanche crouched and leaping. . . .

Strange. Comanches kill silently, but he saw no glint of a knife. . . . He saw Finn crash down, heard the rifle shot and watched them roll. From where he slept, Crete scrambled up, then froze with the click of a gun hammer.

"Hold it right there."

He must be dreaming. It sounded like Will using a voice two times his size.

"All right, drop it."

Cole opened his eyes fully and rose to one elbow. The pain almost blacked him out, but not before he caught a solid side view of Will's young face. What on earth . . . He felt hands and shook his head clear. Abbie. Now he knew he was crazy as a loon. Well, if this were dying, it sure beat the living he'd done these last days.

Abbie tried to rouse Cole, but he seemed to slip back into a stupor. "Cole. Cole, wake up."

She heard Will order the man by the fire to drop his guns and kick them over. He stooped and stuffed both pistols into his belt. "Now strip. Down to your long johns and be quick. Toss me your boots."

The man's voice was gruff and snarling. "You'll regret this. You won't get away with it."

Will waved the gun, and the man obliged.

Abbie looked to where Gray Wolf was disarming the heavy-set one near the string of horses. She prayed Gray Wolf had understood and the limp man still breathed. She returned her attention to Will.

He stood firm, his anger giving him strength. "Kick the knife over." Without taking his eyes or his gun off the bounty hunter, Will tossed the knife into the dirt beside Abbie.

She took it and cut the ropes at Cole's wrists and ankles. He moaned when his arm fell free and reached for his shoulder. Blood soaked the dressing carelessly tied there.

"Cole." She shook him gently.

He opened his eyes.

"Can you walk?"

He appeared lucid. Clenching his teeth, he half rose, barked an ugly cough, then sank to his side. Sweat shone on his forehead in the flickering light. Cole was not a small man, standing at least six feet tall, lean but muscular, and Abbie fought her mounting alarm.

Gray Wolf came to her, and between them they got Cole to his feet. They half dragged him to the horses and shoved him astride the nearest. The men had kept the horses saddled and bridled, no doubt in case of trouble. That made her job easier.

Abbie kept an eye on the man by the fire, who now kneeled in his red flannel long johns on the frozen ground, hands behind his head, face ruddy with rage. He narrowed his eyes and glowered darkly, taking Will's measure but making no move. She suspected he was the sort to bully when the odds were in his favor, but had a streak of cowardice when the cards turned.

Gray Wolf had trussed the other man and removed his boots. The man was coming to, thank the Lord, but Gray Wolf stood inches from his head, knife in hand, should he make a move. Abbie swung onto the bay gelding beside Cole and gathered the reins of the bounty hunters' other two horses, one of them the piebald mare. Gray Wolf leaped astride the black.

Abbie pointed the rifle from the scabbard on her saddle squarely at the man on his knees. "All right, Will." She watched him back slowly toward them. She held the rifle on the gray-haired man who had smacked the rifle into Cole's belly.

Abbie held it steady while Will hung all the gun belts over his saddle and mounted, then she addressed the kneeling man. "You'll find your horses some miles north. Don't you set foot on my ranch again if you value your skin."

Will took the rifle back and waited until the others had started off with a rush, then he swung around and followed. Abbie heard the bounty hunter's hollered curse but kept riding hard and praying Cole would not fall from the horse's back. They would indeed leave the animals ten miles north, but she was uncertain what to do from there.

She slowed as they reached their own horses. She looked at Cole hunched over his horse's neck. He had kept himself astride by grit alone, but his shoulder was bleeding badly, and he seemed more than half dazed. *Give me wisdom, Lord. Gray Wolf calls me wise, but I feel lost.*

She swung down. With Will's help she got Cole onto Whitesock, whom she knew would carry him better than an unknown horse. He tried not to show the pain, but when Will clasped his hand, Abbie caught the look that passed between them. Gratitude and understanding.

Will spoke low in her ear. "We can't go back the way we've come." He glanced up at Cole. "He'll want to clear his name. I think we gotta head for El Paso."

She released a slow breath and nodded. *Thank you, Lord.* She nodded. "We'll circle round and go as far as he can stand tonight." She took Cole's coat and boots from the pack. As she eased the coat over his shoulders, he brushed her hand with his.

The soft touch nearly undid her, and she pulled away. She could not think of his pain or his gratitude or . . . any of the other emotions that rushed in with that one touch. She looked around. Where was Gray Wolf? There, in the night, circling, sniffing the air and listening.

Will helped pull on Cole's boots, and the difference was immediate. She hadn't realized how vulnerable he had looked without them. Now, even though he still hunched weakly, he looked like a man. Will strapped on Cole's gun, then Abbie took the horse's reins and handed them up to him.

One side of his mouth quivered with a smile. She knew what it felt like to be bound and led like an animal. Buck Hollister had shown her. She mounted Zephyr, and with Will leading the packhorses and Gray Wolf leading all of them, they started out into the night.

✦✦✦✦✦✦✦

Cole's coughing jarred Abbie. They had only settled in perhaps an hour before, having made better progress than she'd believed he could stand. But now huddled in the blankets on the bedroll, he breathed in wet, rattling breaths and coughed out the fever that had settled in his lungs. Her own breath suspended each time his caught before staggering into a cough.

They had dared a fire, agreeing to extinguish it at first light, but still Cole shivered uncontrollably. Abbie crawled out of her bedding and put more of the twisted cedar branches on the fire, then moved the water pot over the flames. Gray Wolf watched from where he sat wrapped in a blanket against the side of the hollow.

The water was still hot and boiled quickly. She dipped a cup and added Pearl's remedy for congested lungs to the boiling water. She was thankful Pearl had foisted on her the whole pack of "medicines and cures."

There was scarcely anything in the pack Cole didn't need. One for cuts and swelling, one for infection, another for fever, and this one for coughs. Coughs. It sounded as though his lungs would disengage with each bout.

She stirred the powder in the boiling water until it dissolved and cooled enough for Cole to drink, then dropped to her knees at his side. His eyes flew open. They held a tinge of yellow, but she couldn't tell if that was the fire's reflection or the fever burning there.

With an arm behind his head, she helped him rise up to drink. In the morning she'd doctor his other wounds, but his lungs wouldn't wait. When he'd finished drinking, she put her hand to his forehead and felt the heat emanating before her hand touched his skin.

He startled her when he reached up and took her hand from his head and pressed it to his chest. "I ain't dyin', Abbie. Git some rest."

Whether it was bravado or prophecy, she crawled back into her blankets. The last thing she saw was the glint of Gray

Wolf's eyes shining in the firelight.

◆◆◆◆◆◆◆

When Abbie woke, the sky was dim. The air was keen on her nose and cheeks, and she knew the fire was dead. Will snored softly, no doubt exhausted. But he had proved both formidable and cool-headed. She rolled over and sat up at the sight of Gray Wolf standing over Cole. Something in his stance chilled her as he rose to the balls of his feet, chanting low under his breath.

Her breath came sharply. *Cole?* He lay unmoving, but with irrational relief she heard his tortured breaths. She sat up. "Gray Wolf?"

He didn't turn but stopped chanting.

Abbie climbed out of her bedroll and reached for her coat, then walked to his side. She pulled the coat close in the fresh wind and glanced down at Cole. He slept soundly, a patina to his skin showing the breaking of fever. "What is it? What's wrong?"

"This man. He is Death Rider."

Death Rider? She stared at Gray Wolf, his face set and hard, something . . . savage in his eyes. *Does he mean Cole rides the edge of life and death?* She felt a prickling of fear. "I don't . . ."

"He has passed years, but Gray Wolf knows him."

This was crazy. How could Gray Wolf know Cole? He must be mistaken. Her mind reeled. She knew the Comanche lands were in Texas, and Cole had spent years there, but . . . Abbie recognized then the look on Gray Wolf's face—neither fear nor concern but pure hatred.

This was something she couldn't grasp, something ominous. *Death Rider.* The very sound of it made her quake. "Gray Wolf . . ."

"The Great Spirit demands his life."

Abbie's throat constricted. She stepped between the men,

acutely aware of Gray Wolf's physical power. Did he have a conscience to which she could appeal? She wouldn't believe otherwise. "The Great Spirit sent you to save his life. He made you strong last night and silent as the dark."

He gripped the hilt of his knife. "Death Rider will die."

She saw the tension in his face and neck, the bloodlust in his eyes. *Dear God, please help us. . . .*

Will stepped up behind Gray Wolf with the Winchester rifle balanced in his hands. His face was stern, absent of his boyish uncertainty. He would risk anything for Cole. But she would not risk Gray Wolf. They were bound together by an honor that transcended their races. She must make him understand.

Abbie drew herself up. "Gray Wolf, I know the wrongs done your people. But there were wrongs on both sides. If Cole fought against you, it was to protect his own."

"He is Death Rider."

"Not anymore."

Gray Wolf's eyes turned to flint. Abbie felt them cutting her with all the suffering of the Comanche tribe. But she was right. The Comanches were brutal themselves, shockingly cruel. If Cole had fought them, he was justified. *Please, God. Speak to Gray Wolf's heart, make him see.*

The muscles rippled in Gray Wolf's forearm. His knuckles whitened on the knife, and Abbie saw Will tense. If Cole woke . . . She reached up and opened the neck of her shirtwaist to reveal the string of claws that hung there, given to her by Gray Wolf when she had secreted him to safety.

It was the seal of their unspoken pact. She untied the leather thong and held it out to him, hoping to bargain for Cole's life. She would hold Gray Wolf to his debt and demand his honor.

Gray Wolf's jaw set rigidly; his eyes flamed. Suddenly he thrust his hands out, flat palmed, and knocked the claws to the dirt. "I ride no more with this man's shadow." He turned, strode past Will, and swung astride his horse.

Her heart ached as they shared one last glance, then he kicked his heels and galloped off. Cole jumped awake at the sound, reaching for the gun belted on his hip. The motion made him cough, and he doubled over in its violence. Abbie dropped to his side.

Will stepped close, legs spread and rifle ready, taking no chances with Gray Wolf. He eyed the retreating figure, then crouched beside her. "Now we'll watch our backs for both the bounty hunters and that Comanche."

"Comanche?" Cole wheezed.

Abbie supported his shoulders. "Gray Wolf carried you free last night."

"Thought I was dreamin'. Must be still." He sagged against her arm.

Looking at him, a crushing fear came on her. She didn't want to feel the wrenching compassion the sight of him conjured. The daylight showed everything she'd missed in the dark. His head was battered and cut, his shoulder bleeding, his wrists rope-burned. By the way he moved she suspected internal bruising, and she could only guess at what else.

Cole sat up and coughed again, a wretched, thick barking. Her own chest burned just listening. She kept her voice steady. "You're in no condition to travel, but we've no choice. I'll doctor you first, though." She walked to the fire. The iron pot of water was still warm beside the quenched flames. "Will, please see to the horses. We'll start as soon as I've finished."

She carried the pot to Cole's side, dipped a cloth, and pressed it to his cheekbone. He winced, and she felt an angry satisfaction. *If he had defended himself against Sam, against the bounty hunters . . . if he had not been involved with that . . . Auralee, he'd be safely at the ranch instead of coughing out his lungs on this death trail to Texas.*

He sat silently as Abbie washed the cuts and bruises. Every

few minutes he turned away to cough and held his ribs as he did. There was a dreadful lump at the base of his skull, and through his hair she saw the purple and yellow flesh. No wonder he was dazed. She wouldn't be surprised if there was a crack in the bone beneath.

The water ran red when she dropped in the cloth. Blood. Cole's blood. She unbuttoned his shirt and long johns and peeled them off his shoulder. She bit her lip, forcing herself to focus on the blackened, ugly gash where the bullet had entered and been cut from the flesh.

The ball must have lodged in the sinew and bone near the center of the joint, for they had dug deep. The skin around the wound was angry red and even hotter to the touch than the rest of him, though the fever indeed seemed to be subsiding.

Her fingers shook as she rubbed the wound clean and fresh blood flowed. "We've been here before. I'll need to sew it."

In spite of his efforts, Cole jerked and sucked in his breath as Abbie washed his wound with carbolic acid. It hurt like blazes, but he bit back the cry. The pain cleared his senses and helped to convince him she was real. He watched her take the needle from the box. Her fingers were nimble as she threaded and snipped.

"I don't expect this will hurt anything like what they did last night."

"Go ahead." Nothing could hurt worse than the agony that lodged somewhere near his solar plexus every time she touched him.

Abbie's face was set as she poked the needle through and tied off the stitch, then stabbed it through again and again. He kept the pain from his eyes and fought the cough clawing his throat. She packed the wound with alum and tied on a clean dressing.

He balked when she wrapped his arm tightly to his chest

to immobilize the shoulder, but the look she gave him silenced his argument. The minute she sat back, he let go the cough and fire filled his chest. Whatever she'd given him last night had helped, but obviously the cure was not set.

"I don't suppose you thought to ask for a coat or boots or a blanket."

He was surprised by the anger in her eyes. "Some o' the time I had a blanket."

She turned away. Her breath came sharply, and he saw she was fighting tears. He touched her hand, but she pulled away like he'd burned her. "I can't do this" came her whisper.

"Cain't do what?"

"Love you."

The pain spread from his solar plexus to his throat and put gravel in his voice. "I ain't askin' you to."

She looked at him, her eyes pools so deep a man would never touch bottom. "I don't want to care what happens to you. I don't want to live afraid that one day I'll see you in the back of a wagon. I . . . don't want to feel . . . anything for you." Her voice broke.

Cole's throat was so tight the air hardly passed through. "Fair enough." He pulled the shirt back over his shoulder and fumbled one-handed with the buttons.

She stood and walked away. He kept his eyes from following. If that was how she wanted it, that's how it would be. Wasn't like he hadn't been doing it for the last eight years of his life. He coughed again and pressed a hand to his chest. Then he gathered his strength and stood.

His legs were weak as a new calf's, but he reckoned if he stood a minute they'd come to speaking terms with his head. He checked the gun at his hip, broke it open to see the loads, then slid it home. From the looks of the countryside, they'd continued south last night. Quite a surprise, considering his escort. He'd have thought Abbie would try to take him home,

56

but then, he reckoned that was the last place she wanted him.

At any rate, it probably threw off Crete and Finn. They'd expect him to head any way but Texas. Yet that was exactly what he intended to do. He'd wanted to shake loose of them, but not because he wasn't going to El Paso. He just didn't trust them to get him there.

He took one feeble step. At this rate, he might not get himself there. But he meant to try. If his suspicions were right, if his reckoning wasn't awry, if Sam had ... could Sam have killed Auralee? It pained him to think it, but he knew only too well what a driven man could do. Even a man like Sam.

Cole shook his head. If he was right, he had no choice but to get to El Paso and stand trial for murder. In a way, he figured, he was as guilty as his brother. He glanced at Abbie packing up with Will. What was she doing coming after him with a boy and a Comanche brave? *Guess she feels beholden somehow.*

Well, he'd take care of that. Better to get quits of them now. He joined them resolutely. "I appreciate what you done, but I'll be goin' on myself. You git on home." *Dern.* He bent and coughed. It staggered him, but he steadied himself with the saddle horn and met Abbie's eyes. He would've sooner faced Crete's gun barrel.

"First of all, you won't make it one day by yourself. And second, don't you ever tell me to *git.*" She spun, stalked to Zephyr, and mounted.

He stood like stone until he saw Will's half smile. Why did he suppose the kid knew exactly how it was?

Will drew his horse up alongside. "How're you feelin', Cole?"

"At the moment, catawampously chawed up."

Six

Jenny wrapped her knees with her arms and pulled them to her chest. The valley between her bony knees made a resting place for her chin as she made herself as small and compact as she could. She didn't like the hollow feeling in her stomach. It didn't go away like a bellyache. It just got hollower and hollower.

Even when she woke herself up at night, it was there waiting to gobble her up from inside. She should have known better. She should have never liked Cole so much. Everyone she liked went away.

Jenny pinched her arms above the elbows where they held fast to her knees. *Say it, stupid. He hasn't gone away, he's . . .* But she couldn't say it. She wouldn't. Her folks were dead; there was no denying that. She wasn't sure she remembered her pa. Not much more than his waxy mustache and the smell of his hair pomade.

She remembered Mama. Jenny couldn't squeeze her like Aunt Abbie. Mama wrinkled. *That's silly. People don't wrinkle; their clothes do.* But somehow in her mind she couldn't separate Mama from her clothes. She remembered the feel of hoops and skirts, but had she ever felt her mama?

Stupid, stupid. Of course I did. I was just too little to remember. Jenny knew how Aunt Abbie felt, all warm and smelling of honeysuckle. Even when Elliot was in the secret place and Aunt

59

Abbie's belly was hard and round, she had pulled Jenny close and held her. Aunt Abbie's hugs made Jenny want to laugh and cry together, so she never let it last too long.

What if, just once, Aunt Abbie pushed away first and smoothed the wrinkles? No, better to be the one pushing away. Except for Cole. Jenny trembled. It was scary how much she wanted him to hold her, just like a daddy would. She thought she remembered it. She was almost sure she recalled his arms hard around her, and not just when he had her in the saddle.

She remembered the smell of his neck against her cheek, the roughness of his jaw. How else would she know that if he hadn't held her? Jenny was sure he had. Maybe when he gave her the carved wooden critters. She hadn't called them that for a long time. *Critter* was Cole's word.

The hollow grew harder.

She looked out from the lacework of gray scrub oak twigs to the side of the bunkhouse where the bad men had taken Cole. She hadn't seen them. She had heard Aunt Abbie telling the cowhands what had happened. If she had seen them . . .

A rustling in the crisp, frozen leaves brought her head up. She peered over her shoulder at Elliot crawling through to her. She frowned. He was allowed in her special place, but right now she wanted to be alone.

"What are you doing, Jenny?"

"I'm thinking."

He pressed himself between the trunks in the frozen ground until he was close against her. "Thinking what?"

"What I'd have done to the bad men who took Cole."

Elliot's eyes widened as she'd known they would. "What would you do?"

"I'd have snuck up behind, quiet as a rabbit in the snow, and I'd have lassoed them with the lariat, the way Cole showed me. Then I'd . . ." She hesitated at the sound of a wagon in the drive. "It's Nora."

Jenny released her knees and crept back through the tunnel of branches. She could hear Elliot behind but didn't wait for him. She gained her feet and ran for the yard. Nora had just secured the ox as she rounded the pink stone wall and walked staunchly forward.

"Afternoon, Jenny. Is your aunt about?"

Elliot skidded to a stop behind her, but Jenny didn't turn. "Aunt Abbie is on a dangerous mission."

"Is she, now?" Nora smiled.

Jenny drew herself up. "This is not a laughing matter. She's getting Cole from the bad men."

Nora sobered, but Jenny could tell it was the forced seriousness grown-ups used when they were trying not to laugh and thought they could fool her.

"Are you short of coal, then?"

"I'm speaking of Cole Jasper." Jenny took a step forward and considered her words. She took a tight breath. "My pa."

Nora's eyes widened more than Elliot's. He tugged her arm and stood on tiptoe to whisper noisily in her ear. "He's not your real pa."

Jenny shrugged Elliot off and kept her eyes on Nora.

"I'm afraid I don't understand you, Jenny."

"That's all right. When Aunt Abbie brings him back, you'll see."

Nora looked toward the house. "Maybe I'll just say hello to Pearl and Zena."

Jenny felt the hurt of being doubted. She tossed her head. "You can ask them. They'll tell you the same thing. Aunt Abbie isn't here." She gathered her woolen skirts and ran back around the house. Why did the tears burn now? She wouldn't let them come when anyone could see. She wouldn't.

Jenny heard Elliot's pumping feet on the ground behind like her own shadow. She turned fiercely. "Go away."

He stopped and stood with his look of pained obedience.

Jenny felt the power she had over him, and with it the pang of guilt. She didn't care. She couldn't think about his feelings when her own heart was near to splitting. He had a mama. She had no one to call her own—no one but the man who looked as lonely as she felt.

Her legs flew beneath her skirts, and this time she ran alone.

Nora climbed the steps between the massive pillars. Even after four years she still felt strange approaching Abbie's fine house with its towering portico. In Ireland, wealth like that meant English landlords or turncoat Irish deep in the pockets of the English. She would sooner have spit on the stairs than climbed them to find a friend.

But Abbie was that. They'd grown close as sisters these last years. Aye, she loved her as dearly. And she was grateful beyond expressing to know Abbie returned it. Nora looked up at the looming twin doors. Was Abbie within?

Jenny was such a queer one, people were never certain how to take her. Back home they'd have said the child was fey. Nora didn't believe that. Jenny hadn't the look of one with the second sight. She was normal enough in most ways, just had an overactive imagination and a precocious manner.

She applied the knocker, and James opened the door to her, his grizzled head and shoulders more stooped than ever. "Good afternoon to you, James. Is Mrs. Farrel in?"

"No'm. She gone after Mistuh Jazzper."

Nora stared. She couldn't help it. Hearing Jenny's own declaration from the lips of the old Negro . . . "But . . . who is Mr. Jasper?"

"You come on in now."

Nora followed him in. Here she'd come to brave her news to Abbie, and it was she getting the surprise. Who was this man

Abbie had gone after? Surely she'd not held out on a secret love . . .

She followed James into the parlor, and Zena turned from dusting the mantel. Nora must have looked dazed because Zena put down the duster and came to her. "Don' you worry none. Mizz Abbie, she gonna be fine."

Pearl arrived with tea, and Nora accepted the cup with relief. She sipped the steaming brew and calmed herself. "I feel as though I've stepped into a fairy circle, my head's that spinnin'. What's happened? Where's Abbie?"

The two Negro women exchanged a glance, then Pearl swung her head side to side as she spoke. "She gone after dem bounty hunters. Dey took Mistuh Jazzper off, and him hardly back with Mizz Abbie three days."

"But I don't understand. Who is this Mr. Jasper?"

Zena clenched her hands to her chest. "Mizz Abbie's sweetheart."

"Hush yo mouth." Pearl puffed her cheeks. "He Mizz Abbie's foreman. He come back to work for her."

Nora took another swallow of tea. Why hadn't Abbie told her? Or had she? She had mentioned the man who'd worked for Monte and helped her drive the cattle. But her sweetheart, was he? She tried to remember anything in Abbie's tone or expression that would have betrayed such feelings.

Pearl wiped her hands on her apron. "You set now."

"I'll just be finishing my cup."

Pearl nodded, then left the room with a final dark look toward Zena. The young woman picked up the duster and ran it lackadaisically over the china shepherdess on the mantel.

Nora seized the chance. "Is it true about this Mr. Jasper? Is that why Abbie turned away all the others? Was she waitin' for this'un?"

"I wouldn't know about that." Zena looked sheepishly over her shoulder. "I only know what I seen with my own eyes."

"What have ye seen, then?" Nora raised her brows and fought a smile. She wasn't the least surprised Abbie's help knew her secrets.

"Oh, Mizz Nora." Zena dropped the duster and swept across the room to drop beside her on the settee. "Mistuh Jazzper, he plain crazy 'bout Mizz Abbie. He been that way for years. When she run him off, it like to break his heart, the way she done blamed him for Mistuh Monte dyin' an' all."

"Blamed him . . ."

"It was Mistuh Jazzper brought poor Mistuh Monte's body back home. And him what made her fight back to life." Zena wrung her hands. "After the baby was born, Mizz Abbie fired him straight off. But he come back, an' I knows how he feels."

"But what about Abbie?"

"Well, I don' say for sure." Zena swung her head. "But she went after him her own self with Will an' the Indian."

"The Indian?" Nora was more certain each moment she was in the grip of the little people. She gulped the tea. It tasted real.

"Yessum. A real Comanche buck as a guide."

Nora sat back against the seat. Och, that was Abbie all right. She was always one to up and handle matters herself. But if she had fired the man and gone four years without mentioning him to her closest friend . . . Wasn't that even more a sign than the rest?

Nora's heart leaped. But then she shuddered. Bounty hunters. Comanche guides. What had this Cole Jasper done? Was Abbie's man a scrapper as Jaime had been? Did he burn with the fires of travail? Her chest seized. What would be the end of it this time?

◆◆◆◆◆◆◆

Abbie rode beside Will, each of them leading a packhorse. Cole rode ahead since he knew the way, but he still hadn't the strength to more than keep himself in the saddle. Abbie's fury kindled as she heard him cough, hunched over and weak, and fear for him gnawed at her. Fear tinged with anger.

Three days they'd traveled so, creeping along slowly and arduously, scarcely making eight to ten miles a day before he had to stop and sleep, all the while watching their backs. If the bounty hunters found their trail, they'd run them down with ease, but she guessed now her ploy had worked. The men didn't suspect they'd go on the same way.

Not that she felt particularly gratified for pulling it off. Though Cole had not once looked at her with hurt and condemnation, she knew he felt it. What more did he expect from her? How many loved ones had *he* put into the grave? How many times had *he* risked his heart to have it crushed and sacrificed on the altar of honor?

Honor. Why had that thought come to her? What did Cole know of honor? Was he not mixed up somehow in the murder of a . . . strumpet? Grant's words suddenly rang truer than she had thought. Had Cole spoken one word of explanation? Had he once said, "Abbie, I have no idea what this is all about"?

She studied him as he tried to keep straight in the saddle and bear the pain and chills and fever. *Death Rider.* How much more did she not know about Cole Jasper?

"I think he's better." Will sent her a furtive glance as though he read her angry thoughts.

"Better than what?"

"Than he was."

Abbie tightened her grip on the reins. "What makes you think that?"

"He's not swaying in the saddle so much."

Hallelujah. So her heart should leap for joy now that Cole Jasper was not swaying in the saddle so much. She frowned. The hard shell tightened around her heart. She was sore and weary and missed Elliot and Jenny almost more than she could bear. Why had she come on this . . . rash, harebrained ride?

To keep him alive. To get Cole away from those men who meant him harm. And she'd been right. He might not have made it to El Paso alive. Their digging the bullet out seemed the most they'd done for his injuries. If he was better now, it was due to her doctoring and Pearl's remedies.

She'd made him drink the powder when they stopped to rest the horses and eat cold rations, then watched him stalk from the camp and cough his lungs clear. She'd changed the dressing on his wound and felt the burning of his flesh. She'd watched him sleep fitfully, obviously in pain.

She glanced at him now. Cole did seem a little stronger. At least he wasn't shaking with chills. The air was warming as they left the high mountains behind, and the wind had calmed in the night.

Abbie sighed. He'd never admit it, but he needed her. He couldn't do this alone, and . . . she couldn't let him. Somehow, someway they were bound together until this was over. And then? She shook her head and looked away. There was no *then*, only today.

Seven

Cole coughed, but it didn't rack him as it had a couple days ago. Whatever Abbie put in those cups these past three days took the burn away, and he'd slept like a baby last night. He pressed his ribs. Better. He hardly felt the jolting of the horse.

The shoulder was the worst. It burned and ached and throbbed. He tried to keep it still and let the healing happen. The sling helped, but it was hard to be one-handed on horseback, especially over rough terrain. One thing was certain, his left arm would be no good in a fight for a long while.

His head was clearing, and it was time to decide what to do. Hands down, Abbie was the most determined woman he knew, and she'd set her teeth and dug her heels. But she was in danger as long as she traveled with him. And beyond that, he'd be derned if he'd take her down to El Paso to watch him hang.

The problem was, he couldn't turn back to get her home. Did he dare send her off with Will? What of Crete and Finn? Those two must be carrying a chip the size of Texas, getting bested by a lady like that. They'd be mad enough to whip their weight in wildcats.

And there was the Comanche. Abbie might think she knew this one, but Cole knew his kind better. If this Gray Wolf was half what he expected . . . Doggone it, why couldn't Abbie have stayed where she belonged?

He glanced over his shoulder, then up at the sky. She'd been yapping with Will all day, though she hadn't said a word to him. But it was coming on to night, and maybe she'd be reasonable once they had made camp. Cole turned in the saddle. "We'll stop the night at that stand of pines."

Will nodded. Abbie refused to look his way. Sure as shootin', when Abbie Farrel got something stuck in her craw, she sulked but good. He patted his shirt pocket, dug inside for his tobacco, then shoved it back in. He'd gotten this far without it, he'd gut it out. He coughed. The dern thing wouldn't let loose of him as it was.

Cole swung down from Whitesock's back, slid the bridle off with his good hand, and let him graze. Abbie and Will dismounted. Abbie took a tin plate from the packs and filled it with water from the canteen for the horses.

They'd crossed, then followed the Canadian River nearly two days, but now they were veering west toward Santa Fe, and they wouldn't hit the Pecos for another three or four days of steady riding. It wasn't desert yet, but water was chancy this time of year. Cole cleared his throat. "Go easy with that. We got a ways to go before we find more."

She nodded curtly. Acknowledgment but nothing more. Fine. It would make sending her home that much easier. Will gathered sticks for a fire, and Abbie took out the Dutch oven and the blue enamel coffeepot. Cole almost felt hungry tonight. Guess that was a good sign.

He looked back the way they'd come. The miles stretched long and hilly to the hazy mountain pass. There'd been no sign of Crete Marlowe, and that bothered him. He loosened the cinch of the saddle. Crete was not one to be defeated by losing his boots and walking for his horses.

He motioned to Will, and the boy came. "Tell me what happened the night y'all got me away. It's a mite fuzzy to me yet."

Will shook the hair from his eyes and shrugged. "Gray Wolf jumped the one on watch, and I took the other. Abbie got you roused, then she and the Comanche got you on a horse and we rode out."

Cole smiled sardonically. "That's about what I recall. Now gimme the rest. What was said?"

Will scrunched his brow and chewed his lip. "Well . . . I told the one to strip down, so I could look for weapons. That's how I found his boot knife, same as he found yours." He looked up. "Maybe it is yours. It's in the pack, there . . . an Arkansas toothpick if I ever saw one."

"Go on."

"I told him to toss over his guns and his boots, but mostly my revolver did the talking. I got him on his knees and held him there till the others had you ready."

"What else? Was anything more said?"

"He claimed we'd be sorry, but he was just spouting. Gray Wolf never so much as breathed heavy. Oh . . . Mrs. Farrel, she told them where to find the horses, and never to come on the ranch again."

Cole frowned. "Can you recall how she said it?"

Will kicked the dirt with his boot. "She talked real tough. She said, 'You'll find your horses some miles north.' Then she told 'em to never set foot on her ranch again if they valued their skin."

The sinking in his gut told him as much as anything. Abbie had put them off their trail all right. Not knowing her as he did, Crete and Finn would easily believe she was stupid and sentimental enough to take him back to the ranch, especially when she'd headed that way and left the horses before circling around in the dark. Cole narrowed his eyes out over the desolate land. He wished she'd sent them anywhere but there.

He rubbed a hand over his face. Well, there was no help for

it now. Crete Marlowe would likely add this vexation to the injuries he already carried. But then, Cole had injuries of his own. Memories of his ma flooded in, and the old anger settled at the base of his chest.

So Crete was now hunting bounty. It figured he'd stoop so low. Or was it just him they came after? He could well understand Crete taking a personal interest in seeing him hang. They had bad history between them. Bad history.

"A'right, git these saddles off. I want the horses well rested tonight." Cole patted Whitesock's flank, then joined Abbie at the fire, more sore and tired than he could remember being. He wasn't snapping back as quick as he'd like. Two more days, three maybe, before he'd feel quite himself again, discounting the shoulder.

He watched Abbie pour beans and tomatoes into the pot. Her hair was tied back with a strip of rope. Even trail worn and dirty she was beautiful. But it was no good thinking like that. He might drink in the looks of her so he wouldn't forget, but he couldn't let it get inside where it made him hurt.

Cole crossed the camp and stared out across the land. He smelled the air. It would get dryer still as they pressed south and west. He took out his tobacco and felt the pouch between his thumb and fingers. He breathed the aroma, then clamped his fingers around the pouch and dropped it back into his pocket. His lungs needed all the help they could get.

He felt Abbie at his side and turned. Holding that cup of medicine out to him, she looked like an angel. His heart jumped. *Dern sentimental fool.* He drank it down, handed back the cup, and expected her to leave, but she stood there, working herself up to talk to him. Shouldn't be so hard. "What?" he questioned.

She put up her chin. "I want to know what this is all about."

"Don't we all."

Her eyes flashed. "Don't try to put me off. You must know..."

Cole took her arm and turned her. "Ever seen the sun set over the New Mexico Territory?" He looked out as the bright edge of the winter sun crept away over the brown nubby hills. There was always something in that final moment that made him ponder. He watched the streaks fade from orange to yellow to gray. It created a sadness inside. Or maybe the sadness was there already and moments like this just reminded him of it.

"What are you going to do in El Paso?"

Her quiet query brought him back, but he couldn't think how to answer.

"Who was Auralee?"

He swallowed, but still the words clogged.

"Why do they think you killed her?"

Cole dropped his chin and hooked his thumbs into his jeans. "I don't know. She was alive when I left her." He felt her stiffen next to him. What did she think, that he'd lived thirty-six years without meeting another woman?

"The men who took you said she was a..."

"She was a saloon girl, Abbie."

She made no move, but it suddenly felt like she'd put miles between them. "Did you love her?"

He could answer that simply, but the narrowing of her eyes and the jut of her chin betrayed her double meaning. She'd already judged him, and heck if he'd try to change her mind. He turned and met her gaze squarely without reply.

Abbie looked away. "What was she like?"

"Purty. Red hair, green eyes. Had a spark to her ... it reminded me of you." For two short weeks he'd thought Auralee could make him forget. Two weeks was all it took to see he'd never forget. "But she had a bad streak, somethin' inside that made her mean. She'd take your heart an' twist it if you were fool enough to turn it over."

"Which you weren't, though you availed yourself of her charms."

He looked into the scrubby branches of the cedars. "I ain't the one that killed her."

"But you know who did."

He jolted. "What makes you say that?"

She eyed him with feminine insight.

"Sheez." Cole jammed his fingers through his hair. "If I knew that, would I be ridin' to a rope?"

Her lip trembled. "I don't know."

He took hold of her arm. "Abbie, I want you to go home. I don't know how this'll turn out. I gotta go on and do what I must. But if it comes to it, I don't want you out there when I swing."

He saw her breath come in short gasps.

"Go home to your young'uns."

Angry tears sparkled in her eyes. "Jenny is torn apart over losing you. Did you read her note?"

"What note?"

"I put it in your coat pocket."

Cole reached in and pulled out the paper. He frowned. "You know I cain't read."

She took the paper from his hand and unfolded it. " 'Dear Cole, Aunt Abbie says not to tell you, but I pretend you're my pa. Please come home.' "

The pain flared up in his heart. And he'd thought Abbie was the only one who could put it there. *I pretend you're my pa.* He couldn't meet Abbie's eyes. What had he done to make Jenny think a thing like that? No more than offer a kind word and understand her need.

Abbie's eyes were honed blades. "How do you think it'll be if I go home without you?"

The tightness in his throat kept him from speaking. He cleared it dryly. "I reckon it'll be hard on her. I never meant to . . ."

"You don't understand a single thing about love, do you? It's not something you make happen. It just does."

He understood more than she thought.

A flicker of hurt showed through her anger. "Jenny needs you. And here you are throwing your life away."

"I don't know what you—"

"Oh yes, you do."

He swallowed down the argument. There wasn't any use. "I thought you meant for me to go on down there."

"I do. But to defend yourself."

"What makes you think I ain't?"

"The way you're talking about a rope. The way you're muttering and gazing around like you might never see things again. The way you wouldn't fight Sam."

She was hitting too close. "So?"

"I know you, Cole. Is it Sam you're protecting?"

He kicked his boot in the dirt. "You're thinkin' crazy."

Her eyes glittered dangerously. "Am I?"

He nodded toward the fire. "Them beans are gonna burn."

Abbie's chest rose and fell. Her hands balled at her sides, and he thought for a moment she'd hit him. Then she turned and walked away.

Cole stared after her straight back. Was his mind a window to her? She'd voiced what he hardly dared to think. Was it Sam who killed Auralee? They looked enough alike that someone could mistake them, especially in the dark as it had been when he'd left her.

Had Sam known? Had he seen her carry on? Had she baited him, tormented him with it? Back at the Lucky Star there'd been a familiar look in Sam's eyes when he pounded Cole's face, a purely murderous look. One he'd seen in their pa's face.

If Auralee had pushed Sam over the edge . . .

Cole's throat went dry. Abbie was right. He'd do whatever it took for Sam. Cole jammed his hand into his pocket and felt Jenny's note. His groan made him cough. He looked up at the darkening sky. What in heaven's name was he supposed to do?

♦♦♦♦♦♦♦

Abbie wrestled with her bedroll, then drew its blanket around her. She knew that inside, too, she was sealing herself off. This journey was something she had to see through, but she would not let it cost her. She was beholden to Cole Jasper for all the times he'd helped her in need, but she would not risk her heart. This was duty. Monte would say honor. Either way, she owed a debt.

Hadn't he ridden down Templeton Gap to ransom his life for hers, expecting the rustler's bullet at any moment? She had known that day that he loved her, more so than when he asked for her hand in marriage two years before. The love in his face that day when he had taken the rope from her wrists had been raw, sacrificial love.

Abbie frowned. There was no indication that a trace of that remained. And she was thankful. When he'd kissed her on the plain it had been for his own pleasure. She knew that now. She'd seen him with the saloon girl, Lil Brandon, and could imagine him with Auralee Dubois. *All the time I'd thought he cared, he was . . .*

No, that wasn't fair. Hadn't she sent him away? Hadn't she despised him, hated him even? Didn't she still? Abbie looked at him sleeping by the fire. Cole Jasper was the only man she knew who could sleep the minute he lay down and wake faster than lightning.

She rolled over. But then, how many men had she seen sleep? *Monte.* She remembered his voice growing drowsy, and how she'd rest her head on his chest and he'd curl his arm around. She remembered the gentle rise and fall of his breath, the low drum of his heart. It seemed too far away and long ago. Now she just felt empty.

She watched Will toss about in his blankets. He reminded her of Elliot when he would pad into her room and climb between the covers, then wiggle and squirm until he had every possible part of him against her before he promptly fell asleep.

Oh, Elliot. Every day away was one she'd never have again. Her only baby growing week after week without her there ... Monte's son. The ache of separation was no longer debilitating—the panic and nightmares had only come once since she'd set out with Will—but she yearned for her little boy.

She missed the way he slipped his soft hand into hers, the sound of his laugh, the quirk of his eyebrow, so like Monte's ... Was it possible she had thought of Monte just now without the dreadful ache? Had healing begun? Maybe, just maybe, she would soon be at peace.

Cole coughed, and her heart wrenched. What was she thinking? She was lying out in the New Mexico Territory with bounty hunters searching for them, and only God knew what waited at the end of the trail. How was it in one breath, Cole could steal her chance at peace and replace it with such wretched ...

Abbie heard a low raspy rumbling, and in the same instant Cole's eyes opened. She saw him move under the blanket and knew his hand went to his gun, but he hadn't lifted his head. She felt her own pistol in the pocket against her thigh, but could they risk a gunshot? Anyone within miles would know their location. Will slept on soundly.

She caught Cole's glance and confirmed with her own that she had heard the sound, as well. Slowly he raised his head and folded the covers off, then sat up. She listened. Nothing except her breathing and Will's. She raised her head and saw movement beyond the clump of piñon pines.

Zephyr snorted, and the other horses stamped and tugged at their ropes as they whiffed too late the downwind scent. She caught the glow of eyes reflecting the firelight like flat fiery disks. Cole stood and took up a stout stick with his one good arm.

A flash of tawny hide confirmed her guess, and her heart rate quickened. The cat kept its distance. That it braved their camp at all amazed her, but the fire was no more than coals, and the animal's gaunt condition bespoke its hunger. It limped past the cluster of pine trunks. It was old and mangy, but that didn't make it any less dangerous.

What could Cole do against a mountain lion that size? He'd have to shoot. He couldn't ... Slowly Cole lowered his boot onto a twig and snapped it. The cat's head swung around. He raised the stick.

For a long moment they bound each other with their eyes. The cat's muzzle peeled back from its fangs. With ears flat against its head, the animal wore the scars of too many battles on its face. Abbie's fingers were on her gun, but she dared not move to bring it out of her pocket.

Cole stood, legs spread, slightly crouched and ready. If the lion jumped him he would have no chance, one-handed with a stick. But the cat was wary now, as though only realizing its predicament. A cornered animal was twice as fierce, and this one looked nearly starved. Would it be so brazen?

Abbie lay mesmerized as the two of them held their stance, neither backing down, neither showing fear. What was Cole thinking? What did he feel? He looked hard and ... deadly. Slowly, so slowly she hardly saw at first, he raised the stick and inclined his shoulders. She held her breath. He was challenging the animal.

The rumble in the lion's throat took on a raspy yowl as it took one pace back, then opened its mouth in a low hiss. The horses strained against their tethers, and Will stirred. In a flash the cat spun and bounded into the night. Cole stood unmoving, and Abbie felt frozen by the sheer force of his will.

A moment later Cole lowered the stick, and her breath returned. She sat up as he hunkered down beside the fire pit. He held a hand over the remainder of the coals, then gave the coffeepot a testing touch. Satisfied, he poured a cup of coffee and breathed the steam.

Trembling, she pulled on her coat and joined him. The rock she sat on was hard and cold through her skirts, but sleep was as far away as the dawn. She glanced at him curiously. "How did you hear that first sound in your sleep?"

"How did you?"

"I wasn't asleep."

He drew a slow sip. "How come?"

There he was, turning things back on her. Well, she could give a little to get a little. "I was thinking. Of Elliot."

He drank. "You must miss him somethin' fierce."

She nodded. "It's not as bad as last time. When we first started out on the cattle drive, I thought I'd never survive, it hurt so much."

"You didn't let on."

Abbie shrugged. "You just thought all my pain was from the horse."

His mouth quirked. "You ride a mite better now than you did three months ago."

Cole's teasing smile tugged her heart, but she clamped it down. She pulled a bur from her stocking. It clung to her finger, and she flicked it away, leaving a tiny prick of blood. She felt her throat work around the words that wanted to come. She drew a shaky breath. "Why do the Comanches call you Death Rider?"

Cole stared into his cup until she thought he wouldn't answer. Then he slowly raised his head. "Gray Wolf told you that?"

She nodded.

He looked out into the night. "I ain't proud o' some things. That's one of 'em."

She waited, and at last he spoke. "Livin' in Texas, you expected run-ins. Apaches, Comanches. Most times they settled fer stealin' food and livestock. If you stood your ground they tended not to bother you much, though some were wicked mean. Others seemed peaceable enough, but folks bein' what they are . . ." He swirled the coffee in his cup, then drained it and set the cup on a stone.

"Samuel and I had a healthy respect for our scalps, but we weren't afraid to do a bit of tradin' now an' then, mainly with the Comanches. Got to know some of the camps pretty well, got to understand their ways some, too. Beyond that, the Comanches left us mostly alone. Guess they figured we weren't much of a threat."

Cole rested his forearms on his knees. "We'd gone prob'ly a year without a single raid on our ranch. Samuel was twenty-one, and I'd just turned nineteen. Then a man by the name of Crete Marlowe sold a wagonload of whiskey to the Comanche camp. Samuel an' I were workin' at a neighboring spread when they come."

Abbie heard his voice thicken.

"They hung our ma from the tree by her arms an' set her dress afire." The muscles rippled on the side of his jaw. "While she burned, they shot her full of arrows and ran on to the next place and the next. Thirty-one dead, mostly women and children, tortured, raped, and disfigured. Babies with their heads crushed in."

Abbie felt the horror rise inside.

"When I saw her hangin' there, somethin' snapped. I wanted to kill."

"What did you do?" Her voice was scarcely a whisper.

His answer was low and cold. "I joined the rangers."

"You were a Texas Ranger?"

"One year. Went on a campaign of revenge, ridin' with others who'd seen the butchery. The Comanches come to know when I was ridin'." He bowed his head. "I didn't care how many I killed. I kept seein' my ma hangin' there ... prayin', Abbie, that they'd burned her before they'd done worse."

She felt his pain like a knife to her heart. What had she said out on the plains of Kansas? That he'd never suffered anything to compare to her loss? She felt paralyzed. She wanted to drop to her knees beside him, take his hands in hers, and cry. But she couldn't move.

"I burned Crete Marlowe's cabin to the ground. There was enough liquor in there to shoot the blaze halfway to the stars. Then I beat him a hair's breadth short of hell and hoped he'd die when I left."

She hated what she saw in his face. This was a Cole Jasper she had never guessed existed. This was Death Rider, and his bared anguish awakened her own. Too much death, too much pain. She couldn't bear it. She turned away.

He stood up from his crouch. "Better get some sleep."

She heard his steps on the frozen ground, heard him pull his blanket aside and lie down. She crept to her bedroll and curled up with a dry, hollow ache inside.

Cole could be brash and insolent, cross and infuriating. But underneath he was loyal and kind and steadfast. Was he also capable of a rage that spurred him to such destruction? *Vengeance is mine, saith the Lord.*

Abbie closed her eyes, remembering the horror she'd felt when she killed the young rustler. She recalled Cole's penetrating gaze that horrible night, his words, *"You done what you had to."* He had understood only too well what she felt. Though he tried to hide it, there was agony behind his telling tonight. He was indeed not proud of his name, Death Rider.

Eight

"Aunt Pearl! They's two men in the yard a hollerin' for Mistuh Jazzper. They knocked Mistuh Matt senseless, and they's comin' for the house."

Pearl spun to face Zena. "Lawd ha' mercy." Hadn't she had a premonition all morning? She swooped down on Jenny and Elliot at the table with their fingers in the bowl of sponge cake batter. "Take the chillen down Mastuh Monte's wine cella'." For once she felt thankful it was there. She shoved them toward the door at the end of the kitchen.

James rushed in. "They gonna break the door down."

"He'p me here." With James, Pearl pushed the walnut cupboard in front of the cellar door. Then she sat him at the table and stuck a napkin in his collar as the pounding on the front door ended with a mighty crash.

James pushed back from the table with his gnarled hands. "What's all this? I can' eat, not with . . ."

"Hush yo' mouth." Pearl ladled a bowl of chicken dumplings and set it before him. She stuck the spoon in his hand.

The kitchen door burst open and two men filled its space. Pearl plastered her fists to her hips and scowled her fiercest. "Who are you? Why you bargin' in my kitchen?" She took up a broom and started toward them. "Get out. Get out where's you belong."

The younger man backed out, but the second grabbed the

81

broom from her and threw it. "Where's Cole Jasper hidin' out?"

"Mistuh Jazzper ain' here. He been took off."

The men looked around the room. The older one jutted his chin. "What's that in the pot?"

"Chicken dumplin's."

"Sure a big potful for one old man."

Pearl held her tongue. If ever there was a time for falsehood this was it, but that was how the devil worked, and these two were the devil's own.

"Don't stand there gawkin', woman. Dish us some. And be quick." He pulled a gun. "'Fore I shoot off this old man's head."

Pearl ladled the bowls, muttering. It was a crying shame to waste her dumplings on trash. For once she wished she made them heavy as old Esther's. They'd hang in their bellies like stones. She smacked the bowls on the table, but the men didn't sit. They gobbled like hogs, spooning the food into their mouths with the bowls held to their chins.

The younger one finished and wiped his mouth on his sleeve. "You got whiskey to wash it down?"

Pearl jutted her lower lip. "I got no use for the devil's tool."

The other man took James by the shirt. "How 'bout you, old man? You got whiskey?"

"The massuh got some."

Pearl held her piece. James always spoke as though poor Master Monte was still master.

"Git it now."

Pearl watched as James stood and walked stoically to the parlor. The men followed, and she stayed close on their heels. Now that they were out of the kitchen she meant to keep them out.

They shoved past James to the cabinet. The younger one eyed the elegant room. "Whooee. Looks like Jasper got hisself a fancy position."

Pearl scowled when the older man pulled the stopper and drank from the decanter. Master Monte's whiskey had no right in that man's belly. It had sat in that cabinet four years now, except on the rare times Miss Abbie offered it to a gentleman caller.

He passed the bottle and the other man drank, then he took it back and slammed it on the cabinet shelf. "Finn, you take upstairs, I'll take down. Tear it apart till we find his hidey-hole."

"Mistuh Jazzper ain' here. I tol' you."

The men separated. Pearl heard the crashing and smashing. She backed toward the kitchen as the gray-haired man started that way. She rushed in ahead of him and took up the marble rolling pin Master Monte had brought her all the way from Italy. "You break somethin' in my kitchen, I'll crack yo' skull."

"What's that door?"

Pearl's heart pounded. She turned, then almost gasped with relief. "Tha's the washroom." She huffed over and opened the door to reveal the pantry shelves and the washtub with the small stove beside it. "They's nothin' there. Mistuh Jazzper, he gone."

"What about the missus?"

"What missus?"

"The girl what sprung him loose with that Injun."

So they'd gotten Mister Jasper free. Pearl felt elated but didn't let it show. "Mizz Abbie ain' here neither."

"Where is she?"

"I don' know." And that was God's truth. She worried sick when each new day failed to bring Miss Abbie home.

The look in his eyes near froze her marrow. This man was the devil's own for sure. He turned and bellowed, "Finn!"

Finn bounded down and followed the first man back to the parlor. They shoved the whiskey and the brandy into their shirts. Pearl held her tongue. Good riddance and she hoped it rotted their bellies. The older man took up the lamp.

"Whatcha doin', Crete?"

"Repayin' a favor." He smashed it against the wall. The oil splattered down the lace curtain and over the carpet.

"No!" James hollered as Crete tossed the match, then knocked James to the floor.

Crete and Finn ran from the house as the fire rushed up the wall. Pearl took up a rug and beat it against the flames. The fire jumped from one curtain to the next. James staggered up and ran. "Mistuh Matt! Mistuh Curtis, come quick!"

Pearl's arms ached, and tears streamed as she beat the flames. In the spreading flames she choked and swung the rug with all her strength. What would Miss Abbie do now? Lawd A'mighty! That woman had troubles in this world.

Down in the cellar Elliot pressed into Zena's arms, but Jenny made a small ball of herself. With each smash and thump she tightened until she imagined herself growing smaller and harder like one of Cole's animals. Where was he? Had Aunt Abbie found him? Did she give him her note? Did he know how to pretend?

She pressed her eyes shut and saw him. He could be her pa. Of all the people she knew, she liked him best. She couldn't say why. It was something in the way he smelled, the way he smiled at her, the way his voice got growly when he said something nice.

It wasn't easy to be nice. Not for Cole, and not for her. He didn't have to be. He could grumble and holler, and she'd even heard him swear once when he didn't know she was there. She wouldn't tell, though, because sometimes she wished she could be just as ornery.

But she had to be nice. If she wasn't nice, bad things happened. Hadn't she teased Elliot this morning? She'd made him cry, not that it was hard to. She'd told him maybe his mama wouldn't come back at all. She'd wanted to hurt him. Now the wickedness of it made a hard ball in her tummy.

She'd made this bad thing happen, made the evil men come. Would her mean words ruin everything? What if Aunt Abbie never did come back? What if she couldn't get Cole? What if there was no one, no one but Elliot left? What if she was alone . . . again. . . . Jenny stared into the reddish candlelit darkness.

The shelves of dusty bottles loomed over her. Was this what it was like to be buried? They'd buried her mama. She knew that. That grave was far away, but her pa's grave was right here on the ranch.

She didn't remember him, except . . . his mustache. It had hard ends that curled up, not soft like Cole's. At least she thought Cole's was soft. She could almost remember him holding her, remember it brushing her cheek when she wrapped her arms around his neck. Yes, she was almost certain that wasn't pretend.

Jenny drew a long soulful breath. At least that's what Zena called it when she breathed like that. Soulful. It helped the knot in her tummy, and she took another one, then smelled smoke. She shot to her feet and stared at the door at the top of the stairs.

Nothing showed in the darkness, but she smelled it stronger and started to shake. Every part of her felt tight and wobbly at once. If she burned now, she'd go to hell and burn forever. She saw her grandmother's face, heard the words. *"That child will scream herself straight to hell."*

Jenny clamped a hand to her mouth. She mustn't make a sound. Not a sound.

Sam had given him ten days. Time enough for any man to own up to his obligations. He'd never known Cole to shirk before. He'd trained his brother better than that. But he had waited in that hotel too long, and today was Judgment Day for Cole Jasper.

Sam reined in and squinted. Smoke was pouring from the front of the fancy house. He made out two men beating the flames that climbed the tall white pillars. Neither one was Cole.

It wasn't his business, but . . . Sam spurred the horse into the yard. He leaped down, grabbed a gunnysack from the pile thrown in the dirt, and beat at the pillars. "Anyone in the house?" he hollered over the ruckus, but he saw for himself a moment later.

Inside, a Negro woman rushed past the window just as the glass exploded. She fell clear, grabbed up her rug, then beat out the flames licking the window frame. Another figure, a Negro man, staggered behind her.

Where in tarnation was Cole? Where was the lady . . . Sam straightened. He took one step and hurled himself through the shattered window. He gained his feet, but the Negro woman raised her rug and swung.

Sam tumbled over and rolled. "Wait! Stop! I'm here to help." He clutched the gunnysack as proof.

She took his measure with a hard eye, then went back to beating the flames. He worked beside her. "Is anyone else inside?"

"Dis fire ain' leavin' dis room. You want to he'p, he'p here!"

Sam quickly eyed the doorway. The paint was blistering, but no flames showed past it. He ran over and scanned the hall. Smoke, but no flame. He shut the paneled wood door, then stomped and ground the fire at the edge of the thick rug, swinging the sack into the worst of it.

The old man was wheezing, his gnarled fingers scarcely gripping the broom he swung at the flame running along the ceiling molding. Any moment he'd ignite the broom and spread the fire worse.

Sam rushed over. "Here, get clear." He grabbed the broom and swung at the ceiling, pounding out the flames even as they sprang up anew. Sweat poured from his skin, and he felt his lips burning. He plunged the broom up again and again.

The old man hunched against the wall—a good sign. If it was cool enough to support him, it wasn't likely to ignite. This house was well built. Plenty of lathe and plaster. Sam beat the broom against the wall, then into the thicker flames at the window, his arms aching with each whack.

He turned. The big rug was smoldering, and he lunged to it and rolled the end until the would-be flames suffocated inside. He covered his face with his arm and choked. A wrenching groan brought him around, and he watched the elegant portico come crashing down outside. One of the men leaped free, and Sam suspected he'd purposely brought it down to keep the fire from jumping over the stone face to the wood siding above.

The dark-haired man cast a bucket on the pillar flaming in the yard. The other followed suit, running from pump to pillars, but they were salvaging only. The danger was past, unless . . .

Sam yanked open the parlor door and staggered down the hall through the smoke. If sparks or embers had blown through . . . He cleared the haze with his arms, keeping one wall at his elbow. The place was massive. He felt a warm body behind him and made way for the woman.

She pushed past like a nursing cow on her calf. He followed. They barreled into the kitchen, and she flung open the door to a washroom and then an outside door. Cold air rushed in, and the smoke swirled. The woman came back and put her weight to a cupboard. Sam caught her intention.

He shoved with her until the door behind was free, then yanked it open. A waif stood at the foot of the stairs, still and solemn in the column of daylight. Sam stared through the smoke at the child, and she stared back.

Then she opened her pinched little mouth. "Cole?"

The voice was plaintive, and he eyed the young Negro behind the child, holding a tiny white boy on her chest. He saw their hopeful eyes. They were looking for Cole, and mistaking him in the smoke. He swallowed hard. "Come on up now. The fire's out."

The little slip of a girl came by herself. She stepped onto the slate floor and swiped at the smoke. She blinked, then tightened her lips and brought up her chin. "You're not Cole."

"I'm Sam. Cole's brother, Sam." He heard the heavy woman mutter and turned. "Is that everyone?"

"Tha's all."

The other two came up from the cellar and the small boy stared at him with incredible eyes. Sam had seen eyes like that, only angry . . . that lady must be his ma, the one who had held a pistol to his head as cool as you like. The child's eyes teared in the smoke, or maybe he was scared.

Sam faced the woman who had felled him with the rug. "Where's Cole? And the lady?"

The Negro woman puffed her lips and scowled but kept her peace.

"Look, I don't mean to make trouble. . . ."

"Mistuh, you brung trouble."

Sam looked from one face to another. They could've hardly been more hostile if they were Comanche squaws. He slouched against the cupboard. "My brother and I had some personal business, but this is different. I got word there are bounty hunters . . ."

"They done took him off. An' Mizz Abbie, she gone after him."

Sam frowned.

"Now they come back lookin' for him again. Who you think lit that fire?"

Sam ran a hand through his hair. Was he getting this straight? "The same ones that took him came lookin'?"

"They was hoppin' mad Mizz Abbie got Mistuh Jazzper loose."

Sam stared at her, not certain if this was some tale meant to throw him or . . .

"If you're Cole's brother, how come you hurt him?"

Sam turned to the little girl and met her angry stare. "That's his business an' mine, little miss."

Her fists clenched at her sides. With one swift stroke, she swung her shoe into his shin, clearing the boot by an inch. "Aah!" The pain shot up his bone.

She turned and fled out the back door. The little boy ran after, and the young woman after him. The large woman folded her arms across her chest. One look into her face and Sam felt decidedly unwelcome.

He reached up and realized his hat was gone. He nodded, turned on his heel, and went back to the damaged front room, hoping it hadn't been trampled or burned in the ruckus. He'd been two years training that hat, and it was just now the best fit he'd yet accomplished.

He saw it lying against the wall where he'd rolled from the woman's first blow. He scooped it up and put it where it belonged. He wasn't about to make the long, fast ride with a hat that didn't fit.

Nine

The terrain they'd covered that day had been thickly treed and hilly. They had forded the Pecos River and camped on its far bank. Abbie stirred the thin beans in the pot, wishing for corn bread or biscuits, anything to properly fill their stomachs. They were at the end of their provender, and they'd soon be scrapping for roots and rabbits.

She glanced to where Will sat with his knees poking up like grasshopper legs. He'd sleep with a rumbling stomach tonight. But he seemed cheerful enough as he watched Cole with something close to worship.

"You been through this way before, Cole?"

Cole nodded. "More or less. I've taken herds along both the Santa Fe and the Chisholm trails, among others, from the time I was seventeen. Some herds up to three thousand head."

"Was it difficult driving the big herds?"

"Every drive's difficult, Will. Every drive's different. You never know from one trip to the next what you'll encounter by way of weather and trouble."

"What sort of trouble?"

"All sorts." Cole's eyes took on a faraway look. "The first time I drove a herd as boss foreman, I thought I knew all there was to know on the trail. I was twenty-three years old, and half the men in my outfit were twice that. But I was a cocky son of a gun and had wheedled the job from old man Black."

Cole rubbed the dust from his boot. "We'd gotten word that some herds ahead of us had turned back for lack of water. Well, I knew the land and figured those herds must have been driven by less experienced men. I didn't reckon on the last summer's drought. But that's what it was."

He ran his fingers over the tracery on the leather. "Once we'd crossed the Colorado River, things looked pretty scaly. Where there should have been water, there was mud. We dug wells, but they scarcely filled up enough to satisfy our saddle stock. There was none for the cattle."

He shook his head. "The heat was fierce and sapped our strength. Dusters twisted 'round and stung us fierce. But I knew the way clear and figured we best push on. The herd could go some days, though their tongues were hangin' out and they were bawlin' like babes. They wouldn't lay down, and they wouldn't graze. It took every man ridin' twenty-four hours straight to keep 'em from turnin'.'"

Will whistled low.

"By the fourth day, the cattle were millin' so bad we spent more time breakin' up the circles than movin' forward. Then they turned. We snapped our whips and shot our six-shooters, but they kept comin'. One bull trampled clean over a calf like he'd never seen it. And I realized they were blind. There was nothin' for it but to let 'em get back to water."

"They were really blind, Cole?"

"It wasn't permanent if their other senses could get them to water in time. We couldn't drive 'em. All's we could do was try to contain them as they trailed on back."

"Did they make it to the water?"

"Well, nature smiled on us. The next night it rained, comin' down so fierce it sounded like nails on the hard ground. Kept on all through that day and the next. The cattle, they stood and licked at the water round their hooves like they'd never tasted it before."

Cole shook his head. "It was a sight to see. Come mornin' of the third day, we felt right hopeful that the streams were runnin' good enough to see us through."

"Had you lost any cattle?"

"We lost two that gave up and keeled over less than one hour before the rain begun. But in roundin' up the strays, we gained a number of range mavericks, as well. Times bein' what they were, we let the extras stay, no charge."

Abbie caught Cole's slanted grin as she handed Will his meager plate.

Will nodded his thanks. "You mean you rustled them?"

"No, sir. I never rustled a steer in my life. 'Cept down in Mexico, where they're free for the takin' if you've guts enough to face down the vaqueros."

"What's a vaquero?"

"Mexican rancher. It's kind of a give-and-take across the border. They raid ours, we raid theirs. Most times you hardly know what rightly belongs to one or the other anymore, and it's like a game—only a hazardous one if you ain't quick and quiet."

"But isn't that rustlin'?"

"Not if you're takin' back your own with a few unfortunates mixed in."

Will whooped. "Tell us another one, Cole."

Abbie slopped the beans into the tin saucer and handed it to Cole.

"Thank you, Abbie." He turned back to Will. "Talkin' of rustlin' puts me in mind of the time we met a band of true cow thieves at the crossing of the Brazos. I reckon I'd been trail boss two years or so, and I hadn't had much trouble of that sort to speak of."

Cole took a bite of beans and chewed slowly. Abbie sat down and watched him. This was the most talkative he'd been the entire trip. Of course the cough was nearly gone, and his strength was returning.

"We'd got word from a previous herd that rustlers had set up at the crossing, and sure enough, as we neared the river some fellas came along claimin' to be cutters. Well, I gave the orders to start the herd across before I asked what brand they were searchin'."

"How come?" Will wiped his mouth with his sleeve.

"That way if these men caused us trouble, we'd have the river behind us to catch our herd. Well, they sparked good at that, but I told them I had a job to do and didn't want to risk the river risin'."

Cole chuckled, obviously enjoying his tale. "Once across, they started claimin' cattle that they recognized as this outfit's or that's, and always the brand was close to another or maybe blurred some. Anytime we contested, they demanded we throw it. Bein' of a tractable sort, I obliged, throwin' the steers in spite of my suspicions."

"And?"

Cole swilled his bite down with his coffee. "Once we cut the hair away, our road brand was as clear as day. The fellas acted embarrassed, but I could see they was riled. I told them to take what they had and shove off."

Will's eyes shown. Abbie saw the signs of true adulation as he hung on Cole's words.

"Well, they'd only cut six head of the brand they were scouting, and they were mighty peeved. Their lead man scowled somethin' fierce and acted like he'd been wronged."

Cole fixed Will with a steely gaze. "We figured they'd try to stampede the herd come nightfall, or come back with gunmen and put up a fight. So we night-herded the cattle and kept a scout on through all the watches."

Will's eyes were aglow. "What happened?"

"Nothin'. Next mornin' I sent a man out, and he come back

with the answer. And a mighty grizzly one at that."

"What?"

"Apaches. A war band met up with them on their way to us. Passed within six miles of our herd and never knew we were there."

Abbie released her breath, caught up in the story in spite of herself. "That was lucky."

Cole shrugged. "We felt kinda gypped. Seemed hardly fair the Apaches got all the fun of the fight we picked." He winked at Will.

Will laughed heartily, but Abbie frowned. There again was a peek into Cole's character. As though shooting it out with ruffians was a pleasure to be sought.

Will wiped the brown drizzle of bean juice from his chin with his thumb. "Cole, you got family in Texas?"

Cole swirled the coffee in his cup, then took a swallow. "I got my brother, Sam, but I ain't sure where he is just now."

"Are your parents dead?"

Abbie tensed, but Cole stirred the fork around in his beans. "My ma is. Ain't seen my pa since I was ten years old. But I reckon he's somewhere in hell."

Will nodded slowly. "My pa was killed in a fight when I was a kid."

"You're still a kid. Barely more than a colt with wobbly legs."

Abbie bit her lower lip. Cole was certainly a master at diverting the subject.

"I had my twenty-first birthday the day we crossed the Canadian River."

Abbie glanced up. "You never said. I'd have managed something special for supper."

Cole frowned. "Such as?"

"Well . . . beans." She met his eyes and suddenly laughed. "With a whole side of beans." She liked his answering grin and felt the tightness between them ease.

"We'll be comin' on to Santa Fe by sundown tomorrow. We'll get stocked there."

Abbie nodded. Cole talked as though this were no more than another trail. Try as she would, she could not get one word from him as to his plans once he got to El Paso. Would he turn himself in? Would he clear himself of the charges?

Surely he had some explanation that would clear things up, but she had an ominous weight on her spirit. It was fear. Fear that he had no intention of clearing things up. Fear that he would not defend himself. Fear . . . of losing him?

"What if someone recognizes you in Santa Fe?"

"You an' Will can go into town. I'll keep shy of it."

Abbie swallowed her bland bite of beans. "So we load up there and go on to El Paso?"

"Should find most anything you need there, if you don't need nothin' fancy."

She sighed. "I can't say I wouldn't mind a fine Lucky Star beefsteak just about now."

"That's your own doin'. I've sent you home twice now."

"And I've already told you, we're going all the way with you."

Cole glowered at his plate.

Abbie felt a stab of anger. Why did that disturb him unless he expected the worst? If he thought he'd be turning around and coming home free, wouldn't he be glad for the company? "Have you given thought to your defense?" There, she'd said it. "We could wire Grant and . . ."

He set down his plate, stood, and walked away. So that was his answer. Well, she wasn't about to accept it. She slapped her own plate down on the ground and followed him. The night sky was like jet set with diamonds. She saw only his dark form against the black hills.

If Cole heard her approach, he ignored it. His stance was

firm, stubborn. Abbie felt her irritation rise. Why did he get under her skin so? She stepped around and faced him. "I think we should have a plan."

"I think you should quit meddlin'."

"You're just stubborn."

"Like you ain't?"

She felt the tendons tighten in her neck. "I want to know what you intend to do in El Paso."

"How can I tell you that when I don't know m'self?"

She put a hand on his arm. "You must have . . . an alibi. Grant says if a person has an alibi . . ."

"I was with Auralee the night she died."

Abbie felt as though a rock hit her stomach. *With Auralee?* She pulled her hand from his arm. "But you didn't kill her."

He set his jaw. "I a'ready told you that."

"Then someone else must have been there . . . when you left." After completing the business he had with a saloon girl. . . .

It could almost be a smirk on his face. "Leave it alone, Abbie. The subject's distasteful to you."

She hadn't meant to show her displeasure. But she couldn't help recalling his hand under Lil's fingers. Why would that burn itself on her memory? It wasn't as though twenty men a day didn't do as much and more. But she'd expected better from Cole. Even if Auralee was a red-haired beauty.

Fury and a feeling of . . . jealous dismay burned up inside. She turned and stalked back to camp. What had she been thinking? How could she have thought she cared for him? He was a rake and a scoundrel, as far from the man she thought him as . . . as from the man Monte had been.

Will looked up from his perch by the fire. His eyes were worried. "He didn't answer?"

"He's a bullheaded . . ." Abbie closed her fists at her sides. "If I ever come to you again on Cole's behalf, tell me I'm plumb crazy!" She flounced to her bedroll and climbed in.

Cole stood in the dark. The moon was a sliver amid the stars swarming the sky. He'd have liked to lie on his back and let his gaze search out the farthest pricks of light. He'd have liked to have Abbie beside him, searching out the same stars with that look of wonder she got sometimes over the littlest things.

But she was angry as a polecat, and he'd done it on purpose. Sure he didn't want her prying, sure he hadn't a decent answer, but more than that, he needed to shake her loose. It was eating away his resolve to have her with him. Every day that passed made it harder to keep his focus on what he meant to do.

What did he mean to do? Could he save his neck and Sam's both? If Sam killed Auralee in a fury, was it right to stand in for him? It was, if Cole was the cause of that fury. He'd seen it building, but he hadn't known how to stop it.

Those first two weeks in El Paso he'd been like the blind cattle, feeling nothing but the water on his belly, tasting a lick or two as though he'd never drunk before. He'd spent three and a half years secretly looking after Abbie from wherever he could make the most money, hoping she'd call him back, hoping she'd need him. But she hadn't called.

So he'd gone home. He'd thought to look up Sam, maybe find some of the boys. He'd thought to go down Mexico way and drive a herd for old times' sake. He'd thought to put his feelings for Abbie behind him once and for all. But he hadn't reckoned on Sam loving the one woman who caught his eye.

Auralee Dubois was poison in a silk gown. How Pablo Montoya got hold of her, he'd never know. She was as out of place in La Paloma Blanca as a fish in the desert. With her fair skin and red hair, she stood out, but it was her fire that caught him cold.

He had wanted a woman who'd fight him, a woman who'd exorcise the memory of blue eyes and creamy skin and a tangle of brown hair. For two weeks he had eyed and baited her, until the blindness passed and he saw Sam's face. By then it was too late. Auralee was up to the challenge and not to be put off. That he refused only fueled her fire.

Cole drew a long breath. Sometimes a body just couldn't get it right.

Ten

Nora looked at the wooden walls rising up from the piece of property Davy had acquired. It was no mansion he built. Not like Abbie's fine house, and she was glad. She would never be at home in so much glass and polish. This one would suit her better.

It was near enough to town for Davy to travel to and from the smithy each day, yet far enough out to support a small farm. A half-day's ride from the mission made it impossible for her to look in daily on Maggie and Father Paddy, but Mary Donnelly's mother was to live there when she left.

That was a good arrangement, though Nora felt a twinge at leaving her sister to Father Paddy and old mother Donnelly. Father Paddy was too busy to keep an eye on Maggie now that she was eighteen and as bonny a lass as ever turned a lad's head. Her young sister had enough fire to keep them at bay, but nary the will to do it.

Nora carried the steaming pot of coffee to where the men worked. Though the weather had warmed after the brief snow, there was still enough chill to be chased by the hot brew. And Davy preferred coffee to tea.

He looked up from the architectural pattern he held and smiled. Her heart warmed, though she wouldn't show it. She gave her head a coquettish tilt and met him with the coffee.

"I've something to keep you goin'."

"That you have." Davy's smile broadened, and he reached a hand to her hair and tugged. The coppery coil sprang back from his fingers.

"I mean the coffee, ye daft man."

"Who are you calling daft? Don't you see the walls rising to your house?"

"Aye. But will they hold the roof, I'm wonderin'?"

"They will that and more. They'll hold the family we'll be growing inside them."

Nora flushed. "And if you propagate as well as you boast, where will we put them all?"

"We'll add on as we need to." He took the coffeepot. "Cups?"

"Aye." Nora pulled them from her shawl, one cup for each of the men—Davy, Alan, her brother, Doyle, and big Connor.

The others smelled the coffee Davy poured and left their places on the walls. Alan pulled off his hat, though Davy had no more than tipped his, western fashion. "Mornin', Nora. A bonny day made bonnier."

Nora smiled, his soft speech warming her further. Like his cousin, Jaime, Alan had the way of words that turned a woman's head, though it was only banter built of habit and growing up together. She held up her own side with the retort, "I'm knowin' why Glenna put up nary a fight when you came callin', Alan O'Rourke."

She noticed Davy's frown and regretted the words as soon as they were out. She hadn't meant to spark his jealousy, nor remind him how long it had taken him to win her. It was only that Alan and Jaime had been so close. Part of her linked them together always, and she knew no other way to be with Alan.

"Glenna had never your stubborn temper." Alan said it gently, but she felt the barb. "Davy's the man for the job."

"Aye." Nora tucked her arm into the crook of Davy's to assuage his hurt.

Alan clamped his shoulder. "It's a walk you're needin', Davy lad. A stroll in the winter sunshine with your betrothed."

Davy rolled the plans and slid them into the tube. He slurped his coffee with gusto, then set down the cup. "A walk it is, then."

They headed out across the land. Davy tossed the hair from his forehead as he walked. "Here's your vegetable garden and the plot for potatoes. Over yonder's where we'll pasture the sheep."

"And who'll watch them, I wonder, while you're beating iron into nails and I'm seeing to our home and garden?"

"They don't need to be watched all the time. In case you haven't noticed, there are no rocky cliffs in the vicinity, no roaring falls or flooding torrents. But I have been thinkin'."

"Och, Lord save us."

Davy took the gibe with grace. "I wondered how you'd feel about Mariah staying with us. Ma and Pa haven't had a year to themselves, what with Mack coming so soon and the rest of us following after. Ma's aged so since Blake and Mack..."

Nora held her breath. Davy never spoke of the brothers he'd lost. She'd learned more about them from Abbie than him.

He shrugged. "I was just thinkin' Mariah could help you in the house and watch the sheep some. She's good with animals, and it's not likely she'll marry. Not the way she is. Not..."

"I'll have your sister, Davy. It'd be an honor."

He stopped in his tracks, and she was shamed by his surprise.

"Did you think you'd have to fight me for it?"

"I..." He shoved his hands into his pockets. "Guess I didn't know."

"Alan's right. I've always had a temper and more stubbornness than suits me. It takes the likes of you, Davy McConnel, to have your way with me."

He stood a long moment, then took his hands from his coat and pulled her close. He kissed the crown of her head. "I love you, Nora."

"Aye." She pushed back. "And soon enough you'll be sorry for it."

"I won't be sorry."

She sighed and allowed him to take her hand as they walked again. "I hope Abbie will be back for the weddin'."

"Truth be told, I hope she's not."

Now it was her feet that halted. "Why?"

"Abbie's bad luck to us McConnels."

"Sure an' that's the Irish in you to say that."

"It's just the way it is. Mack would never have gone if Blake hadn't put him up to it. And Blake was tryin' to win Abbie's heart with gold."

"Then it was his foolishness."

"You've seen what she hankered for. You've been in her fine house, crossed the miles of her land. How could Blake compete with that?"

"It wasn't the things Abbie wanted. T'was the man. She loved Blake, but not enough to stop her from lovin' Monte."

"Is that how it is with women? Is there always one who keeps you from loving any other?"

Nora felt the heaviness weigh her down. Her throat was as dry as the ground she tread. "Not always, Davy."

"Just my luck, huh?"

She dropped her gaze to the brown dormant grass. "I wasn't speakin' of me."

"But it's the same, isn't it? You love me, but not enough to stop you wanting Jaime."

Hearing his name spoken aloud jarred her. So Davy did know, and he felt justified throwing it at her. Nora's voice trembled. "What's the use of wanting someone from the grave?"

"No use. But you do, don't you?"

"Aye." The whisper escaped before she could stop it. Nora raised her eyes to his face. "Is it off, then?"

Davy clenched his hands at his sides. "No. I just wanted to know where we stood." He wet his lips as though he'd say more. But he only shrugged and started to walk back. "If Mariah will come, we can start a flock in the spring. Just a few ewes and a ram."

Nora nodded, allowing the change of subject to cover her shame. "You'll stay on at the smithy?"

"What else? Pa needs me. He'd planned on Mack, or maybe even Blake. They had the shoulders for it."

"Seems to me your shoulders are plenty broad themselves."

Davy walked silently. She wished she could take back her words. Did she want Jaime back from the grave? What would she do if he crossed her doorstep, all afire for the cause? Could she sit and listen to him speak his death again and again as she had once?

Nora glanced at Davy plodding beside her, his heavy brogans placed solidly step after step. His big hands were gentle, his dreams close to home. He would be a good father, a fine husband. If only she could let Jaime go.

◆◆◆◆◆◆◆

Santa Fe was a quaint cluster of pole and adobe buildings and dusty streets filled with burros, wagons, and a saddle horse or two. Dried red peppers hung from the whitewashed houses, and Abbie drank in the unhurried bustle and the flavor of things foreign. After the miles of travel, Santa Fe looked as welcoming as any place she'd been.

Abbie searched the street for a bathhouse, but the only hope was the low hacienda with a sign on the front that said, *hotel y cantina*. "Will, I can't do anything else until I've washed."

"I wouldn't mind a bath myself."

"I know Cole's waiting, but I won't get supplies until I've scraped the grime and dust and—"

"I know exactly how you feel." Will smiled boyishly, and Abbie almost hugged him. How good it was not to knock heads with someone. Cole was worse than ever since she'd questioned him. He almost bit her head off when she suggested shaving his mustache and disguising him so he could come to town and have a decent meal.

"We'll wash and have a hot meal without a single bean on the plate."

"Sounds too good to be true."

She curled her hand into Will's arm and saw him blush. It made her feel young, and she realized she was. Twenty-six was not near old enough to feel as dry and bitter as she'd been.

Minutes later, Abbie sighed blissfully as she slipped into the tub. She wished she could have seen Nora before she left. Her friend would have told her straight and clear she was crazy to even think of doing this. And what if she hadn't come? Would Cole still be trailing along with the bounty hunters, more dead than alive? Though he was not yet at the top of his strength and the shoulder troubled him, he was mostly hale, thanks to her.

She splashed the soap down into the water of her bath and rubbed it furiously between her palms. Would she have told Nora all the reasons she came after Cole? Would she have admitted what passed between them only a month ago?

Abbie lathered her arms. No, she would have spoken of her duty, her debt. But she would not have admitted the traitorous feelings that almost led her into more heartache. Thankfully Cole's own behavior had put that to an end.

When she had thoroughly scrubbed in the small galvanized tub, she brushed the dusty skirt and shirtwaist and donned them. She would never take her back-room bathhouse for granted again. When she got home she'd bathe every day without fail, maybe twice a day if she felt like it.

Abbie met Will in the hall. He had used the twin tub on the other side of the canvas wall and looked as though he'd squeak when he walked. Even his nose had a shine. She laughed. She couldn't help it. Then she thought of Cole, dusty and worn back at the camp, and felt a pang of remorse.

Well, he could have come with them. There were few enough people in town to worry about, but he'd been stubborn . . . again. She raised her chin. She would not feel guilty. Will deserved a good meal, and so did she. She stalked to the large room that housed the cantina, determined to dine at leisure.

The meal was hardly worth sitting for, and not without beans. They were mashed and fried in grease with hot peppers, served with beef so tough Abbie suspected they'd been served a leggy longhorn cow. It stuck in her gullet, seasoned with re-morse. They should have gotten their supplies and headed back. Cole would be hungry and cross, and they'd wasted plenty of time.

She would make it up with special purchases—canned smoked oysters if they were to be had. She knew Cole had a fondness for them. And perhaps a sweet or two. With her con-science eased by good intentions, she and Will hoofed it to the general store. She stopped with dismay at the closed sign in the window.

"Closed. How can they be closed?"

Will rubbed his cheek where he'd been nicked by the bar-ber. "I thought the town looked a little sparse. Let's try some-where else."

Nearly every door and window they passed was barred and locked, shades drawn. Will drew his brows together. "Maybe they're havin' a siesta."

"According to Cole, that's over the noon hour, not in the evening."

Will caught her arm and held up a finger. "Hear that?"

Abbie listened. She did hear a commotion and turned toward the sound. It seemed to be coming from a corral behind the livery. "What is it?"

"I don't know." Will started walking, and she followed.

An immense crowd around and inside the corral seemed frenzied. They hollered and gesticulated, made coarse jokes and spat. Will self-consciously shielded Abbie as they drew near, but she climbed the low roof of a lean-to and peered over their heads. A terrible shrieking filled the air, and she caught a glimpse of feathers amid the dust.

A cockfight. Abbie's anger and disgust grew as she caught snatches of the activity through the men's backs. Each time the cocks flew apart, their owners snatched them up and threw them back at each other. She turned her head away from the crazed, bleeding birds. Such cruelty for sport was inhuman.

"Maybe we better wait back at the store." Will lifted her down, and she went mutely, though many choice words perched on her tongue. He shook his head. "It won't be a long wait. They're almost at an end."

Abbie hung her head. She'd wrung enough fowl necks to have little sensitivity toward the creatures themselves. What bothered her was the delight the men took in violence for its own sake. They were more like animals than the creatures they pitted in the ring.

She sat on the bench outside the general store window and closed her eyes. When the proprietor arrived, keys in hand, he tugged his vest and smoothed wisps of hair across his pate. "Sorry to keep you waiting, Señora."

Abbie stood with all the hauteur Monte's late sister, Frances, might have managed and walked inside. By the time they purchased their supplies and had them packed onto the horses, the sun had set. It was dark before they made it back to camp. Cole did not greet them. Was he hiding, fearing foes?

The fire was banked, and Abbie felt a vague disquiet.

"Cole?" Even as she spoke, she knew he wasn't there to hear it. She released a slow breath and closed her eyes.

"You reckon he went on without us?"

Abbie slipped down from Zephyr's back and walked to the fire. He had buried the coals to keep them warm without leaving them free to blow. And at the side of the fire ring, he'd lined stones in an arrow toward the direction of home. For a man who couldn't write, his message was clear. Why did she feel so betrayed?

Eleven

Cole pressed on through the darkness. Whitesock was pretty near stumbling, but he wanted as many miles behind him as possible. These last days he had intentionally misled Abbie as to his condition. He'd kept on at a diminished pace, making more of his weariness than need be in order to slow them down and see to it they finished off their provender before Santa Fe.

It was the logical point to split up. She and Will could gather supplies and head home before the going got really rough. And Abbie wouldn't suspect the distance he could put between them.

Cole felt a twinge of guilt and even more concern, but he didn't figure they'd meet with trouble if he wasn't with them. Will had a good head on him, and Abbie ... well, even Crete Marlowe was no match for Abbie with her back up. Besides, she'd likely thrown Marlowe so far off the trail, he'd lost interest.

She'd get home safe. He had to think so. He'd tried and tried to send them off before this. Now Abbie just had more miles to cover than before. He had few qualms about leaving her to Will. The kid was solid stock. He'd look out for her.

As for himself, Cole shrugged, he'd eat what he found and make his way. He'd done it before. He headed southwest toward Albuquerque and long past sundown he reached the banks of the Rio Grande. He was as stiff and weary as the horse when he swung down.

He pulled the bedroll off and unsaddled the gelding, wincing at the painful strain it put on his shoulder. He'd unslung his left arm as soon as Abbie was out of sight. He had to. There was no way he'd cross this territory with one arm hobbled to his side. Cole tossed his bedroll to the ground and lay down. By morning, Abbie and Will would start home, and he'd work his way down to El Paso.

It was chilly this high up, but he'd do without a fire. He wanted nothing to give away his position. He'd left coals for Abbie and Will. They'd be all right. They'd be . . .

The muffled sound of hooves on turf brought his hand instantly to his gun. No one rode this time of night without ill intentions. Cole sprang up and faced the gun barrel at the rider in black. Every muscle, every nerve was alert, ready.

The rider stopped short. "Easy with your gun, cowboy. I didn't see you there with no fire. I've come a long way this night."

Cole sized up the man and eased only slightly. "What're you doin' ridin' past dark?"

"I could ask the same of you, brother."

"I'm doin' the askin'."

The man took his broad-brimmed hat from his head. "I'm Brother Lewis, bearer of good news and preacher of the truth. I've just quit a camp of evildoers who cared little for the light. I am unashamed to admit they drove me from their midst. As the Good Book says, I shook their dust from my feet, and it shall not fare well for such as they on Judgment Day, for they received not the Lord's messenger."

The rider's pointed features eased into a handsome, charismatic smile as he swung out of the saddle. His face was cleanly shaven; his dark hair cut neatly. Cole couldn't tell in the dark whether it contained streaks of gray or whether the starlight tricked his eyes.

The preacher inclined his head to the side. "Mind if I water my horse?"

Cole appraised the man, sizing him up at about five foot ten and none too brawny, then nodded toward the bank of the Rio Grande, just visible in the moonlight.

"Thank you kindly." Again the stranger's smile flashed.

Cole wasn't sure why he'd agreed. It wasn't from any fear of Judgment Day, nor any hankering after the truth. He wasn't looking for company, and he wasn't eager for talk. This fella seemed right likely to want both.

After watering the animal, Brother Lewis staked his horse and joined him in the grassy hollow. "I appreciate your hospitality. It's always a pleasure to find companionship along my road."

"What's your road, mister?"

"Circuit rider, preacher of the Gospel."

"I meant your direction."

"Wherever I'm called."

"Where'd you leave the evildoers?"

"About seven miles east. A camp of men bound for trouble by the quickest route—greed."

"How many?"

"Eight, plus a deaf mute."

Cole breathed easier. It wasn't Crete, and they weren't anywhere near Abbie and Will.

"Which way were they headin'?"

"West for California."

Cole nodded. "And you're headin'?"

"Wherever the Lord points me."

Cole eyed the man. Underneath his well-defined brows, the preacher had a wide-eyed exuberance, but Brother Lewis was no fool. Cole could feel himself being sized up, as well.

"Are you versed in the Scriptures, Mister . . ."

"The name's Cole."

"Very well, Cole. This place beside the river puts me in mind of the prophet Amos. 'But let judgment run down as waters, and righteousness as a mighty stream.'"

Cole narrowed his eyes and kept silent. What was this talk of judgment? Did the man guess he was wanted by the law?

"Doesn't it awe you to cross the wilderness and suddenly come upon a flowing river? The water seems to have a life of its own, rushing onward like the river Jordan, or the very river of life. To drink your fill when your throat has first known thirst is to find riches and joy."

"I reckon so." He was a spellbinder, all right. Cole wondered if he was as sincere as he looked, or if he was one of them that made his living fleecing the unwary.

"Our God is mightier than our need. 'I will bless the Lord, who hath given me counsel: my reins also instruct me in the night seasons. I have set the Lord always before me: because he is at my right hand, I shall not be moved.'"

Cole felt his pocket for the cigarette papers and pouch. The urge lodged at the joining of his ribs. He needed a smoke and the cough was nearly gone, but he rubbed his hand down over his chest and resisted. "That ain't one I'm familiar with. More like, 'Wherefore I abhor myself, and repent in dust and ashes.'"

The preacher betrayed mild surprise, but Cole simply shrugged. "My ma had the book of Job by memory. It was closest to what she lived."

Brother Lewis nodded. "The world can be harsh to our sisters."

Cole wasn't about to tell him how harsh.

"But have you read—"

"I cain't read, nor write more than my own name."

The preacher pursed his lips. "Yet you live by your wits. I knew that at once. In my travels I've seen many an intelligent man with scant learning and many a learned man with scant intelligence."

Cole half grinned.

"The Lord endows what he sees fit. It's up to us to use the gift or bury it."

Cole stared at the darkness around them. He reckoned he'd buried a portion of his, but maybe he'd done the best that circumstances allowed. He drew a long breath and relaxed. He was tired and had a long ride ahead. He couldn't sit jawing with a preacher all night.

"You're welcome to share this spot. I'm turnin' in now."

Maybe he ought to warn the man that he was a fugitive and others might be coming on them with less honorable intentions, but he didn't want to provoke a sermon. So he lay down and went to sleep.

◆◆◆◆◆◆◆

In the cold morning light, Abbie tightened Zephyr's breastband and rear saddle girth before turning to Will. "Do you know what way Cole meant to take?"

"Not exactly. But it's purty obvious what way he meant us to take."

She brushed the hair back from her cheek. "We've come this far. I've no intention of turning back now."

Will nodded. "Till now we've roughly followed the Santa Fe Trail. I expect he'll keep on that way."

"Then so will we. He has a start on us, likely a good one. But he has no supplies beyond his canteen, some jerky, and hard biscuits. He'll have to provision himself somehow, and that'll take time."

"If Cole wants to keep shy of us, he'll do it."

"Maybe so, but even if he gets to El Paso ahead of us, I'm going down there."

"What can we do?"

115

"I don't know. But I mean to find out." Why? Why not go home to her children? Cole wasn't her responsibility. Hadn't he made that clear by leaving them behind? He wanted to be free of her. He wanted to handle this in his lone wolf way. But something inside drove her on.

She searched the ground and found Whitesock's tracks. From the hoofprints she saw that Whitesock stepped more heavily on his right foreleg and kicked out slightly with the left hind. That would help distinguish these tracks from others she might encounter along the trail.

"It seems he's headed more west than south here. Think back to your geography. Doesn't the Rio Grande lie that way?"

"It's along there somewhere."

"Then we'll know if we wander from the trail."

Will looked less certain, but he manfully shouldered the task. In his own way, he was as determined as she to see this through. Was he also disappointed by Cole's departure? If so, he didn't show it. Well, the sooner they started the better.

Their provisions would go far since she'd bought for three, but she wouldn't waste time cooking more than she had to. With each of them leading a packhorse, she and Will set off. The day was cold and clear, with a sharp wind. Abbie wrapped a scarf around her face against the blowing dust and followed the tracks.

Angling southwest, they rode doggedly throughout the day. As the sun lowered to the western rim of land gouged by a great white stone canyon, Abbie saw the river valley. It lay like a long strip of life through a barren, buff-colored land.

The Rio Grande was edged with low yellow sand hills that gave way to flat, bare mesas. Those to the south were arid, cracked mounds of earth bleached and bled by the sun. Those to the north were covered with sage, rolling up to foothills with scattered mounds of juniper and nut pines. In the far distance, almost like a dream, stood mountains, a jagged, misty blue silhouette.

Abbie reined in Zephyr and sat transfixed. Such extremes of landscape and climate left her breathless. Here was God's handprint, unmarred by man. "Have you ever seen such a sight, Will?"

He glanced the way she was looking. "A sight such as what?"

"All of it. This wide incredible stretch of creation."

He shrugged. "No, I guess not."

Abbie wanted to shake him awake. How could anyone lay eyes on something so new, so wild, and not be moved past words? She shook her head. "We'll camp at the river."

"Yes, ma'am."

As they neared the water, they left the sandy hills and crossed a narrow strip of coarse grassy marshland. At the river's edge grew cottonwoods, some twenty feet high, others small, taking root upon the sandbars. Leafless box elder and wild grapevines choked the bank where there were signs of regular flooding. She guessed without the growth, the river would take the valley again and again.

Abbie looked up at the gray trunks and branches of the cottonwoods, draped with mistletoe. It made her think of Frances's husband, Kendal, and his story of Frigga, the goddess of love and her son, Balder, the sun god. She wondered what gods were worshipped in this untamed land and shivered.

None could contend with the true God, but the followers could be hard to convince. Once again she questioned whether she was doing the right thing. Was it only her pride that kept her going? Her unwillingness to give up? She sighed. What would tomorrow bring?

◆◆◆◆◆◆◆

It was obvious the preacher meant to travel with him indefinitely. Cole had allowed the man to ride along the previous day, expecting he'd take a turn soon enough. But Brother Lewis had shown no signs of parting ways.

Cole scowled. He'd wakened as sour as he could remember, and a dose of the preacher's gab was not the cure. "Look, I gotta cut a good pace today."

"Where are you heading?"

"El Paso."

"I'll do my utmost to keep up."

Cole sucked his cheek. "No offense, preacher . . ."

" 'Where two or three are gathered together in my name, there am I in the midst.' "

Cole rested his arm across Whitesock's saddle and eyed the man. "You sayin' if I allow you to tag after, God himself will ride with us?"

"It's a matter for thought."

Cole wasn't expecting a godly escort, and he'd not have chosen Brother Lewis for company at the best of times, but he shook his head and mounted. "Suit yourself."

They rode in quiet long enough to settle some of his annoyance. But then the preacher started talking, and Cole steeled himself to bear it.

"You're a man who travels alone."

He would be, if the preacher had taken a hint.

"I don't just mean out here on your horse. I mean the journey of life, of the heart and soul. I, too, am a solitary rider, but I'm never truly alone."

Cole reached for the cigarette papers in his pocket. He took one out. He could almost taste the tobacco, feel the smoke filling his lungs. Why not? What difference did it make if he spent his last days enjoying a smoke? But he'd be giving in. He crumpled the paper and let it fall.

"If you once take Jesus into your heart, you never walk

alone from that moment on. For as the Good Book says, 'Whosoever shall call upon the name of the Lord shall be saved.'"

Saved. Cole wasn't asking to be saved. He was sticking out his neck to keep another from the noose. Where was Samuel? How many times had Cole looked to him as a kid, scarcely able to keep from bawling when he hurt so bad there wasn't a position he could find that didn't make it worse?

He remembered the day Sam put his own shoulder between him and the board their pa was wielding. He remembered the smack of it and the welt it had raised on Sam's arm. He remembered Sam telling him to run, and to his shame he recalled running.

His ma had brought in the doctor for Sam that time, and his pa had disappeared for six months. He remembered the fury he'd felt when his pa returned. And he knew he'd never run again. No matter that his ma had told him never to raise a hand in anger. The next time his pa came after him with a stick, Cole wrenched it free and wielded it like a club.

"Come on, come on and take me like a man if you got the guts." His pa was too stinking drunk to hold his own against a ten-year-old with the devil in his blood. Old man Jasper had stumbled away, then drunk himself near to death and left them for good. Samuel had taken on his rearing, Sam and Ma, but it seemed like his ma quit caring, and only Sam was left. Cole realized the preacher was waiting for an answer.

"What's that?"

"I said, have you surrendered your soul to the Savior?"

"Mister, I ain't sure I got a soul to surrender."

Twelve

Cole crouched beside the river and looked up where the ridge of land met the strip of turquoise sky in the growing darkness. He'd expected, and now saw clearly in the failing light, the silhouette of the Comanche. Cole knew better than Abbie the limits of her pact with the Indian.

Maybe Gray Wolf wouldn't attack while she was present, but Cole wasn't at all surprised to see him now that Abbie was heading home. He heard Brother Lewis come up from the water beside him. He turned briefly to warn him, but Brother Lewis eyed the line of sky and smiled. "Ah, the close of day. God is good."

Cole drew his brows together. Was the man blind or just stupid? He looked back. The turquoise had shrunk to a thin band above the black line of earth. Pale stars dotted the darkness above. The Comanche was gone.

Not far, or for long, Cole was certain. Glancing up at Brother Lewis's rapturous face, he held his tongue. He wouldn't disillusion the man.

♦♦♦♦♦♦♦

Six full days of Brother Lewis was wearing him thin. Cole had quit responding, quit giving him any encouragement, but the man was like a bad toothache. He wouldn't go away. Cole swung down from the saddle.

"No man who puts his hand to the plow and turns back is worthy of the kingdom."

Cole loosened the cinch and heaved the saddle to the ground, wincing with the strain to his shoulder. If it kept breaking open and bleeding as it was, he'd expect some degree of permanent damage. He led Whitesock to the riverbank.

They'd followed the Rio Grande through the better part of New Mexico without seeing more than the native Indians, who were peaceful enough, and a few fellow travelers. Most of them were drawn to Brother Lewis's friendly greetings, then cleared off soon enough. No doubt his own expression urged them on. A pair of turkey buzzards circled overhead in the dusky light as he watered the horse.

"And there will come a reckoning. Every man will stand before the throne of God and make an account of himself before the Almighty. Don't think you'll escape that, Cole."

The horse drank, and the preacher's mount lowered its head, as well. At this rate Brother Lewis would be screaming fire and brimstone as they rode into El Paso. Cole felt the tendons knot at the back of his neck, and his gut twisted.

The rabbit he'd shot yesterday hadn't gone far between them, but it wasn't hunger that gnawed. It was fear. He might as well face it. Two days' rides would bring them into town. What kind of crazy man walked into a hangman's noose for a crime he didn't commit?

But what if Sam did? Could Cole stand back and let them realize their mistake, when he'd driven Sam to it? No, he hadn't. It was Auralee herself. She knew Sam loved her. She stoked the flames until they roared inside him, then she turned to his little brother instead ... and rubbed Sam's face in it.

Cole shook his head. If he'd seen sooner ... if he'd realized his holding back would so infuriate her, he'd have plunked down his money and done it. How was he to know she'd take it personal that he wouldn't use her? In a million years he'd never understand the mind of a woman.

Not Auralee; not Abbie. The ache that coursed through him now had nothing at all to do with impending death. Why had he allowed her to come so far? Why had he ridden so many days with a woman he'd loved too long? Why had he allowed himself to imagine she cared, to think . . .

"For all have sinned. Not one is without sin. Repent and . . ."

Cole spun, caught the preacher by the collar, and pressed his Colt revolver to the man's well-shaped chin. "Preacher, you make your livin' by movin' this jaw, but if it don't stop now, I'll blow it right up to kingdom come."

Brother Lewis's throat worked, but no sound emerged.

"You just blink if you got my message."

The preacher closed his eyes and opened them.

"Good." Cole released him. He picketed Whitesock and stalked off to gather wood, such as there was. They'd have a fire tonight. The air was cold. He felt it in his bones. He felt it in his innards. He felt it in his soul. Was he doomed to hell?

Was there truly a place of fiery wrath that forever burned those who failed to account before the throne? He lifted a stick and gripped it in his hand. He'd held the stick his pa had used on him just so. He'd wanted to crack it against his pa's head to see him bleed the way he'd made his sons bleed.

It was easier to think there was nothing past this life, that a man died and went back to the earth, that it just ended. If there was a hell, he sure as heck didn't care to meet his pa there. What worse torment could there be than spending eternity with him?

Cole tossed the stick. All those years away, all those years working for Mr. Farrel, he'd scarce thought of his past once. 'Course, there'd been Abbie to hold his thoughts. He didn't like to recall how many nights he'd spent thinking on another man's wife.

He'd tried not to covet, took pride in the trust Mr. Farrel put in him. But he reckoned that wasn't good enough to state before any throne. Fact was, if she'd ever given him the least invitation, he might have fallen as low as the next man. He sensed Brother Lewis behind him.

"Why don't you unburden your soul? Take the free gift of salvation the Savior has won for you."

The man was a slow learner.

"Pray with me the sinner's prayer that will open the gates of heaven."

Cole turned. The preacher didn't flinch, he'd give him that. "The name's Cole Jasper, preacher. You might'a seen my face on a poster, wanted dead or alive for the murder of Auralee Dubois. I'm ridin' to a hangman's noose in El Paso."

Brother Lewis folded his hands over the black book he held to his chest. "I know who you are. I saw your poster in Santa Fe."

Cole fought his surprise. Brother Lewis had knowingly ridden alone and unarmed, day after day, with a man wanted for murder?

"I told you, I ride where the Lord points me. But Cole Jasper was a name known in these parts long before the charge of murder."

Yeah. They didn't consider Indian slaughter murder, did they.

"And I don't just mean your days as a ranger. It's a name many consider a hero's handle. A name many have counted on, looked to, and blessed. In my opinion, you'll have a hard time convincing folks you're guilty."

"Well, I ain't askin' your opinion."

"What sort of man rides alone to face his crime? How many others would flee the consequences? Either your character is rare or you're innocent of the charges."

Cole's jaw tightened. If folks were thinking that, they'd

look elsewhere for the culprit. His anger rose. "I said I ain't askin'."

"You like to depend on yourself, don't you, Cole? But there will come a time when there's nothing left, when it's too late. Don't wait until the rope is on your neck or a bullet finds you in the dark. Throw yourself now on the mercy of our heavenly Father."

Mercy? Since when did life offer mercy? To his ma? To a little boy with welts on his back thick as a washboard from his own earthly father? Cole felt the anger burning. Was it anger . . . or fear? He'd refused to recognize fear the day he swore never to run again. And he'd refused any heavenly balm that rang as false as his pa's apologies.

He saw the preacher's eyes burning with the intensity Cole had seen long ago in his ma's. She'd wanted him to believe. Even after she slipped into that place where she hardly knew him, there were times when her eyes burned with that same hope.

His chest seized. She'd died not knowing if she'd done her job, maybe most of her not even caring. But somewhere inside, the hope burned. Why would this preacher mirror that now? What was it to him if Cole Jasper burned in hell?

Cole reached for his tobacco. He didn't care that the urges had almost passed. He was going to smoke one now.

Brother Lewis put a hand to his shoulder.

Cole's throat went dry. "God help me."

"Oh, He will, I assure you."

◆◆◆◆◆◆◆

Abbie woke to the cacophony of birdsong. Waterfowl of many sorts dotted the river valley: ducks and geese and cranes. Turtledoves flitted from the branches of box elders and welcomed the day with song. The sun rose sharp in the clear air.

It lightened her heart after the dark and tiresome dreams that had filled her sleep.

She stood and walked to the water's edge. The tracks they'd followed were evident in the sand along the river. But now she saw new tracks beside Whitesock's. Her chest seized, and she searched the ground in sudden concern. There was no sign of struggle. Maybe the second traveler had come later, merely watered at the same spot. But the tracks seemed to match in age.

"What you got?" Will's voice was sleepy, but concerned.

Her troubled thoughts must have shown. "New prints with Cole's."

Will fit his foot inside the boot mark beside the hoofprints. "Do you suppose it's a bounty hunter?"

"I don't know." She stood, refusing to let worry take hold in her heart. She followed the tracks up from the water to a spot near where she and Will had slept, then crossed to the broken ground where the horses had grazed. She picked up Whitesock's marks easily enough and saw the second horse's hoofprints alongside.

She let out a slow breath. "They're traveling together, whoever he is. I guess it doesn't matter now. They'll be in El Paso long before we are."

"We could make better time if we started now. I don't mind chewing hardtack and jerky."

Abbie felt the overwhelming futility. The wonder she'd felt coming upon the river was swallowed today by the endless miles, the continuous strain to keep hopeful. "Yes, you're right. We won't waste time cooking." She packed up their tents and bedding while he watered and saddled the horses, and they struck camp in nearly no time.

Will looked thoughtful as he mounted.

"What is it, Will?"

He shrugged. "Do you suppose he did it?"

The question came from nowhere, but she knew what he

asked. Abbie swung up into Zephyr's saddle. "No, Will. Cole did not murder Auralee Dubois."

"One time when I was in town a couple toughs jumped me, tried to steal the wad I'd been savin' up. Cole was on them like a hawk on a mouse. He thrashed 'em so bad they staggered away, thankful for their lives."

Yes, she'd seen that, too, the night he defended her from the assailants in Dodge. Cole was a powerful man, but that didn't mean he was guilty now. She headed Zephyr away from the wetlands to the flat, level plain of the valley that paralleled the river's course.

Will spoke low. "If he was really mad, I mean like outta control mad . . . he could . . ."

"He didn't kill Auralee. Cole would never raise his hand to a woman."

Will shook his head. "You don't know, Mrs. Farrel. Some women aren't . . . ladies."

Lil Brandon flashed before her, the clear disdain—something near hatred—that had been in her eyes with her rude remark, *"You lost, lady?"* "Even so, Will. You know Cole well enough to know he'd never—" She gripped the saddle horn as Zephyr stumbled and nearly went down.

Will wheeled. "You caught a varmint hole." He jumped down and settled Zephyr, then eased her leg up and examined the fetlock.

Abbie slid down. "Is she hurt?"

"Nothing's broke. Let's see how she does."

Abbie led her gently, but the mare resisted, holding her leg gingerly with her hide twitching and eyes wide. Abbie stopped pulling. There was no point forcing the animal. Even if she rode one of the others, Zephyr would have to carry a load. "I guess we'll have to stay here awhile after all."

Will nodded. "Looks that way."

Abbie prepared biscuits in the Dutch oven and roasted the

duck Will shot from the water. She boiled rice with red peppers she'd purchased in Santa Fe and opened the can of smoked oysters. It reminded her that the extra time in town had allowed Cole to get so far ahead. Would it have mattered? She was too vexed now to wonder.

Abbie kept her thoughts to herself, and Will did the same. He seemed to read her mood as easily as the sky before a storm. Maybe it didn't take much to see that she was in high dudgeon.

She set to exploring the land on foot, noting that there were plant and cactus varieties she'd not seen before. She tried to mentally match them with the illustrations in her botanical manual, but her mind was too restless.

What were the children doing? Were they being cared for with the loving attention she longed to give? Where was Cole? With whom did he ride now? Was he in pain, in danger? There was no way to know, and no way to help. She sighed, shook her head, and returned to camp.

Will was whittling a stick of cottonwood into the shape of a duck. It gave her a pang to recall the knife in Cole's hand, forming the wood into fine creatures. His hands seemed to caress the wood as he worked down to the core, bringing it to life.

The sculpture he'd done of Sirocco had been so lifelike it looked as though the horse would leap from the desk, mane and tail flying. Even Monte had been impressed. She'd often caught him studying it as he mused.

Abbie sighed again as she sat on a stump of driftwood beside Will. "Did Cole show you how to do that?"

Will nodded. "He worked with me some. Cottonwood's not good for carving. Not much good for anything, really. Burns like paper, can't be sawn into lumber, can't hardly make timbers from it at all. It's junk wood, worthless."

Abbie looked along the line of cottonwoods. Leafless, they looked worthless indeed, yet ... here they clung where little else could. How often did the river rip them out and churn them along its bed, though they tenaciously reseeded and grew again? It was easy to miss the importance of things, easy to judge by sight alone.

"Well, it looks as though you'll get a duck out of it."

"Yeah." Will grinned. "I might that."

Thirteen

Abbie woke discouraged. The morning light revealed swelling on the base of Zephyr's fetlock. The mare's hide still quivered at any touch near the injury, and she was skittish. Abbie's spirits sank deeper, discouragement weighing like wet plaster on her soul.

She stood and gentled the horse, then dropped her head to Zephyr's neck. "What are we doing, Will?"

"Seeing it through for Cole."

Seeing it through for Cole. What craziness was that? He'd sent them home. He didn't want them. He had his plan, and she had no place in it. Abbie looked at Will's earnest young face. He didn't want her to give up, even if he wouldn't say it. But she was as close to quitting as she'd ever been.

She fought the weight of her thoughts, the drag on her spirit. "I think we'll have to stay put until the swelling goes down."

"I'm afraid so."

Abbie had hoped keeping the mare quiet one day would be enough. Now it seemed something as innocuous as a gopher hole would set them back and cool the trail even further. She felt Cole pulling away, putting distance between them. It brought an unexpected ache.

She raised her chin defiantly. "I'll make a plaster for Zephyr's leg. Let the others loose to graze on whatever they can find in this desert country." The grasses were probably as hearty as those in Colorado. And they had the river. Cole seemed to be staying relatively close to its course.

"Yes, ma'am." Will nodded. She saw the relief pass over his face. What was Cole to him that he should care so?

After a leisurely breakfast, she washed their clothes in the river and hung them to dry from the cottonwoods. Then she sat across from Will and set about mending the tear in his shirt sleeve. He wore his spare while she worked on his favorite. He had worn the elbows thin, but she had no scraps for patching, so she merely sewed up the tear as best she could.

If Will chafed the delay, he handled it better than she. A wave of annoyance passed through her. She turned her thoughts. "So tell me, Will, did you know Cole was sending money to the ranch?"

He flushed. "Yes, ma'am. That is, I never saw it come, but . . ."

"But everyone knew."

"I guess so."

"Everyone but me."

"I suppose Cole should have asked."

Abbie half smiled. "But I would have refused."

"I reckon he saw it that way. We all thought it would be sort of hard for you to accept. Though I don't know that the men could have stayed otherwise. Especially when Sutler and Fredericks set up headquarters. They were paying top dollar."

Will's confession should have incensed her, but now it just added to the weight. Abbie imagined them all with this unspoken pact. In an odd way it pleased her that Will had been included. He was left to himself too much.

Monte had cared enough to give Will the position in his stables when he was just a ragamuffin boy. But in true aristocratic fashion, Monte hadn't thought much past his physical needs. She'd seen to Will's schooling, but she could do little more for a mostly grown boy. Cole had been the one to fill in the gaps.

Though gruff and sharp with the men under his control, he saw things others missed. He was a man of contrasts. He could rile her to the boiling point one minute, then wash it away with unexpected kindness the next.

Abbie shook her head. She was thankful she'd set herself straight on Cole Jasper. A man like that was more dangerous than any sweet-spoken suitor come calling.

✦✦✦✦✦✦✦

Cole awoke to the cold stillness before the dawn. In the dusky light, the grass beside his face was stiffly outlined, and he smelled the remains of the fire, the dry earth, and something else. His ears sharpened, his breath arrested, and his fingers found the cold metal of his gun.

He sensed more than heard the stealthy step. In one motion he threw back the blanket and drew the gun, rolling to his feet. Brother Lewis startled awake as Cole stepped over him and scoured the half-circular ring of scrub.

"What is it, Cole?"

"Hush." His eyes could scarcely penetrate the lingering darkness. A flicker of movement brought him around, but he could see nothing clearly. A bird flitted to a box-elder branch, then mounted to the sky. A moment later Cole released a slow breath and holstered his gun.

That Comanche had intentionally shown himself the other night. He'd known how it would work on a man's mind. But Cole didn't think he'd imagined this. He'd have to wait for daylight to be sure. If he was right, the sun would show the moccasin prints.

Cole rubbed his hands down the sides of his jeans. That derned Indian was toying with him, wearing him down. He glanced at Brother Lewis. The man looked concerned, but not afraid. Maybe it was time to change that.

Cole squatted beside him. "Why don't you get up now, preacher. I've a mind to tell you my Indian name."

Brother Lewis listened to the story without interrupting. Though the preacher blanched when Cole described his ma's death and the reckless hatred that had followed, Brother Lewis sat without comment until he'd finished. Cole spread his hands. "I reckon that lone Comanche thinks it's his solemn duty to send me on to the Great Spirit. And I reckon he won't mind sendin' you, too."

Brother Lewis nodded slowly. "Yes, that would seem to follow."

"It'd be in your best interest if we part paths now. He's only one and cain't rightly track us both."

"That's true. However, as I told you, I go where the Lord leads, and I've not been given marching orders in any other direction."

Cole cocked his head. "Maybe you ain't heard me. I'm Death Rider to that Indian. He won't pause to shake hands before he slits your throat and takes your hair."

"Yes, I'm familiar with their methods. But have you read . . . heard the story of Jonah?"

Cole stared at him. The man was dense as unshorn wool.

"You see, Jonah heard the Lord's call but went the other way. He thought he knew better than God how to spend his time. But God got his attention, had him thrown into the sea and swallowed by a great fish. After three days in the fish's belly, Jonah thought better of ignoring God's call. I can't do any less."

"I reckon you'd be a sight more useful to God alive than dead. Maybe you ain't heard Him right, either."

"That's possible. I am only human. But He'll honor my intention as long as I mean to hold fast to His will."

Cole scrubbed his bearded jaw with the back of his hand.

"What's to keep you, preacher? You've saved my soul a'ready."

Brother Lewis smiled. "Not I. Jesus Christ."

"So your job is done."

Brother Lewis only smiled broader.

"Look, not to be rude, but what good will you be in a fight? You're not even armed."

"Oh, but I am." Brother Lewis reached for the black Bible. "No enemy in the world can stand against God's Word."

Cole felt a stirring inside. As ridiculous as the man's words appeared, they drew a response deep within him. It showed him just how shallow was his own fledgling belief. Maybe his inability to read made it hard to put his trust in a book. Maybe he was too ignorant of God's ways to fully reckon the change Brother Lewis assured him he'd undergone.

He stood. "Suit yerself, preacher. You've been warned."

"Thank you, Cole."

Cole shook his head. There was no figuring a man like Brother Lewis. Maybe the man had spent time in the belly of something worse than a fish. Or maybe he'd never seen anything to scare him enough to run. Either way, Cole felt shamefully glad for the company.

He pulled a hard biscuit from the saddlebag and tossed it to the preacher. "We'll look for game as we ride. I feel the need of a meal."

"Amen, Brother Cole. Amen."

◆◆◆◆◆◆◆

Abbie swung into the saddle at last. Two days of rest had given Zephyr the chance to heal, and it was time to move on. Ever since rescuing Cole, they'd made dismal progress. His wounds and illness had made traveling more than ten miles a day impossible, though he seemed to have taken off like the wind after leaving them in Santa Fe.

Abbie and Will hadn't done so well. The animals were

weary, no doubt contributing to Zephyr's injury. Now she wasn't certain what the mare could do. But even if they couldn't travel as long as before, it was better than sitting and stewing.

She glanced at her companion, tying up his bedroll. Will was more than eager to strike camp and head out. Thank goodness for that, because she felt cross enough for them both.

They'd hardly left the camp behind when she turned at the sound of hooves. A single rider with a remuda of two chestnut mares and one pack mule cantered over the hill and started down. Abbie felt for the pistol in her pocket and saw Will unstrap his.

There was something familiar about the rider, and she realized he rode like Cole—the same motion, the same easy control, the same set expression. *Sam.* Her heart thumped. It was Samuel Jasper.

Her sudden fury surprised her. Sam Jasper, the one who had led bounty hunters to his own brother. The one who pummeled Cole without once asking for an explanation. The man who got them all into this.

He looked fresh, as well he might with spare horses to trade off riding. He'd likely made fifty miles a day that way. Why hadn't she thought to bring a remuda of her own?

He reined in and stared at her. Was it recognition, or just surprise to see a woman? He tipped his hat. "Ma'am."

She raised her chin. "Good afternoon, Mr. Jasper."

His eyes narrowed, and the skin pulled taut around a small triangular scar on his right cheekbone. "You're the lady from the ranch."

She neither admitted nor denied it.

His look darkened. "Where's Cole?"

"Do you honestly think I would tell you that?" She held steady under his gaze.

He turned and searched the land around.

"He's not with us. He was taken by the bounty hunters you led to him."

"I led . . ." Sam shifted in the saddle. "You mean Crete Marlowe?"

Crete Marlowe. Wasn't that the name . . . the man who sold whiskey to the Comanches, the man Cole had beaten and left to die? Surely . . . Could he have been one of the bounty hunters? Was it another personal vendetta? Did it never end?

Abbie tightened her jaw. "I didn't ask their names when we got Cole away."

"You broke him loose of Crete Marlowe and Jackson Finn?" He tipped his hat back and eyed her.

"If that's who they were."

"Oh, that's who they were, lady. So where is he?"

"I don't know. He went on alone. We've been tracking him since, but he's riding with another now. Maybe the law, maybe someone else looking to make a profit on an innocent man."

The furrow between Sam's brows deepened as he scowled. "What makes you think he's innocent?"

"He's your brother and you ask that?"

Sam rubbed the back of his hand across his jaw, a motion so like Cole's it gave her a pang. He looked out along the broad Rio Grande valley. "Looks like he's headin' to El Paso."

She nodded.

"And you're followin'."

She didn't deign to answer.

He almost smiled. "How far ahead is he?"

"Far enough."

Sam raked his eyes over her, but with curiosity more than insolence. "I ain't caught your name."

"I haven't given it."

He nodded. "I reckon we started out wrong. I'm Samuel Jasper, but you already know that. Are you Cole's woman?"

Abbie felt Will stiffen beside her. "I beg your pardon?"

"I didn't mean that how it sounded. Are you the one who's kept him busy these last years? The widow?"

Her blood pounded in her ears. "I'm Mrs. Farrel, and yes, my husband is deceased."

Sam nodded. "I addressed an envelope he sent off to your foreman. The money he sent."

Abbie felt her ire rise. Did everyone in the country know? "I never asked for Cole's money."

"Don't I know. He said you'd be mad as a peeled rattler if you ever got wind of it."

Abbie turned away. The air carried a dusty film that settled on her cheeks like talcum powder. She was amazed how little the money mattered now. She just wanted to be done with this. "If you'll excuse me, we have a lot of ground to cover yet."

"You sure you want to go on?"

"Why wouldn't I?"

He fixed her with his green eyes, too like Cole's for comfort. "I figure you ought to know Crete Marlowe don't take kindly to meddlin'."

"I don't care a fig about that."

"You might care to know he set your house afire."

Abbie spun in the saddle, her heart caught in her throat.

Sam raised a hand. "Don't fret. Your folks're safe. We got the fire put out."

"We?" Her breath was tight and thin.

"I got word Marlowe was huntin' Cole and went to the ranch to settle things. Got there in time to beat out the flames."

"I don't understand. You led them to him . . . the day you came. Why would . . ."

"I had fire in my blood to take Cole down myself and pound him square, but I never brought Crete alongside."

"But they came right behind you. They . . ." Abbie shook

her head. She didn't know what to think. It was all too com-
plicated, this life of Cole's. How could she help him? How
could she possibly make sense of it? Where was Crete Marlowe
now? What about the children? A cold fear snaked down her
back.

She had to go home. She had to turn back. *What if Crete
returns, what if he . . .* She gripped the reins with white knuckles.
She felt Will's concern and turned to meet his eyes. He
wouldn't tell her one way or the other, but his need was to see
it through for Cole.

*Oh, Lord, help me. I don't know what to do. My heart's divided,
torn in two. My children . . .* She looked back over her shoulder.
Everything cried out to flee for home, to see for herself they
were safe and to keep them that way. But a still, small voice
said *Trust me.*

Trust God? Fear closed around her heart. She couldn't.
How could she? She had lost too much, suffered too much.
*"It's honor, Abbie. Doing what you must, even when your heart is
against it."* She heard the echo of Monte's ardent drawl.

Her breath made a slow escape from her throat. *Oh, Monte.
How can I?* But she had to. She owed Cole a debt of honor. She
owed Cole her life. The edges of her teeth met as she turned
her head back toward El Paso.

Sam brought his horse alongside. There was something in
his expression, some measure of . . . esteem in his eyes. He
slowly tipped his hat. "Seems we're travelin' the same way."

Abbie glanced weakly at Will. By his expression, he was no
more eager to have Sam join them than she, but maybe this
way they could keep an eye on him. If he still meant trouble
to Cole, they'd know it soon enough.

Fourteen

Jenny stared up at the blackened front of the house. Without the tall portico it looked naked, like a face without a nose. The wide stone steps still led to the door, but the pillars lay on the ground beside the house.

She didn't know why the sight frightened her. She had never liked the pillars. They reminded her of Grandmother's house, and she hated Grandmother's house. But somehow, lying on the ground, blackened and peeled, they looked worse, far worse.

Jenny turned away from the house and studied the long field beyond the yard. Her breath made a cloud when she sighed. It was cold and gray, but the snow wouldn't come. It hung in the sky, but wouldn't fall. The dry air had cracked her lip, and she chewed on it. She felt lonelier than she could ever remember.

Pearl would not drive her over to play with Katie. Pearl was afraid to leave the house unguarded, but Jenny knew if the bad men came back they couldn't stop them doing more bad things. Elliot cried in his sleep. The last two nights he'd woken up hollering.

Jenny clutched her hands together. She wished Aunt Abbie would come back, though she didn't tell Elliot so. He cried if she talked about it. She searched the empty range. If Aunt Abbie had found Cole, why didn't she bring him home?

She frowned. She felt little and helpless, like the rabbit dragging its leg she'd seen in the scrub oak. She was sad and scared and angry, and she couldn't do anything about it.

Jenny kicked the dirt. "Why?" Her voice was hoarse, but she didn't know whom she asked.

Pearl came out of the house with her great-uncle Josh. They carried bundles of hers and Elliot's things. Her heart jumped unsteadily. Something was happening. She turned sharply. "Where are we going, Uncle Josh?"

His smile crinkled his eyes, and with his graying beard he looked the perfect grandpa. Elliot's grandpa, not hers. "You're to stay in town awhile."

"In town?" Jenny's stomach tightened. "Where in town?"

"With your Aunt Marcy and Uncle Grant."

The tightness became a knot. She opened her mouth to argue, but Aunt Selena appeared in the doorway, with Elliot grasping her hand.

"Hold on, Selena. That stair's uneven." Uncle Josh deposited the bundles into the buggy and assisted her great-aunt and Elliot.

Jenny fought the angry feelings the knot was making inside her. Had she been bad . . . had she said something wrong? Why were they sending her to Aunt Marcy? Were they punishing her? She turned to Pearl and saw the old woman soften.

"You be fine in town, chile."

She didn't want to be with Aunt Marcy. Especially if it meant being away when Cole came home. Jenny searched the land again as though he would suddenly ride up in time to save her. She felt Uncle Josh's hand on her shoulder.

She mustn't complain. She mustn't . . . He lifted her into the buggy and she waited while he helped Aunt Selena and Elliot up to the seat. Then he squeezed in beside her and took up the reins.

She watched the first tiny snowflakes swirl in the air

around them. The horses bobbed their heads as they pulled, and she watched the flakes catch in their manes. Uncle Josh clicked his tongue and the pair quickened their pace eagerly. Maybe they wanted to hurry out of the coming snow.

Jenny blinked against the thickening flakes, but she was in no hurry. She glanced at Elliot. He seemed quiet, too. He wasn't chattering as he usually did. Aunt Selena looked worried. She probably knew things, things they wouldn't tell her and Elliot. Grown-ups didn't know it was scarier having to guess.

The snow kept on but didn't worsen as they neared the end of town where Uncle Grant and Aunt Marcy lived. She saw the glow in the windows of the house. It had grown dim outside and the windows would have looked welcoming, only she knew better. She was amazed the snow dared to land on the walk without Aunt Marcy's permission.

Jenny drew a shaky breath. "Why can't we stay with you, Uncle Josh?"

"You'd be welcome, but this way you're close to the school." He climbed down and reached for her.

She rested her hands on his shoulders as he lifted her down. "You could bring me in with Tucker."

"It's more practical to have you here."

He meant safer. He thought the bad men wouldn't come to Uncle Grant's house. This was all Pearl's fault. Jenny had heard enough through the door to know Pearl had been worked up to a tizzy after fretting for two days over what to do.

Jenny'd been plenty worked up herself when Zena had hidden her and Elliot in the cellar. After kicking Cole's brother, she had run and run, but it hadn't helped. She still smelled the smoke, still feared the flames. The flames that burned the house . . . and the ones that burned her heart. Those she couldn't outrun.

143

She looked up at the door where her great-aunt Selena waited with Elliot. Aunt Marcy had yet to open the door. Then Jenny would have to face her cousin, Emily Elizabeth, as well.

She liked Emily Elizabeth far less than her adopted cousin Tucker. Tucker could spit through the knothole in the barn wall. Emily Elizabeth tattled when he did. Without realizing, Jenny had pressed close to Uncle Josh on the porch while they waited. He smelled good. Not the same as Cole, but clean and comforting.

Cole didn't wear pomade or wash with the smelly green soap Curtis and Matt used. When she grew up she'd have nothing to do with dandies or men who washed with smelly soap. She'd marry a man like Cole who smelled of horses and the range. Her belly suddenly hurt again.

The door swung open, but it was Uncle Grant who smiled down at her, then tussled Elliot's hair. "Hello there. This is a surprise."

Aunt Selena stepped forward. "Sorry to get you from supper."

"You haven't. We've just finished." Grant motioned them in.

It was warm inside, and the clock chimed prettily on the mantel. Jenny watched it, ignoring the low voice with which her great-uncle asked his favor. She held her breath, hoping Uncle Grant would say they couldn't stay. She snuck a glance.

He looked concerned, but she guessed it was more the news of the burning as they discussed the matter. He was not the one who would refuse them. Maybe Aunt Marcy. Oh yes, if her aunt had her way . . .

Marcy came into the room, all pinched and pouty. She would be pretty if she didn't always look like she'd sucked a chokecherry. But she put on a smile and swept her skirts behind her. "Well, well. Nothing's the matter, is it?"

Jenny scowled when Aunt Marcy fixed her in her gaze as

though any trouble must naturally be her doing. She stood silent as Uncle Grant explained the request. Jenny felt like a young foal at auction, only she wasn't sure anyone truly wanted to bid.

She looked at Elliot. He seemed happy enough. But then, Aunt Marcy liked him. He put up with Emily Elizabeth's airs. Jenny eyed the plump and dimpled four-year-old who pushed in behind her mama. Jenny bristled automatically. She couldn't help it. Emily Elizabeth was prissy and altogether spoiled.

Jenny turned her thoughts back to Aunt Selena, whose next words sealed her fate. "Are you certain you can manage?"

Jenny held her breath, hoping.

But Aunt Marcy smiled her molasses smile. "They'll be fine, I'm sure. Emily Elizabeth sees so little of her cousins, with Abbie always running off somewhere."

"Now, Marcy..." Uncle Grant patted her shoulder. "She hasn't exactly run off."

"Traipsing after some outlaw cowboy isn't what I'd call responsible. Trouble will come of it. Mark my words."

Uncle Josh cleared his throat. "It may not be what we'd have advised, but Abbie did what she thought right."

Aunt Marcy looked like a crow swallowing a worm when she jerked her nose up in the air. "I would never leave Emily Elizabeth in this kind of danger."

"Not even to save me?" Uncle Grant gave her a playful pinch.

Jenny appreciated his joke more than her aunt.

"Hah. As though you'd be mixed up in something so vulgar. Why, I—"

"Well, now." Uncle Josh replaced his hat. "I think we'd best try to beat this storm home."

Aunt Marcy followed his gaze to her and Elliot as though suddenly remembering they were there. Jenny wasn't fooled.

Aunt Marcy meant for them to hear. She wanted them to think badly of Aunt Abbie . . . and of Cole.

Jenny jutted her chin and met her aunt's gaze. "Aunt Abbie isn't afraid to leave us. She knows we can take care of ourselves." She wrapped Elliot's shoulders in her arm.

"There's no need for that." Uncle Grant stroked the top of her head. His eyes were like brown sugar drops. They soothed her temper when she didn't want to be soothed. "We're glad to have you stay with us."

Jenny's heart sank when Aunt Marcy stiffly agreed. It seemed that was the final word. Her aunt turned and fussed with Emily Elizabeth's hair bow. "Now run along and play, sweetheart."

Emily pranced over and took Jenny's hand. "I want to play castle, and I'm the princess."

Jenny resisted making a face. "All right." She used her sweetest tone. When they were alone, she'd announce her role—the wicked, fire-breathing dragon.

Selena climbed into the buggy with the aid of Joshua's strong arm. The snow had mostly stopped, but she agreed with his timely interruption. What was Marcy thinking speaking so carelessly in front of the children? Did her animosity never cease? Nonetheless, Abbie truly was trying the limits this time.

Joshua patted her knee as he joined her on the seat. "What do you think?"

"I wish I could feel settled about all this."

"So do I."

"I've sought the Lord time and again. Perhaps if I understood . . ."

He slapped the reins. "She's following her conscience."

"But to abandon the children . . ."

"Not abandon, Selena. Abbie left them in the care of those she trusts. Pearl and James and Zena . . . and us."

"And now Marcy and Grant."

"They'll do right by them."

Selena knew that. It was only . . . the little ones suffered so. Didn't Abbie realize how they needed her? Jenny's brave front and defense of her aunt had not dispelled the haunted look in her eyes. She was too young to be deserted so regularly, whether or not Josh considered it desertion.

And Elliot . . . Selena sighed. Perhaps it was too much to expect Abbie to settle down like other women. Grant had tried to warn her, but she was always one to throw caution to the wind. The town still buzzed with it all—thanks to Marcy, no doubt—particularly the incredulous news that Abbie had gone with an Indian guide.

Selena half smiled. *Oh, Lord. You do work in mysterious ways.*

"I know that look."

She smiled up at Joshua and saw the answering mirth in his eyes. "I can't help smiling each time I recall poor Ruth Bailey fainting clean away, right in the middle of Marcy's parlor, when she heard Abbie'd gone off with a Comanche."

"Bet that was a sight."

"And Judge Wilson. Do you suppose he'll ever forgive Grant his wayward sister? I suppose it's God's mercy Darla passed on before hearing the news."

"A man's got to choose his in-laws with care. It's a package deal when you set your eye on a pretty face."

Her smile faded, and she sighed again. "I never wished any of this on Abbie. I thought with Monte . . . God's ways are higher than ours, but I wish He hadn't seen fit to take Monte so young."

"God has a plan for our girl. You can rest assured of that."

"But will Abbie stand still long enough to see it?"

"Maybe it's not a standing still sort of plan. I think God's equal to catching her on the run."

Selena laughed softly. "How you do comfort a mother's heart."

Joshua chuckled back. "Would you really want her any different?"

Would I? She'd seen Abbie lose her spark. She'd seen the light go out of her eyes, the spring from her step. She'd watched the bitterness set in and the hollowness follow. Cole's return had seemed such a boon. Then this.

Selena shook her head. "I don't know, Joshua. It seems all these years I've been trying to mold her in ways she just can't go."

"Maybe it's time to see her as she is."

Selena linked her gloved fingers together. "Maybe it is."

"After all, we're none of us perfect."

"No, indeed." *For none is perfect but the Father.* Whose better hands in which to entrust her daughter . . . and the children, and the rest of them—especially Cole.

Fifteen

Not for the first time, Cole wished for a good Sharps rifle. Heck, he'd settle for any rifle. Bringing down an antelope with nothing but a handgun was next to impossible, and once again he had to set his sights on a long-legged jackrabbit. Cole returned to the camp.

Brother Lewis had the fire ready and a spit rigged. He must have expected small game. "I'll skin that. It's the least I can do toward your providing."

Cole held out the rabbit by the feet. He'd spent two bullets catching it, and he'd replace them shortly, once he'd cleaned and oiled the weapon. The shots would have given their location to anyone handy, and he wouldn't be caught with less than a fully serviced gun.

He pulled the chamois from his pack and laid the gun upon it. Beside him, Brother Lewis worked the meat free of the hide. Cole noticed his ability with frank interest. Maybe the preacher hadn't spent all his days with books. "You handle that knife right smartly."

"I've had cause to procure victuals along my trail."

"How? Without a gun, I mean."

Brother Lewis paused in his work and glanced up. "A snare."

"What sort?"

"Whatever I can come up with. Rope and sticks and bait."

Cole raised a skeptical brow. "Sounds chancy at best."

"Can be." Brother Lewis sliced the skin free of the hind leg. "But if the good Lord means me to go hungry, I accept that. More often than not He sends a creature my way for sustenance."

Cole eyed him curiously.

"You see, Cole, God isn't interested in our souls only. He oversees every part of our lives, spiritual and physical. He knows we need to eat, and He provides."

"Well, I'd've preferred an antelope to this here rabbit."

"It's not always what we want that's best. In fact, I've stopped setting expectations whenever possible. What God chooses to send my way is fine by me."

Cole eyed the rabbit as the last of the hide fell free of the knife. The preacher made it sound simple. It was hard to get disappointed if a man had no expectations. He ought to be thankful for the rabbit. Food had been meager enough these last miles, and a man could only go so long.

His stomach rumbled confirmation, and he tried not to think of Abbie's corn bread or biscuits or apple dumplings. Right now, anything she made would be welcome. He refused to envy Will. That only opened up a whole passel of thoughts best not dwelt upon.

Brother Lewis looked up from the spit on which he'd skewered the rabbit. "If you fill my small pot with water, I'll brew some coffee to go with this hare."

Cole nodded, took the blue speckled pot from the preacher's saddlebag, and headed upstream. The water beside their camp was slow, and he walked to where the river narrowed and plunged a scant foot or two. He stooped and dipped the pot into the flow, then flipped the lid down.

The scent came on him like a storm. His senses reeled, and he dropped the pot and spun. His hip felt empty even before he reached, and he pictured the Colt .44 lying on the leather cloth beside Brother Lewis at the fire ring. Cole faced the Comanche bare-handed.

Gray Wolf wore ceremonial paint on his face and chest. His legs were spread and bent, his arms parted, his knife gripped in one hand. Cole eyed its razor edge. That the knife wasn't already lodged in his back was some tribute to the brave. Likely he meant this to be a contest, giving his deed greater honor.

Gray Wolf wove to one side and stepped to the other. Cole followed the motion, imitating the crouch, but kept his eyes on the knife. The Indian thrust, and Cole dove, rolled, and slipped his own knife from his boot. That evened the odds a bit. Gray Wolf's eyes narrowed but showed no surprise.

They circled. Cole feinted left and swung right with the knife. Gray Wolf dodged, then returned the swipe. They were fairly matched. Cole had an edge on the Indian in reach, but his shoulder wound would cost him if they went hand to hand.

Cole dodged a thrust, but Gray Wolf swung out with his leg, and it caught the back of Cole's knee. At the same time, the tip of the Indian's blade cut his side. Cole hissed sharply at the pain, then forced a swipe at Gray Wolf's chest. The brave avoided him easily, but Cole had backed him off and regained his footing.

From the corner of his eye, Cole saw the foliage move. Brother Lewis crouched in the reeds, his Bible clutched to his chest. Cole frowned. If the man had to grab something, why couldn't it have been the gun?

Gray Wolf's knife sliced his shirt sleeve and drew blood. Cole made a poor jump and lost his balance. He went down and rolled as the brave dove and gouged for his eyes with clawed fingers. Cole kicked Gray Wolf in the side with his boot, but the Indian gained his feet and spat.

"The white dung fights like a woman."

"I have no quarrel with you, Gray Wolf. What's past is past."

"My people are dead."

"So are mine."

Gray Wolf lunged, slamming his head into Cole's belly and knocking him backward. Cole fell with the Indian on top. The brave's teeth bit into his collarbone while he gripped Cole's wrist and smashed his arm to the ground. His knife flew free and lay in the dirt.

Cole grasped Gray Wolf's arm as the Indian blade swung toward his throat. His left arm was perilously weak, but he caught hold with his right hand as well and forced the blade back. He brought his knee up with all the force he could muster and shoved the Indian aside.

Gray Wolf sprang to his feet and kicked dirt in Cole's eyes, then jabbed with the blade. Cole rolled. His breath came hard and angry. He was bleeding and his shoulder burned like fire. He saw Gray Wolf's guard drop and shot a right hook to his jaw.

The brave staggered back, and Cole dove for his knife. Gray Wolf sprang like a cat, but his thrust went wide and his knife plunged into the ground. Cole pressed his knee to Gray Wolf's wrist as he fought to free the blade. He felt the bones shift and delivered a punch to the brave's face.

Blood spurted from Gray Wolf's nose, and he seized Cole's arm and yanked him over. Again he tugged his knife, and it came free. Cole kicked it from his hand and it flew, glistening, end over end toward the water. Gray Wolf lunged after it, and Cole threw himself onto the brave's back.

They splashed down together and rolled, sputtering to their feet. Gray Wolf's knife sank beneath the muddied current. Cole tossed his to the shore near Brother Lewis. "Hand to hand, Gray Wolf. Your strength to mine."

"You have no strength. You are wounded."

"That's my misfortune." Cole's blood was up, and no words

from this Comanche were going to cheat him of this scrap. "Come on!"

Gray Wolf's chest heaved with his heavy breaths. He narrowed his eyes like a stoat. "This day you will die."

Cole answered in Comanche. "Then it is a good day to die." The Indian saying registered in Gray Wolf's expression. It seemed to feed him, and he leaped without warning.

Cole caught the full force of the man's weight on his left shoulder and went down. Gray Wolf pressed his head beneath the water. Straining for breath, Cole thrashed free and used the brave's own power to plunge him into the water. His shoulder throbbed and the arm felt numb as he yanked Gray Wolf up. He concentrated his strength and smashed his fist into the brave's right temple.

Gray Wolf went limp, stunned, and his open eyes rolled back. Cole gripped him by the hair and held the back of his head to the surface of the water. When Gray Wolf's senses returned, Cole held him there firmly. "If I were Death Rider, I'd have drowned you like a dog. Because I'm not, and because of your service to Abbie, I let you live. Our score is settled." Cole let him go.

Gray Wolf caught himself from sinking into the water. His black hair was carried by the current as he held himself up by his elbows and returned Cole's stare. Cole saw the vein pulse in his neck and waited. He knew the Comanche temperament well enough not to turn his back.

Gray Wolf shook his head as though just now coming to. He pressed his hand to his temple. "Death Rider has fist like a bear."

Cole lurched to his feet. The current tugged at his calves. He waited while Gray Wolf scrambled up. "Maybe that's a more fittin' name to wear now." He roughly translated "fist like a bear" to Comanche.

Gray Wolf eyed him. "You speak the tongue of my people.

153

Yet you return to the land of death."

Cole bent and pulled his hat from the shallows. "Is that your concern? You worried that I've come to bring harm to your people?"

"My people are no more."

"Oh, there are Comanches yet. Plenty of 'em. Just none you want to run with."

Gray Wolf scowled.

"I reckon you were a renegade before your clan was broken up. You're a man who rides alone. I recognize it." Just as Brother Lewis had recognized it in him. Cole glanced toward the bushes. Brother Lewis was on his feet now.

Gray Wolf drew himself up. "My people were strong, their ways good, until the white man came to their land."

"I won't argue that, though I know the Comanche ways. I've set aside my fight." He waited. This was the man who had saved Abbie's life, who had helped to save his, unknowingly. Perhaps Gray Wolf's need to avenge was understandable. But Cole wanted no more of it.

Gray Wolf nodded slowly. "I will contend no more with Fist Like a Bear."

Cole felt his tension ease. Gray Wolf's use of his new name signified more than it would to a white man. In the Comanche's eyes, he was still a fighter, but perhaps no longer a killer. Cole clasped his hands in front of his body with the back of his left hand down. After a moment, Gray Wolf returned the hand sign for peace. At least for a time, the brave would honor it.

Gray Wolf turned and strode to the gelding with the Lucky Star brand. Cole noted the slitted ears and the overall gaunt and shaggy condition of the animal. One day he'd ask Abbie how Gray Wolf came by the horse. If he ever had the chance.

The brave mounted and held his head erect. He drew a breath and spoke in Comanche. "Perhaps tomorrow will be a good day to die." He wheeled the horse and pressed with his knees.

When the dust settled, Cole turned to Brother Lewis. "I'm not certain I'd choose you for my corner, preacher. That was a little touch and go. Did it ever occur to you I might need help?"

"From the very start."

"You just didn't mean to give it?"

"Indeed I did."

Cole felt his side where the shirt clung to congealed blood. "My mistake. I must've missed it."

"You may not have heard, but God did. I beseeched Him on your behalf the entire time you fought. I'm certain He gave you strength."

Cole swallowed his laugh, then pictured Gray Wolf, dazed, in his hands. In truth, the power of that punch hadn't seemed to be his own. He eyed Brother Lewis sharply, then bent, dug the coffeepot from the shallows, and refilled it. That rabbit must be just about cooked.

◆◆◆◆◆◆◆

Abbie drew the canteen from the water and twisted the lid tightly. She raised her face and let the slight breeze cool her brow. They had dropped down out of the high country, and the approach of the southern climate was evident.

All along the river valley they'd seen Indian pueblos rising like queer formations of the earth itself. Dwarf corn had grown in patches of land trenched with ditches to bring the river to the roots. Though the fields were harvested of their bounty, she could see they'd been productive. The Pueblo Indians had watched but not harassed them as they passed. They seemed a garrulous, uncomplicated people.

At Sam's direction, they had stopped briefly in Albuquerque, but skirted Socorro. Its reputation was such that he wouldn't risk it. The place attracted the worst sort of Texas cattleman and too many others looking to live by the end of a gun.

He'd said bringing her there would be like holding a beefsteak before a pack of wolves, and to Abbie's dismay, she'd blushed furiously. He was as incorrigible as Cole in his understated sort of way. She glanced up as he joined her now at the river's edge.

In physical characteristics, he was more like Cole than she'd noticed when he first descended on the ranch. As they'd ridden, she'd noted features and expressions, intonations and motions that all betrayed their kinship. Were they close?

Cole talked as though they had been, but now . . . was Sam still bent on revenge? And was he as dogged in that as Cole could be? Did revenge run in their blood? Was it bred in this rough, desolate country where mile spread upon mile without end?

She shook away the gloomy thoughts. Whatever Sam had in mind, she'd have something to say about it. Just as she would concerning Cole's intentions, which he had left unspoken when he deserted them. She frowned and dipped the last canteen into the river.

Sam nodded her way. "Fill everything we have. In a few miles our route will leave the river."

She was instantly suspicious. "Why?"

"Well, you see, this road we've been on is the *Camino Real*. Been here since the Spaniards came lookin' for gold. Runs all the way from El Paso to Santa Fe. But along here the river changes course and runs through some wicked arroyos, so most travelers keep to the old bed."

"For how long?"

"Some ninety miles."

"Ninety miles! That's days without fresh water."

"There are a couple of springs, though one is frequently

run dry. The other's full of arsenic, but so many have drunk from it in desperation that the stretch of road's known as *Jornado del Muerto*. The journey of death."

Journey of death. Abbie glanced uncomfortably at Will. And they were following Sam into it. How Sam had assumed leadership of their small band, she wasn't sure. Like Cole, he had simply fit the role.

"Will we have enough water for us and the horses?"

Sam shrugged. "We'll have to go lightly. We don't have the blistering heat this time of year, but it's still desert. Whether there's water at the spring depends on how many have used it before us. There's enough traffic on this road to deplete it, and plenty who've counted on it are bleaching their bones now."

Will shouldered past to face Sam. "Did Cole go this way?"

"I reckon so."

"You don't know?" Will's tone was almost belligerent.

"The trail we're trackin' has been chancy ever since we hit the road. But it don't matter. Either way gets you where he's goin'. This way's just shorter and easier."

"It doesn't sound easy with all this talk about bones and arsenic."

Abbie touched Will's arm to quiet him. "I think we need to trust Mr. Jasper here, Will. It's his risk, too."

"Not if he means to get himself through and leave us to die of thirst."

Abbie saw surprise and offense color Sam's expression.

If Will saw, it didn't keep him from continuing. "How do we know you haven't joined up to keep us from reaching Cole?"

Sam held his ground and wisely kept his cool under Will's insult. Abbie did not intervene. Sam could answer for himself. "You can travel on yourselves if you think you can get through better without me."

"And have you at our backs?"

Now Sam did bristle. "I'm neither a sneak nor a backstabber. You best learn to govern your tongue, son, or a better man might govern it for you."

"If you think . . ."

"Will." Abbie caught his arm. "We're all on this road together. We may as well see it through to the end."

Sam turned his attention to her. "It's plain foolishness your comin' this way at all. The road only gets worse. There's bandits and ruffians and all manner of things a lady don't want to meet in the night."

"Well, unless you know yet another way, I'm afraid we'll have to chance it. I intend to reach El Paso and see Cole freed."

"You'll reach El Paso, maybe. As for the rest, who can say."

"God will stand by a just man."

Sam frowned. "Depends how you define justice, lady."

Abbie raised her chin but refused to argue. "Now, then, Mr. Jasper, are we equipped to proceed?"

"Oh yes, ma'am. I'm certain the very sands will part for your righteous journey. I just hope you don't find your trust misplaced and call down the wrath of God on us all."

◆◆◆◆◆◆◆

Abbie, Sam, and Will alternated riding the remuda horses with their own. Sam was wise to have brought them, as it eased the burden of the beasts through this desolate stretch. In places, the river had flooded, then receded, leaving stagnant alkaline water that bred hosts of mosquitoes. Abbie slapped at their stinging bites but kept her complaints to herself.

She watched a striped water snake slither into the quagmire to her right. On either side of the stranded pool the land was white with poison and cracked. There was nothing to recommend the place at all, nothing but the fact that it led toward the goal.

Her righteous fury had burned to ashes inside her. Her

trust in Cole was nearly as sapped. She glanced at Will. Funny how he'd taken up the cause as she'd felt her own wane. Now she kept on because it was all she could do. They were wrapped up in this to the end, but somewhere along the way she'd lost heart.

Sam rode in surly silence. What strange twist of fate had brought him to them? Or had he merely followed a path known to both him and Cole and found them upon it? Abbie's throat was thick with thirst, and she forced her thoughts away from cold, clear mountain streams.

Two days of travel had nearly emptied their canteens. Every swallow now was precious, not to be taken without need. Desire had no place in survival. Her voice rasped even when she cleared the dust from her throat.

Sam glanced her way. There was concern in his eyes, but he didn't voice it. If they spoke of their thirst it would be worse. He shifted in the saddle. "Not long on past that bend is the spring. With any luck it'll be more than mud."

"I don't depend on luck, Mr. Jasper."

He gave his smile a quirk. "Then I hope you brought your staff."

Abbie turned away. His mockery would not divert her, though her prayers had dried up like the land around them. The horses plodded on. They rode and rode but the land never changed. Distance made sport of progress.

She was scarcely aware of the motion any longer. Her legs and backside were numb, her mind torpid. The landscape became a blur of bland desolation. The sky seemed to merge with it. Part of her was aware of falling, the rest just didn't care.

Abbie tasted the dust in her mouth as she settled into a heap. Then even that was gone until she felt the metal pressed to her lips, the grip of a hand behind her head. She shook away the clouds and drank. The water coursed down her throat, not a single meager swallow, but a flow, gulp after gulp of paradise.

She opened her eyes. For an instant Sam's green-eyed stare was Cole's. Then her mind corrected. He drew the canteen from her lips, but gently. She looked from him to Will, standing just behind, then back to Sam.

"It's all right, Mrs. Farrel. There's water in the spring."

She pushed herself up to her elbows, then sat.

Sam steadied her, then removed his hand. "We'll rest here, though we'll have to be on guard. Anyone on this road will head for this spot. And out here the six-shooter is god."

Abbie half smiled. "Even here, Mr. Jasper, there's only one God."

Sam nodded toward the water filling a shallow pool. "You may be right, ma'am. But I'll keep watch nonetheless."

Abbie curled into the shade of a ragged cut in the land. The water had revived her, but still her thoughts were dull. How much longer could she go? Surely they must be close to the end. "How much farther, Mr. Jasper?"

He settled cross-legged on the ground a short distance from her. His rifle lay across his thighs. "Should reach the river again by noon tomorrow. We'll be nearer the Organ and Franklin Mountains. Two days' journey between them and the river brings us into El Paso."

His voice gruffed as though the thought of reaching the town pained or angered him. Abbie felt a flutter inside, as well. Her thoughts had been so focused on completing the journey, she'd not yet figured her plans once she got there. Much would depend on how she found Cole.

A flicker of fear stirred inside her. What if they came too late? She straightened. "I'm quite recovered now. We should continue."

Sam gave her a slow look down. "I'm glad to hear that. But we'll let the horses drink their fill and rest a bit. There's a dry stretch yet to cover."

She felt like a schoolgirl who'd just received a dressing

down. Who was Samuel Jasper to speak to her so? It must run in the Jasper blood. Cole, Sam—they both thought a good deal too much of themselves. Abbie turned away without a word, though her heart seethed at the low chuckle she was certain she heard.

Sixteen

El Paso-Juarez looked much the same to Cole in the slanting evening rays—low, flat-roofed, plastered adobes with arched doorways and square columned galleries across the fronts. The smell of dust and refuse and even the tang of the river filled the air.

He heard the Ysleta Mission bell some ten miles away and imagined the padres making their silent way through the arched adobe passage. Now theirs was a life free from trouble. But no—hadn't two of them been killed several years ago, when Mexican bandits came after a wounded man they'd sheltered?

The town had been outraged, but that was no help to the two who were buried. Maybe there was no escaping the evil of the world. Maybe it just swept a man up, whether he liked it or not.

Though he looked straight ahead, Cole sensed Brother Lewis's calm presence beside him. He didn't feel much different since praying with the preacher or taking the river dunk that the man set such store by, but it had stopped the sermons some. Strange, but with his innards twisting the way they were, he wouldn't have minded a word or two now.

Brother Lewis straightened in the saddle as though reading his thoughts. "Remember, Cole, in this world you will have tribulation. But be of good cheer, for the One who holds your soul has overcome the world."

Cole didn't answer, but the words had a settling effect. He'd just ride it out. Soon as he walked into the jail, it was out of his hands anyway. They passed the first buildings.

From the corners of his eyes, he saw faces turned his way, folks pausing in their business to watch him pass. One short fella held his hat to his chest, funeral-like. Ignacio Perez, the mule skinner who treated his animals like children and trusted everyone. He'd been the butt of too many jokes, and Cole had taken him under his wing a number of times.

At the end of the block, a woman stared with grief in her face. Cole recognized Sonja Bjork, the Swede's widow. Cole had pulled her young'un from a well. His jaw tightened. He didn't want to put names to the faces, though he likely knew most everyone on the street.

Cole kept his focus at the end of the street. Already a small crowd gathered at the jail's door. Texas Ranger Captain Henry Gates stood at the front. Cole swung down from the saddle and handed Brother Lewis the reins. "Would you find some way to return this horse to the Lucky Star in Rocky Bluffs, Colorado?"

The preacher nodded.

Cole turned and faced Captain Gates. "I hear you got paper on me that says I'm wanted for murder."

The ranger cocked his jaw to the side and nodded. "Got an eyewitness, Cole."

Cole drew a slow breath. So he was right. It must've been Sam if someone thought they saw him do it. The crowd parted as Cole stepped forward and held out his hands.

Gates cuffed him. "I'll question you inside." He kept his face expressionless, but Cole saw something soft in his eyes. Cole couldn't let regret and old times keep Captain Gates from carrying out his duty. Not when that duty kept Sam safe.

They went inside the square, stone building. Two Mexican *caballeros* argued in the center cell. Cole understood most of the words, though they spoke fast in their anger. They broke off to watch darkly as Gates motioned him to a chair. Cole sat.

Gates fixed him in his sights with one brow lowered. "I had no choice but to follow through on the testimony of the witness. You know the law, Cole. But it does me no pleasure to bring in one I served with."

Cole was silent.

" 'Course, it's her word against yours. If you have an alibi that can stand up, prove her wrong—you're a free man. Where were you the night of August ninth?"

Cole wet his throat with a swallow. "I was with Auralee Dubois."

The ranger stood and leaned a hand on Cole's chair. "And what happened?"

Cole stared down at the cold metal cuffs on the skin of his wrists. The truth, and they'd be removed. The truth, and he could go back to Abbie. He drew a slow breath and answered. "We fought. You figure out the rest."

Gates swore and circled his desk. "Give me something, Cole. The last thing I want to do is hang you for the death of a—"

"Lady?"

"That's not the word I would choose to describe Auralee Dubois."

"Don't matter."

Gates lowered his face near Cole's. "Are you tellin' me you did it?"

Cole pictured Sam's eyes aflame with rage and ... gut wrenching grief. "You got your witness." It came out a dry croak, all the more convincing. His thoughts went back to the night he left El Paso, to Auralee's whisper in his ear, begging—or as close as she'd come to it—for him to come up.

He'd thought she was in trouble, needing something, but she'd tried every wile in her bag once she had him alone. She'd wrapped him in her arms and pressed her body close, offering more than what she did for a living. Offering her heart—something she never included in the price.

Cole was probably the only man in town who hadn't paid to prove his love or his lust. Was it her need to conquer him, too, that made her eyes so bright, made her lips like coals against his? He still felt her slap when he'd pulled away.

He should have walked out then, should never have tried to explain, should have left his love for Abbie buried deep in his heart where it belonged. But no, he'd dragged it out, confessed it to a woman who would never understand unreturned devotion. She'd gone cold like the edge of a knife, dug her nails into the back of his neck and tried to force a response he couldn't withstand.

But he'd come to his senses and got clear. Had Sam known? Had she taken delight in tormenting Sam with her version of their moments alone? Had she pushed Sam too far? Pushed him to murder? If any woman could bring a man to murder, it was Auralee Dubois.

Gates turned from the window where he'd been waiting for a response. He was a good man, straight and mostly square. He wasn't above a little rowdy blowing of steam, but he kept control. They'd had some good times.

Cole cleared his throat. "I reckon you'd better choose me a cell."

Gates expelled his breath in an exasperated whistle. "This is no different than the Comanches, Cole. That woman had men tearing each other's throats out. I figure you did the town a favor."

"But that ain't the law." Cole felt his pocket. No bulge of tobacco pouch, no crinkle of paper. He'd tossed them away after praying with the preacher. Kind of a private acknowledgment of his leaving the old self. *Sheez.*

"Listen to me, Cole. Most of the folks out there owe you a debt of gratitude for one thing or another. They want you to walk out of here. They'll buy you a drink, slap your back, and welcome you home." He leaned his head to Cole's ear. "Give me something that will satisfy the law, and you can walk away."

Cole sat silent. *Walk away.* He'd ride to the Lucky Star and explain it all to Abbie. He'd tell her how he felt, how much he cared, how he loved and needed her. He looked into the ranger's face, his friend, a man he respected. Gates wanted that word, his testimony against that of the witness.

Cole again dropped his gaze to his shackled hands. Gates was itching to unlock them. This was sure different than the treatment he'd had from Crete Marlowe and Jackson Finn. And a whole lot harder to take.

Where were Marlowe and Finn now? He felt a grim satisfaction at having cheated them out of the bounty reward. But he reckoned they'd be along to see him hang. At least Abbie would not.

◆◆◆◆◆◆◆

Abbie saw El Paso with the afternoon light beating on the white-plastered adobe walls. Most of the town lay on the far bank of the Rio Grande, or the Rio Bravo, as it was called from the part of town across the river. El Paso del Norte, or Juarez Chihuahua on the Mexican side, was connected by a ferry at the crossroads.

Nearer at hand, a U.S. mail coach drawn by six mules clogged Santa Fe Street while men and women in colorful woven shawls and ponchos pressed through beside it. They had an air of dogged independence and camaraderie that stung her heart. These were the people who would condemn Cole.

Abbie studied the flat, rounded features, the gaunt faces, the smiling, the bronze, the proud aquiline countenances. This conglomeration of peoples were those who had called for justice against Cole. Yet they seemed oblivious, busy with the details of their daily lives.

Abbie shivered. A few cottonwoods stood bare in the cold, dry air, casting small inkblot shadows at the base of their trunks. In two weeks it would be Christmas. The children would spend it without her. She was too weary to hurt.

Under Sam's direction, they'd made it in the time he'd said. She glanced his way. He'd grown silent and introspective as they neared the town. Even Will's enthusiasm failed to provoke a response.

Abbie looked back over the town. There were the usual taverns, blacksmith, livery, and corrals. Her gaze rested briefly on a sign marked *El Paso Sentinel*, leaning against a wall, but its use as a newspaper office like Pa's must be past. She sighed. They had reached their destination. But what could she do now? She felt staggered by the helplessness, lost in the miles, and so, so tired.

"I reckon you'll go straight to the jail?" Sam's voice startled her.

"The jail?"

"You said Cole meant to turn himself in."

"Well, I . . . I'd hoped he'd clear himself." She still clung to it, however foolishly.

"Maybe he did. If you'd rather go to the hotel, I can ask around."

"No." Abbie was suddenly certain she'd find Cole behind bars. She searched the street and found the jail at the end. Raising her chin, she determined to let Cole Jasper know exactly what she thought of his predicament.

She tapped her heels to Zephyr's sides and pulled ahead of Will and Sam. She would do this alone, and she'd do it before any renegade emotions kept her from speaking her mind. She swung down, dust billowing from her skirts. She must look a sight, but she didn't care.

She stepped onto the creaky boardwalk and reached for the latch, but the door swung open, and the stocky man who opened it stopped short. He wore a cropped beard and mustache, mostly gray, but the hair that hung to his shoulders was brown beneath the gray Stetson he hastily removed.

"Afternoon, ma'am. I'm Captain Henry Gates. Can I help you?"

"I'm looking for Cole Jasper." She dared to hope he'd tell her Cole was gone.

Instead he eyed her with fresh interest. "Well, ma'am, he's inside, but I hesitate to let you in there."

"I assure you it's nothing I can't handle."

Captain Gates scratched the side of his beard. "I dunno . . ."

"May I ask on what evidence you're holding Cole?"

"On the testimony of an eyewitness, and his own failure to discount her."

Abbie raised her brows. "The witness is a lady?"

"Well . . . uh . . ."

"I see." Abbie frowned. Good heavens. With how many saloon girls was Cole involved? "If you'll permit me, Captain Gates, I've come a long way. I want a wash and a good meal. But first I want to see Cole."

"Yes, ma'am." He pushed open the door.

Abbie stepped into the stale air of the jail. She saw the three cells along the back. Cole sat in the one on the left with his head on his palms. He had several days growth of beard and looked as though he hadn't slept in as many nights. She stepped past the captain, and Cole looked up.

She watched surprise, then dismay, then fury pass over his features. It was fury that settled in his eyes. She felt a surge of her own and stepped up to the bars. A catcall and a string of

Spanish vulgarities came from the next cell, but she didn't look. She kept her eyes on Cole.

He stood slowly and jammed his thumbs into his belt. "Abbie, what in the blazes are you doin' here?"

She drew herself up. "I might ask you the same."

He growled something that might have been a word she didn't care to hear.

"Why won't you tell the ranger what you told me? You didn't kill Auralee."

"This ain't your business. I told you to go home." His words were as sharp as the report of a gun.

Oh, he'd sent her home all right. But now he'd see she had a mind of her own. "You didn't really expect me to go, did you?"

"Call me a fool, but yes, I did."

Why did it hurt that he believed she would leave him to face this alone? He would never have left her in trouble. Didn't he realize she owed him the same? "As you can see, I chose to ignore your stone arrow, though I assure you its meaning was clear."

He scowled. "You and Will crossed all that territory alone?"

"And Sam."

His jaw went slack. "Sam's here? In town?"

She turned to the captain. "Cole Jasper did not kill Auralee Dubois." She heard Cole's sharp breath.

"Is that right, Cole?" Gates seemed eager to believe her. Abbie hadn't expected his support.

Cole didn't answer, and she glanced his way. His expression was close to what she'd seen the moment after she'd slapped him on the prairie. He narrowed his eyes and looked past her to the captain. "I reckon you'd better stick with your witness. Mrs. Farrel has a vested interest. She needs me to run her ranch, and she'll say anything to get what she wants."

Abbie felt as though he'd slapped her right back. He made

her sound petty and self-serving, after all she'd been through to . . . Her spine stiffened. "May I see you outside, Captain Gates?"

"Yes, ma'am." He sent Cole a penetrating look, then escorted her out.

Abbie settled her thoughts, determined to speak her mind without letting Cole's insult fester. "It is true that Cole is in charge of my ranch in Colorado. It was from there the bounty hunters took him, quite viciously, I might add."

"Bounty hunters?"

"Crete Marlowe was one of them. We . . ."

"But Cole came in alone, ma'am. Leastwise he came with a preacher, not a bounty man."

Abbie filed that, but it was unimportant at the moment. "We relieved Crete and his partner of their quarry."

His eyes widened, then narrowed. "Who's we?" he asked like a lawman.

"My friend, myself, and a Comanche brave named Gray Wolf."

He shook his head. "You'll forgive me, ma'am, if I don't believe you. No Comanche would come in sight of Cole Jasper without slitting his throat."

"When Gray Wolf realized it was Death Rider he'd rescued, he was more than ready with his knife."

That registered truth to the ranger. Cole's name must be known to him. "But?"

She knew this next would sound incredible, but she prayed he would believe her. "Gray Wolf and I . . . have an understanding. We've both had occasion to save the other's life. He refused to ride farther with us, but, on the strength of our pact, he let Cole live."

The captain looked as though she'd just told him the biggest fish story of his life. No doubt he heard plenty in his line of work. He pulled a handkerchief from his pocket, turned and blew briefly, then turned back. "Well, ma'am, I don't rightly know what to say."

"Cole is not guilty."

"Maybe he is, maybe he's not. I know Cole Jasper well enough to say he's actin' mighty queer. Another man in his boots would be sayin' anything to get out of there. Cole, well, he's settlin' in for the trial, and by law there's got to be one."

"When?"

"Whenever Judge McFee comes through."

"Is there nothing you can do?"

"It's my job to uphold the law. Until he's cleared . . ."

Abbie clenched her hands at her sides. "This witness . . . where can I find her?"

"You can't. She's one of Pablo's gals. He won't let a lady near. Thinks you'll missionize him out of business. His place is off limits to womenfolk."

"What place is that, Captain Gates?"

"The Paloma Blanca." He pointed down the dusty street.

"And her name?"

"Goes by Birdie."

"Thank you." Abbie looked at the two-story, flat-roofed adobe. So Auralee had worked at the Paloma Blanca. The white dove. What a misnomer. How many times had Cole taken her in his arms inside those walls? Had he whispered words of love? No, Cole wouldn't say it unless he meant it. But he'd no doubt shown it.

A dull ache started in her temples. She wanted to go home to Elliot, to Jenny, to her memories of Monte, a man who would never have entered a brothel. A man of honor so solid and deep it was unshakable. *Oh, Monte.* How could she have thought what she felt in Cole's arms might be love?

It was nothing more than the devil's trap, the same that

had ensnared men and women since the start of time. Her heart ached with loneliness, her body with longing, and she'd allowed herself to imagine Cole a hero. She closed her eyes. No more.

Seventeen

Abbie started for the white, two-story building with the square, columned porch. The sign read *Central Hotel*. Zephyr and the other horses were tethered outside, along with Sam's pack mule, as yet still burdened. She crossed over and went inside. Will and Sam were not about, but they had registered a room for her and left a key at the desk. She went up.

She ached with weariness and frustration as she stripped and stepped into the steaming tub. Soaking in the bath, she pondered her options. She could go home and leave Cole to handle this as he so clearly wanted, or she could stay and help, though how, she wasn't sure. Either way, when this was over, she and Cole Jasper would part paths. Her heart had nearly betrayed her. Almost . . . she had almost forgotten Monte . . . and her grief.

She looked up at the tap on her door. "Yes?"

"Mrs. Farrel?" It was Sam. "I was wondering if you'd join me for a meal."

She sloshed as she straightened in surprise. "Where's Will?"

Sam cleared his throat. "He took the horses to the livery, and I reckon he's lookin' around town."

Suddenly she had an idea. Maybe Will could get to Birdie. She felt a twinge at sending someone as young and impressionable as Will into a saloon of that sort. But he was as committed as she to getting Cole free. If they could just keep Sam from interfering . . .

"Thank you, Mr. Jasper. I'd like that, but first I need to speak with Will. Can you find him while I finish here?"

"A'right. We'll meet you downstairs."

She had already hung her dress to straighten the wrinkles. It hadn't had time to do much good, but she pulled it on anyway and brushed her hair until the curls shone. She studied herself in the mirror. She should be distracting enough to keep Sam's thoughts from Will.

Abbie felt a pang of conscience. Surely he was still grieving Auralee. Who was she to think . . . Good Lord, this was all so confusing. Why did Cole have to fraternize with trouble until he had everyone, including his own brother, out to get him?

She shook her head and went out. Sam and Will waited at the foot of the stairs. She didn't miss Sam's look of appreciation, though it quickly passed.

"May I speak with you a moment, Will?"

Sam tipped his hat. "I'll find us a table." He hesitated. "For two or three?"

"Two." Abbie gave him a smile she hoped was innocent enough, then tugged Will's arm. "I need you to find someone. She's the witness who claims she saw Cole. Her name is Birdie, and she's at the Paloma Blanca."

He nodded solemnly, and she was sure he knew the place. After all, he was no longer the boy she tended to think him.

"I wouldn't ask this, but . . ."

"I want to help Cole."

"See if you can arrange for me to meet her . . . somewhere." She prayed it wouldn't be at the saloon where Cole . . .

Will nodded again, and Abbie squeezed his arm, then joined Sam. He stood and held her chair. Again she saw a flicker in his eyes, but it was mixed with pain. Being back in El Paso had surely opened his wounds. He looked as though he regretted asking her to share his meal.

She sat quietly, uncertain how to handle herself. The wait-ress brought the food he'd ordered for both of them, and she looked down at the fried steak and mashed potatoes covered with slightly congealed gravy. Sam cleared his throat and said the last thing she expected. "Would you like to pray?"

She barely kept herself from gaping.

He motioned to the table. "Bless the food?"

Abbie understood now, but still his words burned in her spirit. How long had it been since she'd really prayed and turned this whole situation over to God? And how was it this rough brother of Cole's, bent on revenge, was the one to re-mind her?

She bowed her head. "Father, we thank you for this food. Bless it to our use and guide our steps." *And help me know what to do.*

Sam mumbled his amen and took up his fork. Abbie looked at the crispy fried steak, remembering the meal she and Cole had shared in Dodge the night he told her of his promise to Monte. The night she feared he had let Monte die, maybe even caused it. The night he saved her from her assailants.

"They were closin' the kitchen down till supper. I took a chance you wouldn't mind this choice."

Abbie glanced up and forced a smile, though the hard knot of tears in her throat made it difficult. Would she ever under-stand Cole Jasper? "I like it fine." And she took a tasteless bite to prove it.

"Mind my askin' something personal?"

"I can't say until I've heard it." Her voice came a little more naturally.

"Are you in love with my brother?"

It stabbed to her quick. *No. Yes.* She couldn't be. "Why is that your concern?"

"It ain't, only . . . if you are, I want to apologize."

"For?"

"Messin' things up."

"I would think you'd consider that fair turnabout." Abbie watched the scar beneath Sam's eye stretch and compress as he spoke.

"Maybe for Cole. But it ain't right you should be hurt."

She sighed. "I've grown accustomed to hurt."

"That ain't somethin' a lady should ever say. Not if things are right with the world."

Abbie wondered how Sam had handled his mother's death. Cole hadn't mentioned any but his own need for vengeance. "But things are not right with the world, are they, Sam?"

He startled at the use of his given name but didn't gainsay her. "I reckon not."

"Why do you think Cole killed Auralee?"

"Birdie says so, and I . . . I saw him go up."

"And after? Did you see him come out?"

"No. I left as soon as he went with her. I figured I knew how it would end. But I never suspected . . ." He spread his hands, and the raw pain on his face reminded her of Cole. For two strong men to bare their hearts so . . .

"He didn't do it." Abbie played her trump. "He thinks you're the one who killed her."

Sam's face darkened as his eyes ignited. "What?"

"That's why he's taking responsibility. To keep them from suspecting you."

He slammed his fists on the table. "I would never have hurt her."

"Not even if she loved Cole? If she—"

"You think I'm blind? I saw how she took to him. I saw how crazy he made her." His eyes held their own bit of crazy. "Auralee changed after he rode in. She wasn't . . . even willing to listen anymore. I tried to get her to marry me, to come out of that place."

178

Sam gripped his temples between his thumb and fingers, then let his hand drop and slowly raised his head. "I loved her same as any virtuous woman. I didn't hold it against her that she done what she had to. Most times that life's forced on them by hardship or spurious people. Auralee didn't choose what she was."

Abbie did not agree. There was always room for choice, no matter how bleak the circumstances. But she held her tongue and let Sam pour out his heart.

"Sure, it tore me up thinkin' of her with others. But . . ."

"But she didn't love them." Abbie met his eyes with hers. "Until Cole."

Sam scowled. "I raised him up, cleaned him out of more scrapes, stood beside him when things were bad. Then he came in, and suddenly Auralee has eyes for no one else. Even Pablo saw it. He threatened her with the whip if she didn't stop moonin' over Cole and show the others some attention."

Abbie regrettably understood. Cole Jasper had confidence and charisma—not to mention cocky good looks—that were hard to ignore. Sam was all right in his own, but he lacked Cole's energy.

"I'm sorry," she said softly.

He gripped his cup and watched the contents. "I reckon even if he didn't . . . knife her himself, he brought it on. She turned mean as a grizzly whenever he'd been around. I reckon she pushed someone too far. But it's still Cole's fault."

Again she saw the pain that fueled his anger. What could she say? If Cole cared nothing for the woman, then he had no business . . . seeing her. Especially if he knew how she felt. And she doubted very much he hadn't known. *Oh, how muddy everything gets outside of God's plan.*

Again she felt a pang for what she and Monte had known. Even if she freed Cole, she could never love him knowing he'd held other women so cheaply. She suddenly felt empty. "I am sorry, Sam. I'm sorry for your loss. But I must do what I can to see that Cole is freed of a crime he didn't commit."

"You'd stand by him, knowin' . . ."

"Cole is his own man with his own free will. What he does is his business. But . . . I owe him my efforts after all he's done for me."

"There's nothin' more to it?"

No. Her aching heart suddenly throbbed. "There's nothing more to it." She heard the bell on the door and turned.

Will's slight shake of the head told her he'd been unsuccessful.

She wiped her mouth and laid her napkin beside her plate. Except for the first bite, her meal was untouched. "Will you excuse me, Sam?"

He nodded, but seemed lost in his own thoughts. She took Will's arm and stepped out to the street. "What happened?"

"I can't get in to see her. Leastwise, I can't talk to her without . . . money."

"I should have thought of that."

"You couldn't know. And . . ." He reddened furiously. "This Birdie's one of the high priced ones. You can buy her a drink or even a dance, but you can't talk privately without shelling out hard cash."

Abbie closed her eyes. She didn't want to know, didn't want to imagine . . . "How much?"

He mumbled a figure and she stared. If Cole could afford that . . . but maybe Auralee hadn't been . . . but Abbie knew she had. Cole would set his hat for the best.

Will stuffed his hands in his pockets. "Birdie was tight with Auralee. I found out that much."

Abbie frowned. It would cost nearly as much to see Birdie as to supply their trip home. She took the purse from her pocket. "Can you get in tonight?"

"If her dance card isn't full. I'll try."

"And Will . . ."

He held up his hand. "You don't have to say it. I know what I'm there for."

Abbie squeezed his arm. "How did you grow up so fine?"

"Had a good teacher." He grinned, then sobered. "And I had Mr. Farrel's example. I thought I had . . . Cole's, too."

Anger burned her cheeks. "Everybody fails, Will. But look where it's landed him and consider it a lesson learned." She watched him walk back to get his name on the list and prayed he'd withstand what he saw. After all, he'd had Monte's example. Who had been Cole's?

◆◆◆◆◆◆◆

Cole felt the anger spread across his chest and lodge in his throat. For the first time he understood what it was to choke on his rage. Maybe because, caged up, he could do nothing else with it. Hollering, cussing, or throwing things would only provide a show for the Mexicans, and that wasn't his way anyhow.

Why did she come? Why insist on meddling when he'd told her to leave it alone! But that was Abbie, always sticking her nose where it didn't belong. Hadn't she gotten herself in enough trouble for one lifetime? Now she had to mess with his and Sam's?

What could he do about it? She was out there with no one but Will to look after her, and she'd be more likely to mother him. Worse still, Will would be clay in her hands. Whatever she put him up to, he'd do. And with Sam here in town . . .

Cole swore, then felt remorseful. He guessed Brother Lewis's prayer hadn't took so good after all. The preacher shouldn't have wasted his time.

The door opened and sunlight shot into his eyes. Cole looked up, surprised. *Speak of the* . . . He felt a strange elation watching the black-clothed figure close the door and approach, but he hid his grin. "Howdy, preacher."

"Hello, brother. You're in good company, you know."

Cole glanced at the Mexican bandits and raised a questioning eyebrow.

"The apostles Paul and Barnabas spent much of their time in prison." Brother Lewis pulled up a stool.

"That's real comforting."

"The key is to rejoice in your circumstances." Brother Lewis repeated it in Spanish. He must figure on making his sermon count twice. The Mexicans sneered and gave him a string of foul language in return.

"The Lord will turn all things to good for those who love Him."

Cole waited through the translation and the soiled response. Brother Lewis was undaunted. "Cast your cares upon the water and the One who sees and knows all things will bring you peace." He leaned close to the bars. "And the truth will set you free." Brother Lewis's eyes burned with inner intensity. He saw. He knew.

Cole frowned. *The truth will set you free.* Sure it would. But what about Sam? "Brother Lewis, I want you to do something for me."

"Name it."

"There's a woman in town, name of Abbie Farrel. If this turns out as I expect, I want you to get her clear. I don't want to look in her blue eyes when I feel the rope closin' down. And you can return the horse to her. It's hers anyway. And another thing . . ." He got up and leaned close. "I got some money put away in the bank in San Antonio. I want it to go to Abbie and her kids."

Brother Lewis studied him silently. Cole hoped he wouldn't argue. Cole had looked at this every which way and couldn't see clear to do anything different. Wherever Sam went, he'd pay in his own way for the rest of his life. But Cole wouldn't let his brother swing. All those years ago, Sam had taken the punishment meant for him, and he couldn't do less now. It had to be this way. It had to.

◆◆◆◆◆◆◆

When Abbie viewed the handsome minister making his way purposefully along the boardwalk, she recalled Sheriff Gates mentioning one who rode in with Cole. Glimpsing Whitesock tied to the post behind him, she guessed this was he, though as a companion for Cole Jasper, the minister was as unlikely as she was apt to find.

The circuit rider, as she guessed him by the layers of dust on his boots, appeared to be as ardent and sincere a man as she'd laid eyes on in some time. It only raised her hackles to think of his riding in with Cole. Maybe taking an outlaw to jail was his good deed for the day. She frowned as he removed his hat and held it to his chest.

"Good afternoon, ma'am. Would you by chance be Mrs. Farrel?"

She drew herself up respectfully. "On what do you base your assumption?"

"A fair description from my friend and traveling companion, Cole Jasper." The reverend kept his hat to his chest, his intense brown eyes searching hers.

His friend and companion? "Do you always ride with outlaws, Reverend . . ."

"Brother Lewis." He bowed slightly. "And yes, I would say the majority of my time is spent among the godless, the hapless, and the scorned."

Abbie smiled in spite of herself. "Then I presume Cole found himself in good company."

"He may have doubted that, ma'am, until he came to see the light."

"The light?"

"The saving grace of our Lord and Savior, Jesus Christ."

Abbie glanced down the dusty street to the jail. Was he saying Cole had turned to God? Cole, who had told her himself he knew little of God's ways, who had counted himself sufficient and had stubbornly refused her help? If Cole had turned to God, why did he now live a lie inside the walls of that jail?

"Did you have business with me . . . Brother Lewis?"

"Cole requested I return the horse to you." He waved toward the gelding tethered on the street.

"Thank you." Her ire rose. It should be Cole riding the horse home, Cole keeping his word to help her run the ranch, Cole standing tall and sure before her. Not this . . . this . . . "What kind of preacher are you, not to see that Cole is innocent of these charges? What kind of friend would ride here beside him without convincing him of his error? What—"

Brother Lewis raised his hand. "Please. I understand your concern." The sable fabric of his coat sleeve furrowed at the elbow with a threadbare sheen. "But Cole is walking a destiny laid out for him. Through trial and suffering—"

"He'll end up hung."

The minister bowed his head. "I have given him council to speak the truth. But he finds a greater good in laying down his life. . . ."

Abbie spun and stalked to the post that held the roof over the entrance to the hotel. She raised her chin and closed her eyes, drawing in a sharp, hostile breath. The air smelled of dust, the scent of her dreams.

"Mrs. Farrel, Cole has surrendered his heart to the One who knows. If God calls him out of there, Cole will honor that."

And if not? Once again, Abbie felt the pain of hurting for a man who honored something with which she was at odds. Would honor forever be her enemy? What if it was honor to God? Could she dare stand against it? "You've returned the horse, sir. Was there anything more you needed?"

The reverend held his ground. "At his request, I would, regretfully, ask you to leave town. It pains Cole to face his trial with you here."

Abbie turned with fire in her veins. "It pains Cole? It pains him? What of the rest of us? What of Will and Sam and me? This isn't about him alone. It's about . . ." She faltered. Jenny, the ranch . . . her own half-hopeful dreams. They lay now in the dust, trampled by Cole's stubborn self-destruction. It wasn't God's will he followed; it was his own.

Well, she wouldn't stand for it. She hadn't come this far to turn back because her presence pained Cole. She hoped it pained him fiercely. "You may let Cole know that I'll not leave until I've seen him freed. And as for his supposed surrender to God . . ."

"I baptized him myself in the waters of the Rio Grande. I heard his confession of faith, and I assure you the Lord Jesus Christ heard it, as well."

Abbie matched Brother Lewis's stalwart stare, but she had no words to rebut his assertion. *Will Cole now die in peace?* That was the last thought she wanted to allow.

Eighteen

Jenny darted to the back corner of the house and peered around the side. Drawing a sharp breath, she ran for the stable and ducked inside. Uncle Grant's horse was gone, of course, but the gelding, Topper, was there. Aunt Marcy would be furious, but she didn't mean to take him all the way, only to the ranch to fetch Snowdrop.

Jenny couldn't saddle the gelding or hitch the buggy, and she'd only ridden bareback a score of times when she'd escaped Aunt Abbie's watchful eye. But there was no help for it. Jenny took the bridle from the wall and slid the bit into the horse's teeth. Topper was old enough to accept it without much trouble.

She had to stand on a bucket to get the straps up over his ears. That done, she swung her leg up and tugged and wiggled herself astride. The gelding sidled to the wall, but she collected the reins where they hung and took him in hand.

Topper would get her home, and from there she'd set out on her own horse. She adjusted the pack of food she'd strapped to her back. She wished it held jerky and biscuits like Cole's, but Uncle Grant didn't ride the range, so Aunt Marcy's cupboard held neither. What Jenny had taken would have to do.

She clicked her tongue and the horse left the stall and stable. She kicked her heels, and he picked up his stride. She'd have to reach the stable at home without Pearl or James or any of the men hearing her. Maybe she'd leave the horse and creep in on foot. She could sneak quiet as an Indian if she had to.

Mr. Bender looked up as she passed, and she waved shortly. He returned it and went back to loading bags of grain into the waiting wagon. She kicked in her heels again and the gelding broke into a trot. It was painful with no stirrups, and she urged him to a canter. Once away from town, he could slow down, but she didn't want anyone asking questions.

Just outside the Lucky Star yard, Jenny slid from the horse's back and ran for the bunkhouse. This time of day it would be empty, and it afforded a view of both the house and stable. All was quiet, and she crept from her hiding spot to dart across the yard.

If Will were there, he'd catch her, but Will had gone with Aunt Abbie. Jenny found Snowdrop contentedly munching her oats. Curtis and Matt were doing well looking after her. Jenny stroked the soft pink muzzle and white speckled cheek. The horse blew hay-scented breath through her wide quivering nostrils.

Jenny reached for her own small saddle. She could manage that one herself. She stood on the mounting block and fastened the cinch. Normally Will helped her tighten it, but she pulled as hard as she could, then hung her whole weight and dangled beneath the mare's belly. Snowdrop obliged by not bloating her stomach.

Jenny fastened her food bag and a bag of oats to the saddle, then mounted. The yard was still empty, so she walked the horse slowly and quietly. The men must be out with the herd. James was growing deaf and if Pearl was in the kitchen she wouldn't hear. But Zena might see from a window ... Jenny looked quickly to the house, but all was still.

She walked the mare out the gate and hurried her along. She wasn't sure exactly what way El Paso lay, but she'd ask the travelers she passed. Someone must have seen a man like Cole. They'd notice him for sure, and they'd be willing to help when she told them he was her pa.

Jenny only felt a little twinge now when she said it to herself. He could have been her pa. He should have been. Cole understood her, and he cared. She was now convinced of that. If the bad men hadn't taken him, he might even have told her so. Now he'd have the chance.

She imagined how happy he'd be when she found him. He'd know how hard it was, and how far she'd gone just for him. She pictured his face full of wonder and joy. Aunt Abbie couldn't find him, but Jenny would. She wouldn't give up until she did.

Jenny laughed, and it made a cloud as white as Snowdrop's breath. The cold air stung her cheeks, and she was glad for her heavy woolen coat. Snowdrop would keep her warm at night. She'd snuggle up beside the mare like the picture of Prince Rabadash and his steed, Goldthorn, in her *Tales From Far Lands* book.

When she looked back the first time, the house was small. She looked back again and could scarcely make it out in the vast stretch of land before the foothills and mountains. She'd never been out this far unattended, though she knew the road to the mission as well as anyone.

When she came near the mission itself she'd leave the road and cut over the land, avoiding the homesteads of Miss Nora's friends and family. Jenny wouldn't ask them if they'd seen Cole. But anyone she met after that . . .

Her heart beat quicker. Maybe El Paso wasn't far. Aunt Marcy and Uncle Grant hadn't said how far when she overheard them last night. Aunt Marcy had been whining, of course. She'd said bad things about Aunt Abbie, and Uncle Grant had tried to explain.

Jenny was glad he had because now she knew Cole was in

real trouble . . . hanging trouble. And she knew he was in El Paso. Someone would know where that was. She closed her eyes and imagined him again. That helped her not to be scared.

She pictured the way he rode his horse, so easy in the saddle—like an Indian, Aunt Abbie said. She pictured his walk, his strong stride, his long legs, a little bowed at the knees. She liked that. She pictured his eyes, the color of sagebrush in the spring, with crinkles at their sides.

She pictured the smile he had just for her. It warmed her better than her coat. She raised her face and pretended he tweaked her nose. It didn't bother her when Cole did it. It was affectionate, not teasing.

"Jenny?"

Her eyes flew open. Where had Miss Nora come from? And Mr. McConnel? Her first urge was to kick the mare and run, but that would be no good. Even if they couldn't catch her on foot, they'd send others. No. She had to fool them.

Jenny smiled. "Hello, Miss Nora. Hello, Mr. McConnel."

He tipped his hat and raised a hand to Snowdrop's reins. Jenny felt her heart flip as he took hold.

Nora came close, her hand resting on her hip. "Where be you off to, little Jenny, all by your lonesome?"

"Just riding." Jenny sweetened her smile.

Mr. McConnel glanced around her. "Well provisioned for a ride, aren't you?"

Jenny looked at the food sacks tied to the saddle. "Oh, I just brought a snack for me and Snowdrop."

"And you've ridden all the way from town?"

Jenny looked back to Nora. "From the Lucky Star."

"But I thought you were stayin' with your aunt in town."

Jenny's thoughts spun. "Oh, I was. But now I'm not . . . anymore. Well, I guess I'll just be on my way."

Mr. McConnel tightened his hold of the reins. Jenny's heart fluttered. She felt Nora's hand on her knee. "Suppose you tell us what ye're really about," Miss Nora said quietly.

Jenny felt the blood rush to her face. She'd been caught in a lie. Aunt Abbie would be so shamed.

"Well, I am on a ride."

"That ye are, darlin'. But *why* is what we want to know. And where ye're goin'."

"I'm . . . I'm looking for Cole." Jenny blurted it almost defiantly.

Nora's eyebrows raised, and she glanced at Mr. McConnel. Jenny felt their joined forces. "You can't stop me, because I mean to find him. Aunt Abbie tried, but she couldn't, and I won't stop until I do!" She felt the fear and fury rising up. Worse, she felt the tears.

Miss Nora stroked her knee. "There, there, *aroon*. We're not meanin' ye harm. Has your aunt come back then?"

"No. But she would have if she'd found Cole. She'd have brought him home by now."

Mr. McConnel steadied the mare with a hand to her muzzle. "El Paso, Texas, is a ways away."

Nora patted Jenny's knee. "Suppose we go to the mission and talk about it over a hot cup of tea with cream."

Jenny felt her indignation fading, and with it her hopes of success. "I think I'll just ride on."

"Come and have a cup, Jenny, and we'll talk it out."

Short of bolting, there was no help for it. Jenny allowed Mr. McConnel to lead the mare. Of all the terrible luck, to meet them on a stroll. She should have been paying attention. She'd never have come this close to the mission with her eyes open. Now everything was ruined.

Mr. McConnel lifted her from the saddle, and Jenny walked despondently behind Miss Nora into the warmth of her kitchen. None of the children were there but Maggie. And Maggie was all grown up now. Jenny gave her a weak smile.

Nora bustled past and hung her coat on the hook. "Now,

then, Maggie dear. Pour us a cup, will ye? And one for Davy. He'll be inside in a minute."

As Maggie poured the tea, Jenny noticed her questioning glance.

All Nora said was, "We've a wee visitor, this day."

"Aye. How are ye, Jenny?" Maggie smiled warmly.

"Fine, thank you." But she didn't feel fine. She tried to keep the sorry look from her face, but she knew it was there. Now she'd never find Cole. She'd never get away again. Aunt Marcy would see to that. She imagined all the dark places Aunt Marcy could lock her up.

Maggie slipped a plate of oatmeal cookies under her nose. They smelled of cinnamon and molasses, but Jenny shook her head.

"Och, that's a gloomy face if ever I saw one." Miss Nora caught her chin and raised it. "Suppose you tell me about this Cole Jasper. I think ye said he was your da."

Jenny flushed. "Well, he's not exactly my pa, not in the real pa way. But I pretend he's my pa. I wish he were."

"And why is that?"

"He's . . . well he likes me, for one."

"Of course he does, darlin'." Nora glanced at Mr. McConnel coming into the room. "So does Mr. McConnel and lots of others. Ye're a fine lass."

"But Cole . . . he's different. He needs me." She hadn't meant to say that part. That was her own secret thought.

"Does he, now? And why is that?"

"Because no one loves him as I do."

Miss Nora sat back. "Now, then, I've not seen for myself, but I think yer aunt might have a thought or two for him. After all, she's gone a'lookin'."

Jenny shook her head sadly. "I thought so, too. But I asked her if she'd brought Cole home to be our pa, and she said no." Jenny saw the smile Miss Nora hid.

Mr. McConnel slid to the bench beside her. "That's not always a good indication." He took the cup before him and slurped the tea. "Sometimes grown women don't admit the things they feel. Not to children, not to the ones they feel it for, and not even to themselves."

Jenny watched his eyes. He had kind eyes, but she felt as though he wasn't speaking just to her. "Why wouldn't they admit it?"

"That's something I can't figure, but I can tell you unequivocally that it's so."

"Then you think Aunt Abbie loves Cole?"

"I think it takes a lot for a woman to go after a man in trouble. Most would say he made his own bed, now let him sleep in it."

Jenny frowned. "Cole didn't do anything wrong. Especially not what they say he did."

Miss Nora nudged her cup toward her. "And how would you be knowin' what they say?"

"I heard Aunt Marcy. I don't care if it was eavesdropping. I never get told things, and I had to know. He's in bad trouble. Hanging trouble, Uncle Grant said. And I mean to find him and get him out of it."

"How?" Mr. McConnel's question was softly asked, but it hit her hard nonetheless.

Jenny clutched her stomach, hoping the knot would go away. "I don't know." She fought the tears. Miss Nora held the tin cup to her and Jenny drank. It was warm and sweet. She took another gulp, and a tear started down her cheek.

"It's all right, aroon. It's in God's hands, ye know."

Jenny shook her head. "No. God takes people away and they never come back. My pa and mama . . . I won't let Him have Cole, I won't!" She threw the cup down and tea splashed all over the table and her dress. She tried to stand, but Mr. McConnel caught her into his arms and held her to his chest.

"Let me go! Let me go!" Tears flooded her eyes.

"Now hold on a minute. We're not gonna stop you doing what you must. But you need to listen here."

Jenny didn't want to listen, but there was something in his tone she couldn't ignore. She sniffed. She'd hear him out if it meant they would let her go on.

"Now, you have to think this thing through. El Paso's hundreds of miles away, close on a thousand maybe. You think you can go a thousand miles on that little mare with what you have in the bag?"

A thousand miles? Could it be so far? Jenny shook her head slowly.

"Even sayin' you could, it's a mighty big world out there. How will you know the way? How will you keep shy of people who wouldn't be nice to a sprig like you? What about bobcats and coyotes . . ."

And wolves.

"And supposing you did find Cole Jasper. What then, Jenny?" Mr. McConnel looked as though he really wondered.

If she could give him an answer . . . But what answer did she have? Jenny felt the lump growing in her throat again.

He cocked his head to the side. "It's an awful big task you're takin' on. It'll be gettin' dark soon and mighty cold. Where are you gonna sleep?"

Jenny looked out the window. Already the sky was the color of her velvet dress at home. Soon it would be black. She felt a shiver creep up her back. All her imaginings had dissolved. What could she do for Cole? How could she even find him?

Miss Nora squeezed her hand. "Ye'll need more than ye have in the bag. I've a fresh loaf and apple jelly if ye want it."

Jenny's stomach rumbled. She'd hardly touched the lunch Aunt Marcy put out, so nervous was she about breaking away. But it was silly to think a loaf of bread would go much farther than the things she'd stuffed into her bag. Not for hundreds of miles.

Jenny shook her head again, the sadness settling deep. "I can't go, can I?"

Miss Nora stroked her cheek. "Ye can if ye've a mind to. But ye won't be gettin' far."

She sniffed. "Aunt Marcy will be hotter than a gunfighter's pistol."

Miss Nora gave her a sympathetic smile. "She'll be that and more. But Davy and I will speak a word on yer behalf."

Jenny realized Mr. McConnel still had a heavy hand on her shoulder. She glanced up at him.

He smiled. "That we will."

"I stole her horse, only I didn't keep it. I just rode it to the ranch to get Snowdrop and left it there."

Mr. McConnel frowned. "I reckon you'll catch it on that one. Some things can't be talked past."

Jenny nodded. "I reckon so." She drew herself up. She'd suffer it for Cole. She'd done it all for him anyway. "I better go now. Before it's all the way dark."

"I'm needin' to go that way myself, sprig," Mr. McConnel said softly. "How about we ride together?"

Jenny's heart skipped with relief. Visions of sleeping under the stars beside Snowdrop had vanished with the sun, replaced by ghostly wolves. She nodded solemnly. "I don't mind."

"Wait for me at the front door. I'll just say good-night to Miss Nora."

Jenny nodded again. Part of her hurt, and she figured that would get worse, but just now she felt a little glad Miss Nora and Mr. McConnel had found her out.

Nora's heart was pounding as Davy sent Jenny off, then turned to her. He'd been wonderful with the child, his arms about her, his gentle concern, his honest discourse. He had neither lectured nor scolded, but had taken her need seriously, though Davy saw well its futility. That was one thing Jaime had lacked. He couldn't see the importance of anyone's fight but his own. And he hadn't had time for the lads and lasses.

As Davy eyed her, Nora's heart kept up its dance. She could hardly keep it from showing through the layers of her bodice. He must have sensed it, for his eyes took on a depth she'd seldom seen. She cleared the awkwardness from her throat. "What is it ye're wantin'?"

He stepped close. "Just a proper sending."

"Well, have it then."

He took her in his arms. "Thank you for the walk, Nora." He bent and kissed her.

Of their own volition, her arms wrapped tightly about him. Was she daft to give her mind and heart away so? "You were fine, Davy. With the lass."

He drew back only inches. "And with you? Just now?"

"Aye. That was fine, too."

He kissed her again, and Nora didn't hold back. What was the use against a heart as big as Davy's?

He smiled broadly. "Now, that's a proper sending."

"Be off with ye, then. Ye've taken more than yer share."

"Oh no, Nora. It's all mine. Soon."

"Go on, or the child'll be off to the wolves without ye."

Davy sent her one more smile. "Soon."

Nineteen

Will didn't get in to see Birdie. Her card was full the first night, and Abbie fretted all the next day. Sam had disappeared, though she suspected she'd find him at the town's graveyard if she looked. But she stayed in the hotel, though the walls were starting to close in on her. She wanted to draw as little attention to herself as possible while Will tried to learn what he could.

Now night was drawing on, and still she sat, fully clothed, drowsing in the chair in her room, waiting. The letters she'd penned to the children lay on the table beside her, sealed and ready for the next day's mail coach. There were a thousand things she could have said to them, but she'd kept the notes short and cheerful.

The letter to Pearl told more, but even it held only a fraction of all there was to say. In neither letter did Abbie explain her current plans, nor express a time for her return. She didn't know either of those herself. When the knock came, it jarred her from her dozing. She rushed to the door and opened it.

Will stood sheepishly in the hall. "I hated to wake you, but you said . . ."

"Yes, Will." She stepped out into the hall. "Tell me."

"I saw Birdie. She's a real small thing, but kinda . . . hard, like she's scarcely a girl at all. I think she's scared. She said she wanted money to see you. I told her I already paid, but she said that was for another thing altogether, and she wouldn't see a penny of it herself."

"How much does she want?"

"Twenty-five dollars."

"Twenty-five! How will I come up with that?"

"I don't know. Maybe you could wire for it."

"But . . . isn't there any other way?"

He shook his head slowly. "She said when you had it, I was to have a drink at the Paloma Blanca. She said not to come in until you had the money. She'll meet you outside the back at four." Will swept the hair off his forehead. "That's in the mornin' as she usually . . . works till then." He slouched. "She acted real tough, but . . . I kinda felt sorry for her."

Abbie frowned. He sounded like Cole. Sorry for a brazen minx who demands that kind of money to see her? "Did you ask about Auralee?"

He shook his head. "I didn't want to scare her off. She already thought I was crazy for not . . . you know."

Abbie suddenly felt exhausted. "Would you go with me to meet her?"

He nodded.

"Thank you, Will. Get some sleep. I'll work on finding the money tomorrow." Abbie sighed. Twenty-five dollars. Even if she could find it . . . No, she refused to think about all the things she needed it for.

◆◆◆◆◆◆◆

Samuel stood before the rough chalky stone marker on the edge of the graveyard. AURALEE DUBOIS. That was all. At least they'd marked the grave, though he couldn't read it any longer in the darkness. His legs were like stone themselves from standing so long, his hands loose and weary at his sides.

He couldn't picture her dead. He'd not seen her. He had been nursing a drunk headache the day she was buried. He hadn't even heard she was killed. He'd thought . . . thought she was with Cole. Thought maybe they'd ride off together. Thought no man, not even Cole, could withstand her once she got him alone.

The anger was cooling, but he couldn't let it. Mrs. Farrel had planted doubts in his head, but he wouldn't listen. Why would Cole go after Auralee if he had someone like her to love? But he recalled the night they'd sat together, brothers not yet divided.

Hadn't Cole told him then that Mrs. Farrel would have no part of him? She blamed him for her husband's death. She'd given him the kidskin boot. *Cole tried to forget her with Auralee.* Sam stiffened. Cole would get what he deserved. Auralee was dead because of him. His Auralee . . .

The pain choked his thoughts. Sam dropped his face to his palms. She was never his. He'd never laid claim to her because he wouldn't dishonor her. But she'd only laughed at him and made crude jokes he flushed to recall. She'd questioned his manhood, but she'd never questioned Cole's.

Had Cole used his woman? Sam dropped his hands into fists. Knowing wouldn't help. It wouldn't change things. But not knowing was making him crazy. If Cole had used Auralee, he'd . . . what? His brother was already waiting to hang.

Because Cole thinks I did it. Sam looked down at his hands. How? How could Cole think . . . He recalled the knuckles crushing against Cole's jaw. He recalled the fury, the desire to see him bleed. Sam swallowed the tight lump that filled his throat.

He could have killed. If he had found them together he could have. All these years he'd thought he could control it, the rage that burned inside. He felt again the board ripping his flesh, felt the point of it dig into his cheekbone, saw Cole running for his life. A kid too scared to feel shame. Sam felt again the blood spurt from his ear, the dazed numbness he thought was death.

He recalled the smell of the doctor's fingers, the burn of carbolic acid searing his wounds. For the first time he had taken on himself what Cole had endured for years. For the first time he knew what it was to hate his pa. But he'd never let on. He never told Cole he understood. And they never spoke of the man who walked out of their lives a miserable wreck.

Sam and Cole had each other and their unspoken pact to care for their ma. They'd failed there, too. Cole took that bad. He'd gone a little crazy. Sam drew a long, slow breath. Maybe the rage was there in all of them. Maybe the ability, the desire to maim, to kill, was embedded in a man's soul.

Maybe Cole did believe his brother could kill Auralee. So why was Cole taking it on himself? Sam recalled the look in Cole's eyes when he'd stood at his bedside, staring at the bandages. He'd stopped being a boy that day. He'd been shamed into a man. Was it that shame that drove him now?

Sam felt a wicked satisfaction. Hadn't Cole started it all with Auralee? Hadn't he played her fiddle until she sang for him alone? Hadn't he made her crazy when he changed his tune? Hadn't he seen the damage was done?

Sam shook his head. The damage was done. She was gone. Auralee. His Auralee. Never his. Never again. Never at all. He felt the sob rise up from his chest, and this time he didn't fight it.

◆◆◆◆◆◆◆

Every time the door opened, Cole expected to see Abbie. Every time it wasn't, he felt relieved and hurt at once. He didn't reckon she'd left town, though she hadn't been in but the once. His last sight of her had been her angry response to his cruel words.

What was it that made them spar so? He should have

thanked her, should have told her how much it meant that she would care enough to come. He should have told her if there was any other way, any way at all . . . But doggone it, he'd told her to go home!

Cole stretched and felt the sharp pain in his left shoulder. The wound hadn't poisoned, thanks to Abbie and, grudgingly, Crete's burning knife. Still, it pained him plenty, especially after the tussle with Gray Wolf.

It was closing into a dark, puckered scar that matched the one on his opposite thigh, just above the knee, the one he'd gotten on Abbie's wedding night. That night he'd been hurting worse inside than any bullet hole. They'd had a right purty wedding, and Mr. Farrel had won her fair and square, but that didn't stop the pain.

Cole leaned against the wall. The Mexicans in the next cell smelled, and he figured he'd be the same if he hadn't asked Gates for a basin of water and a shaving bowl. Even in a hole like this it felt good to be clean. He ran his hand over his mustache.

And if Abbie should come in . . . The hours dragged. He watched the Mexicans play cards for stones. He ignored their sneers. Gates had told him they were in for robbery and murder. They would hang. There were witnesses . . . just like there was for him.

Captain Gates returned from his rounds and stopped outside his cell, holding a pack of Genuine Blackwell Bull Durham smoking tobacco, maybe not the best on the market to Cole's mind, but mighty tempting nonetheless. "Smoke?"

Cole reached automatically, then heard Brother Lewis in his head. " 'If any man be in Christ, he is a new creature.' " But there was nothing in the Book about smoking tobacco. That was Cole's own idea, first to help his cough, then to prove he could do without it. Now . . .

Cole withdrew his hand. "Naw. I'll pass." He could almost

taste it, but what he wanted even more was a stiff shot of whiskey, the kind Mr. Farrel kept in the house. 'Course, the whiskey might not be there anymore. Abbie had little use for it.

He pictured the big white house with the pink stone and tall pillars. It was fitting she should have a place so nice. She deserved it and any other comforts that came her way. But it was unsettling sitting around that big fancy table, though Cole felt a pang at the thought of never doing it again. Little Elliot with manners like his pa's, Jenny and her saucy ways, Abbie . . . He felt the darkness descending on him. He might be ready to meet his maker, as Brother Lewis claimed, but it sure didn't feel that way.

The daylight faded from the single small window high on the side of his cell. One of the Mexicans snored; the other tossed pebbles at his boot, gathered them up, and tossed them again. Cole felt the wall grow cold against his back.

Gates brought them their supper. It was decent food—beef brisket and roasted potatoes Gates's missus had sent over. This whole time Cole had been showered with gifts of food, some given anonymously through Gates, others by the hands of those who thought they owed Cole something.

Gates snuffed the lamp and left them as night settled. Cole ate, then set the empty tin plate on the floor by the bunk. He cleaned his teeth and washed his mustache, then sat again on the edge of the bunk. His companion's eyes glittered in the dark. The man was staring his way, and Cole just made out a hint of teeth that could be smile or snarl.

"Hey, *gringo*. You are ready to die?"

Cole said nothing.

"Your preacher, he thinks you are ready. I think you are scared."

Cole shifted his legs up on the bunk and lay back. No, it wasn't fear. Not anymore. More like wondering. He'd sure done a whole lot wrong in his life. He would have liked a chance to do some good. For little Jenny maybe, or others.

He'd helped where he could, but it didn't seem complete somehow. He hated to think of Abbie on that long ride home. Would she grieve for him as she had Mr. Farrel?

No, not like that. Not likely. But she might some. It pained Cole to think of it. But she'd go on. Abbie was a survivor. She was made of stiffer stuff than some men he'd known.

Maybe she'd marry again. She was plenty young yet. She ought to have more children. She was real good with kids. Cole tried not to think they could have been his. It'd be enough for her to be happy. He felt a drowsy acceptance of the way things were. *Thy will be done.*

Strange, it wasn't Brother Lewis he heard in his head. It was his ma saying the prayer that contained those words. *Thy kingdom come; Thy will be done.* Cole understood it now, but as a boy he'd wondered what "thy" was.

What exactly would be done? Something that should be, but never was, at least to his ma's way of thinking. Maybe things were better for her now. They must be. They must be real . . . nice. . . .

◆◆◆◆◆◆◆

Abbie stood outside in the dark, afraid that even after all her efforts, Birdie wouldn't show. It had taken four days to transfer Grant's loan from Mr. Driscoll's bank to the bank in El Paso. Had Birdie forgotten her promise? Will had taken a drink at the bar in the main room, just as they'd agreed, but Birdie had paid him no mind.

Now he stood beside Abbie at the back of the saloon, waiting. The watch that hung on her neck said half past four. Abbie searched her heart. Had she misunderstood? Was she outside of God's will? Had she followed the wrong path? She jumped when the door clicked open and Birdie stepped out.

It had to be Birdie. She was small . . . and hard. More like an old woman than the delicate child she appeared. Abbie guessed her true age between fifteen and twenty, but her eyes said fifty at least. The light from the lantern above the back door of the saloon showed that much clearly.

Abbie breathed her relief. "Thank you for seeing me, Birdie. I was afraid you wouldn't come."

Birdie raised one slight shoulder. "I was busy." She flashed her eyes toward Will and back. "You have the money?" She spoke English with a Spanish accent.

Abbie wondered which was her native tongue. Probably both. She handed Birdie the money wired from Grant, the money Abbie could ill afford to lose.

The girl shoved it down her low-cut bodice with a lewd glance at Will. "So talk. He said you wanted to talk." She thumbed Will rudely.

Abbie looked at the narrow oval face, large dark eyes, and straight black hair hanging loose to her waist. The girl's skin was a flawless olive tone, and she recalled Cole's description of Auralee's beauty. Obviously Pablo Montoya carefully chose his wares.

Abbie's throat tightened. "I want to know about Auralee." She hadn't meant to be so blunt, but thoughts of Cole had brought it out.

Birdie's eyes narrowed. "Who are you?"

"Mrs. Abbie Farrel. I'm a friend of Cole Jasper's."

Birdie looked over her shoulder, then searched the wood-pile and trash heap. "Who sent you? The captain? Does he not believe me? I saw it all." She clenched her hands at her sides. "Did Cole send you?" A brief concern showed, then passed.

"No one sent me. Do you know Cole?"

Birdie raised her chin with a slight smirk. "Of course. Why wouldn't I?"

Why indeed? Abbie wanted to walk away. Pinch that smug smirk from Birdie's face and walk away. . . . She didn't want to know what Birdie had to say. With sheer will, she drew her next breath. "Please tell me what happened."

"I told the captain. Ask him." She turned for the door.

"Birdie."

The girl stopped, and with the light full on her face, Abbie saw she was no more than sixteen, if that.

"Cole didn't kill Auralee. Who did?"

"You are wasting your time. I have told what I know." Birdie reached for the knob.

"Please . . ." Abbie's spirit sank. "I paid you . . ."

Birdie turned with a shrewd eye. "Perhaps if you come to-morrow, I might remember something I forgot. But remember, my time is valuable."

Abbie clenched her teeth against the furious words that flooded her mind. She closed her eyes and felt her breath come sharply.

Birdie's voice was smooth and clear. "Same time. Same price. Tomorrow."

Abbie felt Will's hand on her shoulder and opened her eyes. Birdie was gone, and they were alone in the alley. She felt close to tears but held them back for Will's sake. She glanced up, but he was staring at the door through which Birdie had dis-appeared. "Will?"

He startled as though coming to himself and turned to her. "She's afraid to talk."

Abbie's jaw dropped. He could hardly have said anything more naïve. Her anger flared. "Afraid? She's no more afraid than a . . . a rattler or a rabbit. She's using me. Blackmail, plain and simple."

"What are you going to do?"

"I don't know. But I certainly won't put another cent down her sultry little bodice."

Will flushed, but Abbie ignored him. "Come on. We've no more business here."

◆◆◆◆◆◆◆

Abbie tossed in the bed, more restless than she'd been all the nights sleeping on the ground. She flounced to her side and punched the pillow under her cheek. What could she do? Even if she convinced Sam to tell Cole he didn't do it, even if Cole gave up the charade, there was still Birdie's testimony.

It would go before the judge whether Captain Gates wanted it to or not. It was the law, and it would be Cole's word against hers. What man wouldn't deny a crime that would have him hung? If Birdie was convincing ... and Abbie had no doubt she could be convincing. The little vixen had more tricks than a riverboat gambler.

What grudge did Birdie nurse against Cole? Why would she claim to see him, unless ... maybe she had seen him. Hadn't Cole said he was with Auralee? Maybe Birdie had seen him there, but not seen what happened. Maybe she just guessed or thought to gain something by lying.

Abbie shook her head. She had to get the truth from that woman. She dropped to her knees on the floor beside the bed. *Dear God, help me to find the truth. For Cole's sake and all those involved. Help me to know your will....* What if it was His will that Cole die?

No. It couldn't be. Not the will of a just God. She had to trust. She had to believe. As Cole did? Had he truly surrendered his heart? Was he following God's will? Was she storming the gates of heaven in vain? Abbie shook her head against the despair inside.

Lord, help my poor faith. I trust you with Cole's life. Guide and direct me to accomplish your will. What else was there but God's will? She could either fight it or accept it. Either way, His will would be done.

Father, make me an instrument of your purpose. Use me as you will. Forgive my doubt, my fear, my weakness. Make me strong. Make me wise. Make me obedient.

Abbie dropped her face to her hands. What if that meant she must fail? Could she watch Cole die? Her chest constricted. *No. Please God. I beg you for his life. Even if I never see him again, please don't ask me to face another death.*

She felt ashamed of her faithless plea. Tears stung her eyes. Here she was thinking of herself when Cole . . . *Dear God, he's in your hands.*

Faith.

There it was, the still small voice she had learned to trust from her youth. Peace washed her, and she closed her eyes, then bit her lip with renewed determination. Now that she knew there was no hope of loving Cole, she could help him unselfishly, for his sake and for the will of God.

Twenty

Nora stirred in her sleep, the dream fresh upon her. *Abbie, walking in a shadowland, huddled in a shawl and staggering, uncertain where to turn. Nora saw the path clearly and tried to call out, but Abbie seemed blinded, dazed, and either she had grown deaf or Nora's cries were mute.*

She shook herself awake. What an odd dream, to picture Abbie uncertain of her path—Abbie who always knew what she intended and went forward to it. But that was the way of dreams. It was Nora's own fears coming out. For on the morrow she'd marry Davy.

She'd held out for Abbie to stand with her, but Davy wouldn't hear it. He had overnight become the stubborn Irishman she'd suspected him to be. She had given him a fingerhold the night Jenny came, and he'd gripped it with both hands. And his hands were the size to wield the tongs and bellows at his da's smithy.

The thought of letting Davy McConnel into her life was fearfully wonderful. But the deed was done. She pressed her face into the pillow's softness. Och, it was her own nerves bringing the dream. Surely Abbie knew exactly what she was about. But just in case, Nora lifted a prayer for her friend.

♦♦♦♦♦♦♦

Abbie walked through the field behind the scatter of buildings that made up El Paso. She listened to the burros bray and the group of black-haired children holler and laugh as they scrapped behind the smithy. The confidence of her prayer the night before was greatly diminished this morning. The doubts had crowded in, and she'd sought the solitude of the fields until Will found her there.

He turned to her and took the grass blade from his teeth. "Maybe I could talk to some of the others, see if anyone else knows something about the night Auralee died."

"That won't change Birdie's testimony." Abbie bent and picked up a white stone, round as a marble. "It all rests with her, but I don't know how to get through."

Will hung his head. "What I don't see is why Cole won't tell the truth. I thought he was honest. He lectured me often enough."

"It's not as though he's lied, Will. He just won't say he didn't do it."

"Isn't that the same thing?"

Abbie fingered the stone and closed it in her hand. "I suppose it is. If only Sam would tell Cole he didn't do it. If only Cole knew he didn't have to protect his brother."

"Have you seen Sam?"

Abbie shook her head. "I don't think he's in town."

"Where would he go?"

She shrugged. "I don't know, Will. I just don't know."

At Will's frown, Abbie sensed his concern. "What is it?"

"Just . . . I heard that judge fella—McFee or something—is expected by the end of the week."

Abbie stopped. "So soon?"

"I only heard it. Down at the general store."

She bit her lip. "Then I have to see Birdie again. There's no help for it."

"But . . . the money . . ."

Abbie spread her hands. "What else can I do?"

"I wish I had it."

She smiled up at him. His hair needed cutting again. He always looked in need of a haircut. Abbie reached out and squeezed his hand. "Thank you, Will."

Half an hour later she stood at the window while the teller counted out the money. Grant had left his last loan open-ended, should she need more, and as the integrity of his standing with the bank in Rocky Bluffs was already established, the bank in El Paso would draw the loan against his account, for a slight amount of interest. Abbie had only to sign the note.

Doing this rankled, but at the moment Birdie held all the cards. She trembled to think what would happen if the demands continued. At what price would she value Cole's life? At what point would she stop paying and let him hang?

With a sigh Abbie slipped the cash from the teller into her pocket. She turned from the counter and met Sam's gaze. He must have come in behind her. By the look of his eyes she wasn't sure he'd slept in days, but there was no smell of whiskey, and he seemed sober and lucid.

"Good morning, Sam." Her voice came softly.

He tipped his hat automatically. "Mrs. Farrel."

"Will you join us for breakfast? Will is at the hotel."

"No, I . . . think I'll be movin' on."

Abbie stared at him. "You can't mean that. You won't leave town with Cole in jail, waiting to . . . to hang for a crime he thinks you committed."

Sam dropped his chin. "Cole can stand on his own two feet. It's time he did."

"But he won't if he thinks they'll come after you."

"That's his problem. No one's said anything about me bein' with Auralee. If he hadn't gone up there, he wouldn't be in this fix."

Abbie saw something flicker behind his eyes. Was it a twinge of conscience or a lust for blood? "At least talk to him,

Sam. Tell him you had nothing to do with it."

"If he had half your sense, he'd see that for himself. He knows me."

"Does he?" She felt her anger besting her. "Would he die for a brother who hasn't the guts to stand up for him? Will you let him die because Auralee saw something in Cole that you lacked?" Abbie saw Sam's jaw stiffen, but he held his peace. "Can you live the rest of your days knowing the real killer is living free?"

He spread his hands, then closed them into fists. "It don't matter. It won't bring her back."

"And hanging Cole will?"

"He don't have to hang. That's up to him. He ain't in there to protect me. He's in there to ease his guilty conscience."

"That's not true."

"Ain't it?" Sam's cheek twitched. "Suppose you ask him. Suppose you find out why he took to Auralee."

Abbie's chest constricted. "I know why. Does that mean I should hang, too?"

Sam cocked his jaw to the side and held her angry gaze. "I reckon only you know that." He slowly tipped his hat and walked away.

"Sam!"

He stopped at the door and turned.

"I will free Cole."

He shook his head. "Not likely. Not with the tale Birdie has to tell. Not even you can change that."

Abbie wet her lips. "I've spoken with her once. I'll see her again tonight."

Sam drew his brows together and scrutinized her. "You're messin' with things you don't understand. If Pablo gets wind of your meddlin'—"

"I'll just see that he doesn't. No one knows but you and Will."

"And Birdie."

Abbie thought of the money in her pocket. Would Birdie double-cross her? Did this Pablo put her up to it? Or was Birdie playing a game of her own? "I'll just have to take that chance."

Sam spoke slowly, as though the words came from a recess in his mind that had grown dusty with lack of use. "I wish you luck, Mrs. Farrel." Again he tipped his hat, then walked out.

Sam stepped into the street, and for a moment he envied his brother. Abbie Farrel might be a hard nut, but at least Cole had hope. Maybe that's what hurt the most. There was no hope now, not once a person was gone.

He'd looked that truth in the eye these last days. He'd cried like a baby, holed up in the shack where he'd grown up. He'd been tempted to lose himself in booze. Instead, he'd let the raw pain sear him like a smelting fire. He wasn't sure what was left. Maybe nothing. Nothing at all.

♦♦♦♦♦♦♦♦

This time Birdie seemed edgy. Abbie watched her eyes dart back and forth across the yard, saw her flinch at any sound. Birdie caught the hair back from her face with her fingers and let it cascade over her shoulder like silken thread. The motion was practiced, but her fingers trembled.

"What do you want? Why are you doing this?"

Abbie tried to look determined and not as desperate as she felt. "Because an innocent man will hang unless you tell the truth."

"Innocent? What is innocent? I have men at my door all night long. But they are not there to protect me." Her voice held a bitter edge.

"Protect you from whom? If Cole is guilty, who do you fear?"

Birdie's eyes shot to the door behind her, and Abbie thought she might run. What had happened between now and their last meeting? Had Abbie's questions made the girl consider what she was doing? Or was it something else?

Birdie rubbed her wrists and hesitated, then drew a sharp, sudden breath. "If I talk, I'm dead, too. This life, it's better than lying in the graveyard."

Abbie searched for words of assurance. Could she appeal to Birdie's conscience? Could she—

"We'll take you out of here."

Abbie spun with Birdie at Will's words. What was he doing? What was he saying?

He straightened. "Tell us the truth, and we'll get you out of here safe."

Abbie watched the doors close in Birdie's mind. Her eyes grew dull and hard, absolutely dead. Abbie had never seen eyes so cold, so void of feeling.

"Sure you will, caballero." Birdie's voice was mocking and cruel. "You and a hundred others." She swept the hair in a shimmering stream from her face. "What do you want in return? A little sugar?" She stretched her delicate fingers to Will's shirt, and Abbie watched the shock of it register in his face.

"We want to help Cole." Abbie said it plainly. "And we'll help you, too." She hadn't planned on that, but Will's intent was clear. And it might be the only way. "I give you my word."

"Your word?" Birdie's eyes stabbed her with the same derision she'd seen in Lil's. "Oh, sí, the word of a lady. You know the best part of all this? The judge will take my word." She smacked her hand to her breastbone defiantly, but Abbie saw a confused mixture of pain and hatred in her face.

Birdie narrowed her eyes. "What is Cole to you?"

"A friend."

"You lie."

The words sank deeply into Abbie's soul. How dare this ... this ... woman call her a liar? Was it a lie? Was Cole only a friend? Was he even that? Was he more? How could this person think to know her heart, when she didn't know it herself?

"You think I do not know a lie when I hear one? 'Oh, Birdie, you are the only one. I love you. I will come back and marry you. Just you wait.' "

Abbie swallowed her indignation. One angry word now could ruin everything. At least Birdie was listening. She'd almost admitted her story was untrue. . . .

Abbie drew a long breath. "We will take you out of here."

"Why should I believe that when you lie about Cole?"

Abbie forced her heart to steady. "The truth is I don't know what Cole is to me. I ... care for him, and I don't want him to hang for something he didn't do."

Birdie dropped her eyes. For a moment Abbie saw a young girl, uncertain and ... afraid. Will was right. He'd seen something Abbie's eyes had missed. Birdie's head jerked up, and she whispered, "I cannot tell you. He'll kill me."

"He?"

Birdie shook her head, trembling. "He will knife me as he did Auralee."

"He won't." Abbie held her gaze, willing her courage.

"My room and hers, they join up. I wasn't working. I was sick. I heard ... I tried not to listen, but then he came into my room. He had blood all over him, all over the knife. He asked who'd been with Auralee. I only knew Cole. I had heard them talking just before, arguing."

Birdie shuddered. "He was pleased when I said Cole. He told me to name Cole. Then he ... rubbed her blood on my throat. He said I would be next if I crossed him. I know better than to cross Cre . . ." Her mouth froze in a grimace.

"Crete? Crete Marlowe?"

Birdie moaned. "You must get me away. If Pablo knows I told . . ."

"Pablo Montoya knows it was Crete?"

Birdie's voice rose a pitch. "He knows Crete was last with Auralee, but he said Crete was with me."

"Why? Why would he protect Crete Marlowe?"

"Money. He can make Crete pay for his silence." Birdie gripped the doorframe. "You take me out of here as you promised, or I will swear it was Cole and watch him hang." She heard a step inside and paled. She pointed to Will. "Send him after me in one hour." Birdie pulled open the door.

"*¿Que pasa alli?*"

Abbie heard the male voice, but Will pulled her out of the light and away before she caught Birdie's reply. She held tightly to Will's large-boned hand as they rushed through the alley to the back of the hotel. Then she leaned against the wall and caught her breath.

Crete Marlowe. The one who came hunting for Cole was the one who'd killed Auralee? He had hunted Cole for his own crime?

"You're shaking."

She gripped Will's hands. "What are we going to do about Birdie?"

"I'm goin' for her tonight. I'll take her straight to that Captain Gates, then light out of town. Can I . . . take her to the ranch? I mean, if she has nowhere else to go?"

Abbie felt the pulse in his hands, and they warmed. What had she gotten him into? "I guess so, Will, but . . ."

"Be ready to go in an hour."

"I can't leave until they let Cole out."

Will shook his head. "I don't know . . . that Pablo . . . You didn't see him, Mrs. Farrel. He has eyes like . . . He's a man who will kill."

She rubbed her temples. "I can't leave, not without seeing Cole freed."

"Then follow as soon as you can. And don't let anyone connect you with Birdie. No doubt Pablo will be lookin'."

Abbie was amazed by Will's manly tone. But then, she reminded herself again, Will was no longer a boy. She went up to her room and lay without sleeping. The few hours of sleep she'd gotten before meeting Birdie left her weary but unable to sleep again.

What was Will doing? She pictured him pacing his room, waiting for the hour to pass. But no. He would be packing up, making preparation to travel. They still had supplies from Santa Fe. They'd used little of it since reaching El Paso.

What of a horse? A horse for Birdie? Abbie's thoughts spun. She forced them to still. Will would figure it out. This was his cause, not hers. She must see Cole freed. Abbie sank her head back into the pillow.

With Birdie's testimony removed, they would have no cause to hold him. Cole might even be out that day. Her heart quickened, but not with the elation she might have expected. She pressed her fist to her forehead and closed her eyes. It would mean another good-bye.

Her task was accomplished. Her honor satisfied. Cole would be exonerated and now . . . What? Abbie's breath came in a half sob. *Oh, Lord. Give me strength to do the right thing.* She would be alone, but alone was better than compromising what she knew love could be.

A tear crested and made a slow channel down her cheek to catch in the hair at her temple. If only it hadn't been so right with Monte. Maybe then she could have loved again. Her heart was willing, but her mind, her memories . . . God had given her one perfect love. She could never expect that again.

More tears burned and fell. The short years she'd had with her husband would have to sustain her. And she had Elliot, the fruit of their love, Monte's legacy. She had her memories. What more did she need?

Twenty-One

Cole was jarred awake by the door banging open and a streak of pale daylight. He rose to one elbow as Captain Gates passed in, much too early for any normal matter of business. The captain looked as though he'd been roused in a hurry. Had the judge arrived?

Gates strode forward, jammed the key into the lock on Cole's cell, and turned it. "Cole Jasper, I'm tired of havin' you in my jail." Both of Cole's neighbors stared wide-eyed as the cell door swung open. "Well, go on. Get out."

Cole came fully upright on the bunk. "What the heck are you doin', Gates?"

"Charges against you are dropped. The witness gave us the real story. It wasn't you she saw at all."

Sam. Cole felt his chest lurch. His throat went dry. "Who, then?" The rasp was pathetic.

"Marlowe. Crete Marlowe."

Cole stared at the captain as if he'd spoken some language Cole didn't know. "But you sent Marlowe after me."

"I didn't send him. If he came after you, it was his own doing. Anyway, the warrant's out for him now, and you are a free man."

Cole stood, but he wasn't sure he was awake. "Why'd your witness change the story?" He hadn't bothered to ask who the witness was, but now he had his suspicions.

"Your lady got through to her."

"My . . ." *Abbie.*

"Seems Marlowe threatened Birdie with the same as he did to Auralee if she named anyone but you."

Cole frowned, picturing the little raven-haired wisp. He could hardly blame her. She must've been plenty scared. It suddenly hit him. "You mean I've been rottin' here in place of Crete Marlowe?"

"Looks that way, you stubborn son of a gun. What the heck did you think you were doin'?"

Cole buckled on the gun belt Gates handed him and reached for his hat. "I figured someone mistook me for Sam. You know how he was about Auralee."

"So you were gonna hang in his place?"

"I was hopin' it wouldn't come to that."

Gates quirked an eyebrow. "Ever consider bein' a lawman again? Anyone with your kind of death wish ought to do just fine." He clamped Cole's shoulder. "I could use a deputy."

"I'll think on it." Cole quirked his mouth. "But not too hard."

"I guess not—not with that purty lady waitin' for you."

Cole felt none too sure about that. "Where is she?"

"Guess she headed back to the hotel after the young fella skipped town with Birdie."

"Will?"

"He's takin' her out of harm's way, back to your lady's ranch."

His lady. Cole's heart jumped in his chest, but things were far from settled in that area.

"I got Birdie's *X* on her statement, should we catch up to Marlowe anytime soon. But I may be calling for her if it comes to it."

What was Gates running on about? Oh, Birdie. Little Birdie with a smile of promise and a heart of quicksand. God help

Will. It suddenly sank in what the boy was up to. And what would Pablo have to say about it? This was trouble Cole hadn't counted on. Did it never end?

Cole almost wished he could go back to that sleepy place of acceptance. But no, he was a free man again. His grin probably looked as stupid as it felt. He didn't care. *And the truth shall set you free.* The truth. Could he tell Abbie the truth?

"As for the lady, I wouldn't be looking any further if I were you, Cole."

"I ain't plannin' to. But she's got a mind of her own."

"No mistaking that." Gates clapped his back. "But you're up to it, I reckon."

"We'll see." Cole took a step toward the door and inhaled the early morning air. He cleared the doorway and stepped out onto the walk. Every step seemed a true pleasure. He could direct his feet, go whichever way he chose. He was free.

He eyed the street, the hotel, and Abbie's horses outside it. She was shy a packhorse and Will's bay, but the others stood ready, packed up. So she was leaving. Without word. Or had she wanted him to come to her? Cole started along the walk, hesitated, then continued on. He owed her his thanks at the least.

He stopped outside the hotel door. Should he go in? The eastern sky glowed orange under a hazy pink. It was early yet. What if she'd gone back to sleep? He could wait. He could . . .

She came out dressed to travel in a riding skirt and fitted jacket buttoned to her neck. She looked prettier than any woman had a right to be. But her face was set, determined. He knew that look. It had shut him out more years than he could count.

Cole pulled the hat from his head and forced the lump from his throat. Still, the words were slow in coming as they stood and looked, one on the other. "I came to thank you." He was gratified that his voice showed none of his distress.

Abbie's expression softened. "No thanks are needed, Cole. I only did what you'd have done for me, what you have done in the past."

The past. "You're ridin' this mornin'? Alone?"

"If I travel fast, I'll catch up with Will. Birdie won't be used to the saddle." Her words were frank, her tone matter-of-fact.

"I reckon not." Cole ran his hand through his hair and replaced his Stetson. It was now or never. Could he live with himself if he didn't take the one last chance he'd likely have with her? "I got someplace I'd like to show you before you go, if you can spare the time."

Abbie nodded slowly and none too eagerly. "I can spare it." She motioned toward the horses tied at the post. "Brother Lewis returned Whitesock, but I intended to leave him for you."

"Thank you, Abbie." He took the bags and bundles from her and tied them onto the horse beside Zephyr. "What's Birdie ridin'?"

"Will purchased a mare from the livery with the money I . . . money Birdie had."

Birdie? Unless she'd gotten a whole lot better at pinching wallets, Birdie had no such wherewithal. Abbie must have paid to make her talk. That would have set Abbie back badly, if he knew Birdie.

Cole saw Abbie's flush and knew his guess was right. How much had it cost her to get him free? And why had she done it? Why not? She had a good heart, even if it was as closed to him as it seemed.

Abbie had meant to seek out Cole before leaving, to say good-bye in as sensible a manner as possible. She wanted it to be brief and unemotional. She had not expected to come upon him with the morning sun in his hair and its reflection in his eyes.

She didn't want to know what he felt, what he wanted. It was better for both of them to part friends, without saying or doing anything they'd regret. It was better to leave the possibilities in the dust of El Paso. It was time to go home.

But Abbie couldn't refuse him the simple request, and now she felt the silence grow between them as they rode the horses away from the ferry after crossing to the older Juarez. She fought to keep her emotions from rising to the fore. They were too confused, too dangerous. Yet she was painfully aware of him beside her as they rode the river valley to the edge of town and beyond.

Abbie looked ahead and saw a weathered earthen hut. The door was lost or stolen, and the opening gaped darkly. As they drew close, she saw a piece of canvas hanging from a window like a flap of skin on a sightless eye. The stoop was choked with weeds and likely crawled with things better left undisturbed.

Cole reined in and crossed his wrists over the saddle horn. His gaze looked pensive and . . . pained. Surely this wasn't what he meant to show her, this desolate, forsaken place. But he didn't move on.

Abbie turned to him, confused. "What is this place?"

He swung down and led Whitesock a couple paces forward. "This is my home."

Abbie felt her lips part as she looked at it with new eyes. The heap of rotted wood on the side might have been a barn or shed at one time, and her gaze was drawn to the burned-out stump of a tree. Images of a woman hanging by her arms, flames and arrows . . . Pressing her eyes shut, Abbie shuddered and slowly climbed down from the saddle.

Cole didn't look her way. "Belongs to Sam now, though it ain't worth much. Not like those across the river, stateside. The place was goin' down even before my pa left. Sam and I scratched the ground some, raised enough to fill our bellies.

Ma tried to patch up the place as best she could, but with the floodin' and the droughts . . ."

He spread his hands. "After pa left, she hadn't much to go on, so Sam took jobs where he could find 'em. When I was twelve we signed on together at a spread owned by cattlemen up from San Antone."

He looked along the river valley as though imagining the herds grazing there. "When we weren't workin' the herd, we were drivin' mules and haulin' freight, or raidin' the vaqueros' range and drivin' home the wild horses. At night, Sam taught himself to read and write. I learned to bust broncs."

Cole let the reins hang and rubbed the back of his neck. "Good money in that, but it's hard on your innards. You void blood often enough, you get to thinkin' there must be a better way. Only sometimes no other way shows itself. So you do what you gotta do till you're the best there is. But that don't keep you from makin' mistakes."

Abbie listened. Though the picture he painted was painful, it explained his fierce independence, his gruff and caustic ways, his need to control and his commitment to good. From what she'd overheard during her days in El Paso, the town's esteem for him was unparalleled.

"You were born here, in Mexico?"

"I was born in San Antonio. We moved here when I was five. I suspect my pa was runnin'."

"From the law?"

He shook his head slightly. "I doubt it. Most of his crimes were legal."

Abbie waited, but he didn't elaborate.

Cole stood without speaking, then kicked the dirt. "I've never brought anyone here before."

She heard the vulnerability in his voice and resisted its tug on her heart. She couldn't, she wouldn't . . . Abbie drew herself up. "Not Auralee?" Her voice had an edge she hadn't intended.

"Or Birdie or any of the others?"

"The others?"

"You've traveled around. I imagine there are broken hearts in more than just El Paso."

"I ain't sure where you're gettin' your imaginings." Cole turned to face her. "Abbie, I . . . never had relations with Auralee or any other."

She felt the blood rush to her face. "What?" It came out more breath than voice. "But you told me . . ."

"No, I didn't. You were just so ready to believe it, I didn't argue."

Abbie's temples started to throb. What was he trying to do? "I saw you with Lil . . ."

"You saw what you wanted to see. You marched in believin' the worst."

Now her anger gained strength. "You made very little effort to dissuade me. And how did Birdie know you, then? And Auralee? You said you were with her the night she died."

"I hate to be the one to educate you on how those places work, but there are different levels of involvement. The downstairs is public, just like the saloon in Rocky Bluffs. A man can pay for a drink and a dance and pretend for a while that somebody cares. Least until the music stops."

"And that's all you did."

"The one time I paid entrance to an upstairs room was the night Auralee died."

"Why then?" Abbie's throat cleaved, and her voice came out thin and tight.

"I thought she was in trouble."

Abbie felt her defenses crumbling. She didn't want to believe it, but how could she not? Cole could no more resist helping a woman in need than . . . Her anger stirred. "Why were you there at all, in that sort of place?"

Cole slouched. "Well, Abbie, the truth is a man gets lonesome for a purty smile and a soft voice. With another kind of woman you set up expectations, and that ain't fair. But those in the business, they're just doin' their job."

Abbie heard the gentle compassion he felt for the women who offered him a soft word and pretty smile. The fight left her, and she felt ... ashamed; ashamed for condemning Cole for seeking solace in his loneliness and judging the women who gave it.

It didn't make it right, not by a long shot. Some things were wrong no matter the circumstances. But it wasn't for her to condemn. If Cole had never more than kept company ... How could she know? How could she be certain?

He must have seen her doubt. "Two things my ma taught me—never underestimate a woman and never take advantage of a lady. Some folks draw a line between the two. Me, I consider them all ladies."

Abbie's conflicting shame and relief were swallowed by the sudden pulsing rush that swept her. She couldn't help thinking how much he'd changed from the cocky trail boss who'd told her dancing was just like roping only gentler. But then, maybe he hadn't changed so much after all. Maybe now she just saw beyond his crusty edge.

What had Cole said with that confident grin all those years ago? *Dancin's easier than ropin' cuz every girl wants to be caught.* Abbie fought now to keep from proving him right.

"If you were lonely, Cole, why did you never marry?" It was a feeble attempt.

"I reckon you know the answer to that."

Abbie was sure he must hear her heart pounding from where he stood. She took one step closer, drawn by his green eyes, by his suntanned features, straight nose and jaw, by his firm mouth half-covered with a mustache in need of a trim. She remembered the feel of his mustache. . . .

He didn't move, didn't reach for her.

Her lips trembled. "Aren't you going to kiss me, Cole?"

He parted his mouth slowly. "No, I ain't."

His expression betrayed nothing. Abbie was suddenly young and uncertain. "You don't want to?"

"I want to."

She searched his face, trying to discern what he felt. Anything at all?

"If I kiss you now, it won't stop there. I'll want to kiss you tomorrow and the next day and every day after. I've spent too many years wantin' to kiss you, Abbie. But if you tell me one more time that you cain't love me, I'll walk away now and not come back."

Abbie's heart rushed in her chest. She reached for his hand, firm and strong under her fingers, but he still made no move. His own honor, disguised behind the character of a cowboy, kept him back. He wouldn't settle for less than everything, not this time.

Lord, help me. I don't know which way to turn. Lose him forever or . . . or risk . . . A deep, fearful warmth passed through her, then peace so profound it took her breath. She almost felt the hand of God nudging her onward. Her gaze met Cole's, the waiting evident in his eyes. "I love you, Cole."

Abbie wasn't sure if she'd actually said the words, or if her heart had just thrummed it through her being. But Cole's expression deepened with a look almost painful as he enclosed her hand in his.

"I asked you this a long time ago. Now I'm askin' again. Abbie, will you be my wife?"

His face held the same raw, unconditional love she'd seen the day he meant to die for her. She didn't deserve it, didn't deserve his steadfast devotion. She knew him now. She'd seen into the depths of his soul, his failings and his goodness. He seemed no longer rough but . . . noble.

"Yes."

Cole stood a moment as though she hadn't spoken, then pulled a slow grin. "I'll be. I'd have gone down on my knee if I thought you'd say yes."

Abbie gave him a shaky smile. "You still could if you're inclined."

He drew her close. "I reckon I could. Or I could take care of that need."

"What need?"

"As I recall you were just beggin' a kiss."

"I wasn't begging."

"What then?"

"Offering."

He wrapped her cheek in his callused palm. "I accept." He kissed her long and slow.

Abbie's heart beat a powerful response, drawn in by the call of his own. She caught her breath, then tried to sound frank and sensible. "We can speak with Father O'Brien on the way home."

Cole cupped her face in both hands. "We can speak with the priest if you like, but first we'll have us a ceremony with Brother Lewis. Sheez, Abbie, I've waited eight years."

Twenty-Two

Abbie stood facing Cole under the cottonwoods on the rise above the old cabin. In her blue woolen skirt and jacket bodice, brushed clean of trail dust, she looked presentable enough, but it was hardly what she'd call wedding clothes. Cole had purchased a six-dollar suit that looked as out of place on him as Monte had looked in dungarees.

No, don't think about it. Don't question. Don't doubt. But how could she not? Had her feelings once again held sway over her judgment? Had she only imagined God's blessing? Why else would she now feel so . . . terrified? The December air was cold, but her palms were slick in Cole's hands.

She'd thought to have time to let the decision sink in, to get used to loving Cole, to . . . let go. This immediacy, this . . . finality, the irrevocable words . . . and what would follow . . . *Oh, Lord.* Yes, she loved him, but . . .

Cole cocked his head just slightly, and his eyes narrowed, making fine lines at the edges. The chilly wind ruffled his hair like a cockscomb, and the creases on either side of his mouth deepened. He saw her hesitation; he knew.

No. Yes. Abbie's throat was tight and dry. The wind caught her hair and carried it. She should ask him to wait. *Wait? Until when?* Would she ever be ready? Would it be different two months, six months from now, a year, five years, or ten?

Brother Lewis's question hung in the air, caught away by

229

the wind, but there ... waiting for her reply. *Do you take Cole Matthias Jasper to be your lawfully wedded husband ... until death do you part?*

Until death. Joined until death. Did death part two hearts that beat as one? Was she severed from Monte by the grave? If Cole took her in his arms and loved her, would they join? Would it be the same? Could it ever be the same?

Please, God. But no voice came. Had God already shown her the way? Was it now hers to accept or reject what He had given? Cole waited, impassive, neither forcing nor pleading. Cole Jasper who had been part of her life so long now. Cole who forgave even her ugliest parts ...

Abbie didn't know what to feel, and for once she was glad of that. She didn't want her emotions to make the choice. She must take this on faith, choose to commit her life to this man whom God had provided, no matter how unlikely.

Had Cole truly surrendered to God? She thought for a moment of Gray Wolf. Hadn't God used him? Was it any less likely that Cole was in His hands? She had a hard time seeing Cole submissive even to God, yet ... there was something, some depth she hadn't seen in him before, a humility ... an acceptance. Trust.

Brother Lewis cleared his throat.

Abbie trembled. "I do." It came from her, but her throat shook, bearing witness to her doubt.

The tension in Cole's jaw released, but his mouth kept the same line as he slipped the ring on her finger. His eyes probed, offering ... what? A chance to turn back? Take back her vow?

Brother Lewis covered their joined hands with his. "Cole and Abbie Jasper, I now pronounce you man and wife, and may God guard your promise all the days of your life together." He smiled. "Cole, you may kiss your bride."

Cole bent and brushed her lips with his. There was nothing of his passion in the kiss. It was the seal of their testament, but no more. Abbie waited in surprise, but he straightened, turned to Brother Lewis, and extended his hand.

"Thank you, Brother. It was a fortunate bend that brought our trails together."

Brother Lewis matched Cole's grip. "Fortune had nothing to do with it, Cole. It was God Almighty and His wondrous ways."

Cole turned, and Captain Gates gripped his hand. "Congratulations, Cole." He tipped his hat to Abbie. "Ma'am." Then he and another man Cole had introduced, but whose name Abbie forgot, signed their names as witnesses and strode away down the hill.

Cole took the license from Brother Lewis and tucked it into his vest. It was done, settled and permanent according to the law. Cole and the preacher spoke briefly, saying their good-byes, but Abbie felt rooted to the ground.

Brother Lewis gripped her hands warmly. "God bless you, Mrs. Jasper."

Mrs. Jasper. It jolted her as though she'd been suddenly changed. She was no longer the person she'd been, the person she'd dreamed of being and become. She was Mrs. Montgomery Farrel no more. Her mind closed in, and she felt dazed.

Abbie stood alone with Cole on the hill. He was silent, but his questions, his disappointment shown in his eyes. She offered him a thin smile. What was wrong with her? This man had proved again and again his integrity, his fidelity, his love. An hour ago her heart had pulsed with passion for him. Why did it now beat with fear and uncertainty?

Cole reached for her hand and brought it to his lips, then closed her fingers between his palms. "How much of a start did you give Will and Birdie?"

She felt thick-headed and stupid. "What?"

"Will and Birdie. When did they start out?"

"This morning, before dawn."

"Then I reckon we'd better ride." He kept hold of her hand and started down the hill at a saunter.

Abbie stumbled beside him. Did he mean to go, to leave without . . . would he not consummate their marriage? Didn't he expect . . . "Cole—"

"Mr. Farrel told me something I never forgot. He said when you get a new foal, fresh into the world, you go over it with your hands real gentle. You don't rush and you don't force it. That way it comes to know you and remembers your touch."

What was he doing? Why was he speaking of Monte now? Why churn up old memories, emotions, sorrows?

Cole stopped and turned. "He said he wouldn't touch you until he had a touch he wanted you to remember."

Abbie's heart seized. Was Cole intentionally hurting her, paying her back for her indecision?

He cupped her cheek with his palm. "I reckon now I know what he meant. It has to be right, and here and now there are too many things workin' against us. When you're ready, and when we ain't fightin' time and trouble, then I will love you."

Abbie felt the warmth of his palm on her face. She heard the tenderness in his words. He was giving her time. Without her asking. He knew her heart, and it again surged with love for him. Would she ever get it right?

She touched her fingers to his jaw, felt his wind-chapped skin, smooth shaven for the occasion. Her gaze went to his mouth, to the line of his lips, to the overhang of his freshly trimmed mustache. She felt a quickening, and she wanted his kiss, wanted it badly.

His mouth pulled slowly sideways. "Don't make it hard on me, Abbie. We got a lot of miles ahead."

"Don't you even mean to kiss me?"

"Sheez!" Cole pulled her into a rough embrace and kissed the crown of her head.

That wasn't what she meant, but he set her back and

started down at a quicker pace, tugging her along. "I reckon by the time we're packed up and on our way, those two will be restin' the horses and settin' off again. We'll have to cut a good clip to catch them by nightfall."

"Well, if not tonight . . ."

"You don't know what you're sayin'. You set that boy's foot in a bear trap, sendin' him off with Birdie."

"But surely . . ."

Cole gathered Zephyr's reins and held her while Abbie swung up. Then he mounted Whitesock and brought its head around. Once more he was the cowboy, one with his horse and in control. "Trust me, Abbie. We ain't got a spare minute."

She followed him into town at a canter. His words were clear enough, but she couldn't help wondering if it was Will he feared for, alone with Birdie, or himself.

✦✦✦✦✦✦✦

Cole led the packhorses at an easy lope, with Abbie riding beside him. His wife. On paper at least. It shamed him, the disappointment he felt. What did he expect? He'd rushed her. He'd thought her acceptance was more than it was. Maybe she loved him as she said, respected and accepted him, but her heart wasn't his. Maybe it never would be.

Could he live with that? Cole shrugged away the doubt. He would, if it came to it. She'd made the vow, though it took everything in her to get it out. She could have refused, but she didn't. She took him as her husband, the same as he pledged himself to her. They would build on that promise.

The daylight was nearly spent. If they didn't find Will and Birdie soon, they'd have to camp separately—something he'd just as soon avoid, all things considered. But it was getting cold, and they couldn't go on in the dark. Will had probably stopped already and set up camp with whatever he had.

Abbie had sent them minimally supplied so they could ride

fast. And that was good. Birdie's fear of Pablo Montoya was well grounded. He didn't let his doves loose without a fight. Cole had heard the whispers of a search beginning as he and Abbie packed up and resupplied in town.

So far the runaway hadn't been connected to them, but as soon as she was, Pablo would make his move. Cole looked back over his shoulder. With Abbie's conditioning, they had made good time and spread some miles behind them. The same wouldn't hold for Birdie.

If she'd ever been on horseback, it couldn't have been much. Pablo kept a tight rein on his girls. Abbie had no idea what she'd done in freeing that bird. But now that they were in it, they'd see it through.

"There." Abbie pointed. "There's a fire, Cole."

He picked out the prick of light in the darkness ahead. "You're right. I don't suppose too many folks are travelin' this time of year, but we'll take it slow anyway." He reined to a walk, unwilling to mention all the possibilities of who could be sitting around that fire. They'd see soon enough.

But once the blaze was a discernible glow, Abbie hurried the mare toward the camp.

"Abbie . . ."

She kept on, and Cole matched stride, trying not to take her eagerness personally. Two figures huddled near the flames, one large, one small. Cole relaxed. They'd found their party, but that didn't mean they were out of trouble, from without . . . or within.

Abbie swung down and rushed to Will. "You did it!"

He rose awkwardly and caught her outstretched hands. He grinned like the boy he was, regardless of his size and years. Then something caught his attention, and he stared from Abbie's hand to her face, then to Cole's. "You . . . you got hitched?"

The ring. He'd noticed the gold band with rose-colored

tracery. Cole hadn't meant to make a deal of it, but that Will, he was observant. And there was Abbie with her hands still caught in the boy's, though she was none too quick to explain.

"Yeah, we got hitched. Now, why don't you see to these horses while Abbie cooks up some grub." Cole hadn't meant to sound so gruff. He saw Abbie's puzzlement and hurt. Well doggone, he was only human. How many emotions could a man juggle in one day?

Cole looked at last at Birdie. Her dark eyes were sharp on him, like those of a hawk. She was a twisted-up child with enough wiles to outsmart the nation's governing body. Her gaze went to Abbie, and he didn't like what he saw.

He rubbed the back of his neck and crouched beside the fire. "Pablo got any idea what you're up to?"

Birdie shrugged. "It may have occurred to him by now. He has eyes to see."

"I mean, does he know you took off with Will?"

"I did not take off with Will." Her voice dripped scorn.

"Does he know you're travelin' with us?"

She fanned the glimmering veil of black hair over her shoulder with one splayed hand. "He may. He is not *estúpido*, eh?"

"Did you tell anyone else what you were doin'?"

"Oh sí. I mentioned it to all the upright citizens of El Paso."

Cole felt like shaking her.

"Listen, Birdie, we're in this together. If Pablo comes lookin', it'll take all of us to keep you safe."

"What is it to you?" She turned so the fire outlined her fine profile. "You are free now, regardless."

"That ain't the point. Abbie gave you her word . . ."

"Oh sí." Birdie's chin raised. "Her honorable word." She combed the hair back with her fingers. It was a calculated move. She knew what that hair did to men. She knew how to use her beauty to slice through men's defenses. Pablo had trained her well. "But she has kept it already, no?"

Cole wet his throat. "It's not likely we'll abandon you now." *Unless you're more trouble than it's worth*, he wanted to add.

"How gallant, Cole Jasper. And on your wedding night." She shrugged and both the blanket and blouse slid off one shoulder.

Cole restrained the urge to shake her silly. He stood and helped Abbie gather up the pots and supplies to make their supper. Things could get real difficult if Birdie kept up that chatter in Abbie's hearing. He had a sudden need to hold his wife, but he resisted that as well. *Oh, Lord, you do try a man.*

◆◆◆◆◆◆◆

Abbie waited as Cole spread her bedroll. It was near his, but not touching. That's how she felt, near him but not touching. He kept her at a distance. Was he angry? Had her hesitance hurt him more than he let on? Didn't he know it wasn't him; it wasn't anything but her own disabling fears?

Will and Birdie were at opposite angles across the fire. Will at Cole's head, Birdie at hers. How had adding one slight girl to their number so changed the ease with which they'd traveled before? Will was tongue-tied and fumble-fingered, Cole gruff and short-tempered. He'd barked at Will twice.

But Birdie wasn't the only change. She and Cole were changed, man and wife, though somehow things had gone awry. Why had he insisted they marry at once? Had he thought if they waited she would change her mind? Would she have?

Abbie caught his gaze in the flickering light. When she was ready, he'd said. What if she went to him now, asked him to hold her, spoke of her love? Birdie shifted in her covers, and Abbie glanced over her shoulder. When she turned back, Cole wore his insolent grin.

What he found funny in the situation was beyond her. She

raised her chin and showed him her back, but he took one stride and caught her shoulders. "Good night, Abbie." He kissed her forehead. His lips were warm, his mustache soft.

She raised her face. If he just kissed her, she'd know. He couldn't keep his love from his lips, not if he really kissed her.

Cole tapped her lips with his finger. "Get some sleep." He let her go and waited while she climbed into the bedding and pulled the oilskin cloth over the blankets.

The ground was hard, the wind cold with more than a hint of rain, and Abbie felt a surge of temper. *Lord, what were you thinking when you made men so all-fired stubborn and impossible? I might offer an improvement or two, if you've ever a mind to listen!* She breathed an immediate apology and settled into a dismal mood. If she slept at all it would be a wonder.

Twenty-Three

The bed felt so deep and soft it wrapped itself around her. The flannel sheets were thick as fur, and someone's arms held her. *Cole.* She heard his deep breathing, felt his beard-roughened cheek against hers. With her eyes closed in drowsy content, she reached a hand to stroke his jaw.

Her fingers grew confused trailing over features they knew, only . . . he felt so cold. She ran her hand down his neck, over his chest. Her hand went inside him, and she felt the gore through shattered ribs. *Monte!* But the cold, dead face was Cole's.

Abbie jolted awake in teeth-chattering fear. The blankets slid down as she sat up, trembling. The sun had not yet risen, and the sky was a dull gray. She turned to Cole, but his bedding lay empty. Fear crawled up her spine.

She threw off the covers and stood. The camp was still, the embers low. Whitesock was not with the other horses. Cole was gone. A burning pierced the ice inside her. She felt betrayed all over again.

Abbie stalked to the fire and cleared away the rain-soaked ashes. She stoked the coals beneath with a vengeance and added damp cottonwood to make a sullen blaze. She scooped water from the river into the coffeepot and filled the insert with grounds. She shoved on the lid and set it to heat, then mixed up cornmeal batter.

When the lard was melted in the iron skillet, she poured in the batter and set it to cook. After washing out the bowl, Abbie wiped it dry and set it to be packed when they moved on. She moved with controlled determination, every action, every thought sharp and calculated.

Both Will and Birdie slept through her clatter, Birdie completely submerged in the blankets and likely too sore to move. Will snored like a hog in slop. What did they have to worry about? What troubled their dreams? Nothing. She looked up at the sound of hooves and stiffened.

Cole dismounted and joined her at the fire. "Coffee ready?" He reached for the pot.

She gave him a curt nod.

"Somethin' wrong?" He released the pot.

"No." Abbie turned the skillet to brown the other cornbread edge.

"Then why are you in a huff?"

"I am not in a huff." Abbie shoved the skillet and stalked away. She heard Cole's boots on the crisp turf behind her. She picked up speed.

"You cain't outwalk me."

She stopped, keeping her back stiffly toward him. He wrapped her from behind and rested his chin beside her head. "What's the matter?"

"Where were you?" She knew he could feel her trembling start up again.

"I went to see if we were bein' followed."

Abbie dropped her head forward, fighting the tears. She was unfair in her anger, but it gripped her nonetheless.

Cole turned her in his arms. "I'm sorry. I didn't know that would upset you."

"Well, you ought to have." She bit the words tersely. She couldn't tell him she was ashamed a dream could shake her so, ashamed to dream of Monte still, even if it was twisted and distorted. Besides, he should know better than to sneak off and leave her to wonder.

Cole looked at her with a frown between his brows, as though he were trying to piece her together. Oh, what was the use? Abbie shook off his arms and stalked to the fire. The corn bread was blackened at the edges, cracked and crusty on top. With a wadded cloth, she yanked it from the heat.

Cole bent and poured a cup of coffee, then he nudged Will awake and sent him to graze the horses. The grass was coarse and swampy from the icy rains, which looked to be coming again right soon. He would let Birdie wake her own self, or Abbie could rouse her if she'd a mind to.

He slid Mr. Farrel's Winchester rifle from its scabbard on Whitesock's saddle and checked it over. He'd have preferred a Sharps or something with more kick to it, but the Winchester used the same caliber load as his Colt revolver, so that was one benefit. He hoped it wouldn't see use, except maybe to hunt some meat. But he'd make sure it was in working order, just in case.

When Cole had cleaned and oiled and reloaded it, he did the same with his revolver and saw that Will was caring for his, too. Birdie woke, and he saw the pain in her movements. They'd not get far this day. He would pad her saddle with a blanket and shorten the stirrups some. Maybe that would help. He just hoped they'd have no need to ride hard.

They ate in silence around the fire. It was not Abbie's best effort, but then, he reckoned he'd distracted her. She put out a more frigid chill than the wet wind kicking up off the hills. Well, he'd apologized. It was up to her to accept it.

They rode slowly and made poor time. The rain came and beat on them relentlessly. It would wash clean their tracks, but there was really only one path to take through the desert country. Pablo knew that, and he'd know Birdie's condition. If he was of a mind to claim her, he'd do it this day or the next. Cole chafed. Two women, a man, and a boy were no match for the plug-uglies Pablo would bring.

Will rode up beside him, rain running from the brim of his hat. "You worried, Cole?"

"Does it show?"

"Not to the ladies, I don't think. Birdie's in too much pain, and Mrs. Farr . . . Jasper, well, she's . . ."

"Yeah, I know." Cole eyed Will. He'd filled out plenty these last years. He was what they'd call strapping, and he even carried a decent beard from the whiskers on his cheeks today. Twenty-one years old. Maybe it was time he stopped thinking of Will as a boy.

Cole dropped his chin. "I got a bad feeling. It ain't just that the girl's a valuable commodity, it's that Pablo might take it personal we saw fit to remove her."

Will nodded. "I suppose he would. She was pretty shaken up when we snuck out. That Captain Gates didn't promise anything as far as holding Pablo back."

"Nor could he, even if it was his job to. Which it ain't."

"What do you mean?"

"Well, Birdie's like property. Ain't right, but Pablo's invested in her keep and her clothes and the like. The way he sees it, she owes him, and on account of that, we've stolen from him."

Will shook his head. "She's a person, not a thing."

Cole noted the heightened color and vehemence in Will's face. "Look, kid, maybe you best know a thing or two." He lowered his voice and watched Will color as he explained the ins and outs of Birdie's life as he knew it. "So you watch yerself, you hear?"

Will nodded, but there was a manly set to his jaw that told Cole he might have done more harm than good. If Will took it on himself to conform and win over that vixen, he'd be a man right quick. Luckily, Birdie seemed to think Will had fallen off the face of the earth. Just now that was the best news Cole had.

◆◆◆◆◆◆◆

Under the stormy night sky, Abbie finished scrubbing the dishes in the creek. The rain had stopped long enough to permit a fire, but what wood and peat they could scrounge had burned with a sulky flame, and they'd eaten lukewarm beans and hash. So far, Birdie had not lifted a finger, but Abbie supposed that was due to her pained condition. Abbie remembered how it was but could conjure little sympathy for the girl.

Birdie's tongue was sharper than a viper's, though most of her virulence was directed at Will. The remarks she sent his way made Abbie's hair rise, though most of the time Birdie ignored him as completely as she did Abbie. It was to Cole she looked for everything.

Abbie watched him now, standing beyond the fire's smoky glow, looking out ... for what? Trouble? His stance was solid, his thumbs hooked in his belt, his gun hanging at his hip. She felt a stabbing remorse.

She'd snubbed him all day, responded in monosyllables or not at all. What kind of wife was she proving herself to be? Not that he'd yet taken on his role of husband. Or had he? Wasn't he taking seriously his care and protection of her? But hadn't he done as much before their vows were said?

He'd protected her since the first time he found her dazed in the snow. He'd been checking their safety this morning ... at his own risk. And there it was. The cold, clawing fear. She'd awakened and seen his blankets empty, just as she'd seen the empty bed beside her, morning after morning when Monte ...

The dream images filled her mind—irrational, confused, but potent in their terror. She stared at her hand as though it would actually be red with gore, then clenched it into a fist.

With taut arms, she left the firelight and joined him in the darkness of the night.

"You shouldn't have gone out alone." She spoke with the edges of her teeth joined together.

Cole turned, looking uncertain what to make of her sudden attack.

"This morning. You shouldn't have gone alone. It was reckless and . . ."

"Is that what this is all about? You were worried?" He made it sound childish.

"I don't believe in taking unnecessary risks."

"Since when?" Cole raised an insolent brow. "Since it's someone besides you? Seems I recall plenty of times I pulled your tail out of trouble you dug up yourself, takin' risks."

The fury warmed her. "I don't mean doing what you have to do. I mean . . ." Abbie tightened her hands at her sides.

He cocked his head, waiting, seemingly unwilling to join the argument any more than he had to. His self-control threatened her lack and only riled her more.

"What if they'd been out there? What if there were too many for you alone? What if you'd been . . ."

"Killed?"

Her chest heaved, and he took her arms. His grip was solid, hard. "I cain't promise I won't die. Only that I'll live the best I can until then."

Abbie rested her hands on his chest over the buttons of his yoked shirt, inside the flaps of his tawny duster. She felt his heart beating strong and fast beneath her right palm. His breath was warm, with no hint of tobacco. She suddenly realized he'd not smoked a cigarette since they started. It was different to smell him without it. It was nice.

"Tell me what you want, Abbie."

Her fingers trembled. "I want . . . I want to see you without your shirt."

"What?" His voice thickened.

"I need to see you whole. I have dreams . . . bad dreams . . ." Abbie dropped her head to his collarbone. She wasn't making sense and she knew it. He must think her addled.

Cole stroked her hair gently, his breath coming quick and shallow. "Well, back off, then."

She stepped back. He shrugged out of the duster, opened the yoke of the blue flannel shirt and tugged it over his head. In the darkness, she looked at him, his lean musculature, his smooth skin rising with gooseflesh in the stormy cold, the matting hair that spread across his chest. He was whole, undamaged except for the wound in his shoulder, healing now into a dark, puckered scar.

He shifted, and she watched the flex of bone and tendon. He was beautifully made, her husband. The thought caught her short. Abbie reached slowly, ran her fingers down the muscles of his chest and felt his stomach quiver.

Cole caught her hand hard at the wrist. Tears stung her eyes as she dropped her face to him, and he pulled her close and wrapped her in his arms. "Satisfied?" His voice was hoarse.

Her tears fell silently over his skin, and he pressed her head close and kissed its crown. She felt him shiver. He was cold, poor man. She laughed, then sniffed, and looked up at him.

Cole frowned. "I'm glad you find this comical."

"I'm sorry." She bit her lip against another laugh. "You're cold."

"On the outside, yeah. But you've stoked my furnace good."

Her breath caught jaggedly. "Kiss me, Cole."

"No, ma'am. We're in what you'd call a precarious situation. I need my wits about me."

"One kiss."

"Doggone it, Abbie." He pulled her close and kissed her soundly. "Now, let me keep watch in peace and with my clothes on, if you don't mind."

Twenty-Four

Cole dozed as he sat with his forearms to his knees, rifle ready across his boots. His eyes were closed, but his ears stayed wary. He could keep it up this night and maybe the next. After that he'd have to sleep.

He'd expected Pablo before this. But he knew in his gut it wouldn't be long now. With the Jornado Del Muerto less than a day's ride ahead, they couldn't risk the barren stretch where ambush would mean certain death. And if they stayed beside the Rio Grande they'd traverse rough and pitted country, scored by cliffs and arroyos that would make progress slow, if not impossible.

Again he wondered what chance they'd have against Pablo's men. Cole felt his innards twist up with concern. What he needed was a plan, but for once no possibilities seemed to come. Too much rested on this to take a chance he might have otherwise considered. Now he had Abbie to think of. His wife.

He felt wholly inadequate for the job. He'd saved his own skin plenty of times, even on occasion stepped in for Sam or one or another of his men. But he'd never had to risk what he now risked with Abbie—his heart and soul. *His soul.*

What had Brother Lewis said? To put his trust in the One who held his soul? Cole turned it over, but what good was that in a practical sense? Hadn't Brother Lewis had an answer for that? He'd sure filled time with all his sermons. Cole rubbed his brow.

Ah yes. The preacher had said God had charge over all the circumstances of his life. His physical as well as spiritual needs. Well, if Pablo came along armed as Cole expected, they'd sure as shootin' have physical need. Cole pressed his eyes with his right palm.

Lord God, you haven't known me long—leastwise, I haven't known you. But I reckon I need you now even more than when I was sitting in the jail. It ain't just me now. It's the ones in my care, and especially the one you gave me to love. I'd sure consider it a personal favor if you saw fit to get us through this somehow.

He peeled open his eyes and gazed along the line of the river in the dawning light. The storm had passed in the night, dropping rain and hail pellets that left the ground wet and surfeited. The water ran high. Storms had glutted the banks.

Abbie, Will, and Birdie slept beneath their oiled muslin tent covers. The hail had stung but not injured as it might have. They were none the worse for it. They'd move on at first light. He was edgy to get going even now. What kept Pablo?

Cole stood up stiffly. As he worked the kinks from his back, he scanned the distance. Heavy clouds met the earth at the horizon. Another storm would slow them, but it would work against Pablo, as well. The ground was slippery; it had been too dry underneath to receive the rain gracefully. Instead it rushed across the surface, filling the ruts and gullies.

He dropped his head back and stretched his arms, then yawned. He needed coffee. He could make it himself, though he'd gotten spoiled on Abbie's. He turned, but something caught his eye. He squinted out across the land. There it was. Birds.

Several things could raise a flock like that, but Cole knew better than to wonder. He stooped and took up the rifle, gauging the distance as he did. The rain last night had precluded a fire, but even if it hadn't, he wouldn't have allowed one. Now it looked like he wouldn't have coffee this morning, either. Cole gave Will's foot a kick with his boot, then squatted to wake Abbie.

She opened sleep-glazed eyes, then reached for his hand and held it between both of hers. "Pablo?"

Cole nodded. There was no use pretending they weren't up against it. He'd return Birdie before he let any harm come to Abbie or Will. But he'd give Birdie his best shot, as well . . . for what it was worth.

Abbie sat up, and he cupped her cheek in his palm. He had to be careful touching her, so potent were the feelings it kindled. But this morning it was comfort he wanted to give, comfort and courage. She'd need both before the day was out.

"Come 'ere." Cole caught her close to his chest.

After the episode with the shirt, she'd seemed less touchy, but he knew there were fears inside Abbie that he had no way to control. Today might prove her worst ones true. Cole almost wished he'd loved her when he'd had the chance.

He buried his fingers in her hair, and she raised her face to him. Her lips were soft and full from sleep, and he felt drawn beyond his resisting. He leaned close.

"Should I rouse Birdie?" Will's voice was as thick as his head. Hadn't the boy any sense of timing?

Cole drew back. "Yeah. We'll have company before long." He watched Will hesitate before touching Birdie's shoulder, then saw him sag when Birdie shoved his hand away. At least the kid was safe as long as she chose to spurn him.

Safe? They were none of them safe yet. He needed a plan, but his head was as thick as Will's this morning. No tobacco, no coffee, no sleep. And he'd missed his chance at Abbie's kiss. It was working into a sorely trying day.

Birdie sat up, looking scarcely all of her sixteen years and more like she wanted a paddling than saving. She gave him another inviting, almost pouting, smile. Cole turned away without response and stood.

"Listen up now. I reckon we got maybe an hour to decision time." He saw Birdie stiffen. "I don't mean decidin' *whether* to resist Pablo, but how." Cole ran his hand through his hair. "Ain't much use movin' out. Birdie's sore, and there'd be no outrunnin' them. May as well save the horses the trouble."

Abbie stood and pressed her hands to her lower back, shaking out her rumpled skirts. "What do we do, then? There's little cover here."

"That may be, but the country just ahead ain't the sort you can hurry through." The sound of hooves reached him at the same time he felt the vibration faintly in the ground. He stepped around Abbie and stared. He'd miscalculated. Or had he? It sounded like a single rider. As he watched, the rider came into view.

Cole raised the rifle to rest in both hands across his chest. His throat felt dry. Was it Pablo come to make his demands ahead of his men? Would he challenge him personally? A matter of honor? Was there honor among his kind?

Cole spoke over his shoulder. "Get down to the bank and hide yourselves in the bushes."

Abbie raised her chin.

He didn't give her time to argue. "Go on."

She shook her head and waved her arm over their camp. "It's obvious by the bedding that you're not here alone."

"I don't mean to fool anyone. I just don't want you in the path of any stray bullets. Now *git*." He saw her eyes flare and regretted the unfortunate words. Hadn't she already shown how poorly she took to that phrase?

Will stepped up and took her arm. "Come on, Mrs. Jasper. The sooner you and Birdie are out of harm's way, the better we can concentrate on the business at hand."

Abbie seemed surprised, then relieved that Will meant to

stand with him. Cole hadn't intended that at this point, but he wasn't going to argue. Especially as it smoothed Abbie's feathers. But he saw her pull the pistol from her pocket before she moved. He'd forgotten she carried it. And she could shoot. That was one more gun to count on.

Cole squinted at the rider, just visible now. He was coming at a good clip, not as he would expect Pablo to ride with a threat on his lips. Suddenly Cole relaxed and lowered the rifle to his hips. The rider drew swiftly closer, then slowed. Cole held his stance. If Sam meant to whip him again, this time he'd find a rival. He couldn't afford to be taken out now.

Sam swung down from his horse and caught the reins loosely with his left hand. Cole met his gaze evenly but let Sam speak first.

"I reckon you know you have trouble on your heels."

Cole nodded.

"I figured you could use a hand."

"You usin' it as a fist this time?"

Sam kicked the damp earth with the toe of his boot. "I reckon that's out of my system."

Cole drew a deep breath. "How many are they?"

"Baker's dozen." Sam tipped his hat, and Cole realized Abbie had come up from the bank.

He turned and drew her up beside him with a hand to her elbow. "I hear you've met Abbie, but I'll introduce her now as my wife." Cole watched the surprise in his brother's eyes to see if it triggered bitterness that could endanger them. Instead, Sam gave Abbie a questioning look, then extended his hand.

She took it, and Sam brought her fingers to his lips, a hint of mischief in his eyes. "Welcome to the family, little sister."

Abbie seemed taken aback, then annoyed. "Not so little," she stated, though she had to look up considerably to meet his eyes. "And if you've any more thoughts of thrashing my husband, I'll still put a gun to your head."

Sam cocked his jaw and grinned. "I reckon you would at that." He looked past her to Birdie coming back up from the riverbank.

Cole shook his head. So much for his instructions. "Well, if you're all done socializin', maybe you'll recall we're in a bit of a bind here."

Will came forward. "How far are they?"

Sam shrugged. "Twenty minutes, maybe, before they get a look at us."

Birdie tossed the braid she'd made of her hair back over her shoulder. "It is a shame we are on the same side of the river."

"They'd see us anyway." Sam eyed the sparse growth on either bank.

"But they would not reach us."

Cole stood the rifle on end and eyed her. "Why's that?"

"Pablo takes us to the river to bathe. But he does not swim himself."

"Why not?" At least Will didn't stammer when she looked his way.

"He is afraid, no?"

Cole snatched at the thought. "Are you sayin' Pablo won't cross?"

Birdie turned her wide sultry eyes on him. "Pablo believes his death lies on the water. It was spoken at his birthing." One eyebrow raised. "He will not cross."

"His men might." Sam turned as the sound of hooves became faintly discernible.

"Pablo will not lose face. If he cannot cross, his men will not."

"How sure are you?" Cole tried to read beneath her practiced bravado. She seemed smugly certain, but their lives depended on it.

Birdie shrugged one slender shoulder and said no more. It

was for him to decide whether to believe or not, and he didn't know which way to go. Crossing the Rio Grande was not to be taken lightly at any time and certainly not with the water up as it was. He glanced at Sam.

Sam tipped his head to indicate the decision was his. Cole looked across the water. It was a chance he hadn't counted on. But it was a dangerous one. *God, I ain't sure here. If you're listenin'...*

Suddenly he thought of Brother Lewis's awe at the sight of the river, his almost boyish delight as he spoke of the water having a life of its own, rushing like the river Jordan or the river of life. This was the same water that had baptized Cole into the kingdom at Brother Lewis's hands. It had ushered him into life once. Maybe it would again.

Cole felt a conviction inside. He'd take the chance. It was all he had. "We'll even out the load on all the horses. Sam, you and I will swim 'em across. Then we'll come back for the others."

He turned to Abbie, expecting support. Instead he saw confusion, uncertainty. "What is it, Abbie?"

Her eyes looked like a young doe's, all pupil and lashes. "I ... can't swim."

Cole's conviction faded. "Not at all?"

"Where would I learn? The most I've done is wade the mountain creeks."

He looked back at the water, then to Will. "Will?"

"I used to swim some. But it's been years."

"Can you hold your own against the current?"

"I swam the Ashley River as a boy."

Cole turned to Birdie. She smiled confidently and nodded. "I had planned one day to cross the river and leave Pablo cursing on the bank. Today will be that day."

Cole nodded. "Let's go, Sam."

Abbie came up beside him as he reworked the supplies onto

the horses' backs. "Could I ride across on Zephyr?"

"Too dangerous. She's never been tested as a water horse, and any of them could cramp and sink without warning. You'd be dragged under without a chance." Cole yanked off his boots and coat and then stripped down to his long johns, stuffing it all into the packs on the horse.

"Cole . . ."

"Don't worry, Abbie. I'll get you across." He gave her what he hoped was a confident smile.

She looked pale and less than certain. Of all the times for her to lose her nerve . . .

Twenty-Five

Abbie watched Cole lead Whitesock into the water. He and Sam kept the other horses between them, carrying the gear. The animals breasted the water and splashed until the bottom fell away and they swam. Cole caught hold of Whitesock's mane and swam beside him.

As they entered the current it carried them a little, but they angled against it and fought to keep a steady line to the far side. The river was wide and angry, fifty yards at least and far more tumultuous and deep than before the rains. Abbie felt fear grip her. Where was her bold defiance? She felt more akin to Pablo at this moment than her own husband.

Was there nothing Cole feared? She saw him reach out to free a drifting branch from the packs on one of the horses. Whitesock veered and almost dunked him, but Cole brought the animal under control and kept on. His hat hung by its cord, floating behind him like an obedient pup.

Abbie could just make out a cloud of dust from Pablo and his men. It would take a dozen horses moving fast to raise a cloud from the damp and cracking earth. Crossing the river seemed their best chance if what Birdie said was true. Looking at the girl, Abbie wondered. But it was Birdie's own neck at stake as well as theirs. Surely . . .

Birdie turned with a smile too close to a sneer. "You are afraid, no? They say to drown is very peaceful. But perhaps the snakes will get you first. There are nests of them. Their poison is swift."

Abbie's chest seized, but the cruelty of Birdie's words emboldened her. She would not be intimidated by a misdirected snip of a girl. Abbie returned her gaze to the river and watched Cole and Sam reach the bank. They shouted the horses up the side, then paused and caught their breath.

Abbie could see them talking together, but no sound reached her. Cole took off his hat and rubbed his forehead. She thought he looked her way, and she stood tall for his sake. She would face this. She would conquer the fear. She would do it for him.

Then he and Sam were swimming back. She could see them moving through the water like bobbing apples. As they neared she saw the strong strokes of their arms and legs. When they climbed up the bank, both men were breathing hard, their chests heaving and dripping, their skin red with cold.

"The current's strong but steady." Sam spoke between breaths.

Cole looked to Will. "Sam'll swim alongside you and Birdie. Shed anything that might hold you down."

Will pulled off his boots, and Cole tied them together and hung them over Will's neck. Birdie nonchalantly stripped down to her bloomers and chemise. She dipped her narrow foot into the water and splashed it up playfully. "It is cold as death."

Abbie shuddered involuntarily.

Birdie entered the water, walked a small way, then dove in headfirst, gliding like a fish. Will rushed in behind with awkward giant steps, and Sam shook his head. "Guess I'm off." He cut back into the water.

Abbie stood on the bank with Cole. Her reluctance was a weight on her shoulders, dragging her down.

He gave her a halfhearted smile. "I'll turn my back if you want."

She glanced up, confused, then caught his meaning. "It's not that. It's . . ."

"I know you're scared, but it won't get better by waitin'." He looked to the riders coming on. There was movement detectable along the valley, and she could make out figures. In minutes they, too, would be visible. Cole had rested, and it was time.

Abbie unfastened her skirt and let it fall. She stepped out of the petticoats and unbuttoned her shirtwaist. Cole was looking out across the river, watching the progress of the others. They were in the thick of the current now. Abbie shuddered.

He turned back and reached for her hand. He kept his eyes on her face, and she felt grateful for that. This was hard enough without feeling self-conscious, as well. He walked her to the edge and stepped in without hesitation.

The water was cold, but not icy as the mountain runoff waters of Colorado. Abbie let him tug her deeper. It climbed to her knees and kept mounting.

"When we get to where you cain't stand, I'll get a hold of you and swim. You just relax and let me do the work."

Abbie nodded. The water reached her waist and she could feel the power of the river, even though they were not yet into the current. Her ribs were engulfed, and she felt each breath against the slap of the water.

"It drops off here." Cole reached for her waist.

Abbie's foot slipped on the decline, and she went down, swinging her arms and grasping for Cole. She heard him holler, but her head went under and she thrashed wildly. She felt him there and clung with all her strength, but he broke her hold, and she panicked.

Cole trapped her arms and hooked an elbow across her

throat, pressing her head back to his shoulder. Her face came out, and she gasped air.

"Don't fight me!"

She dug her fingers into the forearm around her neck and kicked. His muscles were hard, but she fought to break free.

"Stop it, Abbie!" He covered her face with his free hand and pulled her ear to his mouth. "Stop kicking. You'll drown us both."

They went under, and Abbie understood his words. She fought the fear and released her hold. He twisted her to her back and once again hooked her under the chin with the crook of his arm. She went limp, begging God's mercy. They surfaced, and she felt Cole strike out with a powerful kick and his one free arm.

She let him drag her, sputtering when the water splashed into her face. She held his arm with both hands but didn't fight his efforts. She was helpless, totally dependent on him. The fear filled her chest and formed a scream, but the splashing water kept her mouth shut tight.

After some moments she learned Cole's rhythm and tried to relax into it. Then they hit the current. She felt it thrust them to the side. He'd never hold against it, not with her as dead weight. The panic rose again. She twisted, and he tightened his hold. She was strangling, but it was enough to bring her to her senses. *Don't fight; don't fear.*

Abbie forced herself to slacken, and he loosed her slightly. His chest was heaving against her side, the muscles tight and hard. She felt him straining. How could he go on? What if he let go? The water was grasping, demanding, terrifying. It would take her, drag her under, hurl her along until it owned her, body and soul.

Something whizzed by her head and struck the water. Cole jerked, and the river carried them the moment his stroke paused. Again something splashed the water, and she realized what it was. Bullets.

"Take a breath."

"What?" Terror seized her.

"Take a breath!"

Abbie gasped, and Cole pulled her under. He had hooked his arm over her right shoulder and under the opposite arm. He dragged her down, no longer fighting the current but still angling toward the far side. The water was thick and murky. Her lungs burned. She imagined snake nests and slimy things lurking just past her vision.

She pressed her eyes shut, and fought the reflex to breathe. Her lungs were bursting. They couldn't hold it. Cole would drown her. She kicked and kicked again. She felt the thrust through the water and kept kicking. The air was leaving her lungs. She couldn't hold. Bubbles rushed past her ears.

Abbie broke the surface, gasping once before he pulled her down again. This time she kicked immediately and tried to push with her free arm as Cole did. She scraped her knee on something jagged and tangled. She kicked free and kept on.

Her lungs cried for air. Her throat ached as she clenched her teeth against the need to breathe. Her head was dizzy, and she no longer knew which way was up. Her legs were heavy, her arms like lead. She stopped kicking. The air flew in bubbles from her lips as her lungs emptied.

Cole's arm was hard and unrelenting. Then she felt a quick thrust, and suddenly she thrashed and gasped air and water together. She choked and wheezed, crying and coughing and trying to breathe.

"It's a'right. It's a'right now." His voice was low in her ear, soothing.

But it wasn't all right. She was still up to her neck in water. She sucked a hard breath and clung to Cole. Though she felt earth beneath her feet, the water still tugged. She clawed his arm and sobbed, trying to keep her feet and get free of the river.

He spoke again into her ear. "Keep still. The river's dragged us some, but we're still within gunshot."

Abbie coughed and squeezed tears from her eyes, trying to see the horsemen on the far shore. She felt as though half the river were inside her ears and eyes and throat. She couldn't get a clear breath for the wet rasping of her lungs.

"Go ahead and cough it out. If they see us, we'll go under again."

"I can't." She choked and water spewed from her lips.

Cole pressed her head to his neck. "A'right. Try not to move. We've got that bit of sandbar between us an' them. Maybe they won't notice if we're still."

"I want to get out."

"I know you do. But that's what they're lookin' for. And the minute we start climbin' they'll cut us down."

Abbie closed her eyes and let the dizziness pass. The pull of the water made it hard to keep her feet, but Cole held steady. Slowly he backed through the water, careful not to splash the surface. A shelf rose behind them, and he eased her down to sit.

The water lapped her throat, but he hooked her shoulders with his arm and pressed her close to his side. Her teeth chattered with the cold. They'd freeze if they didn't drown. "Cole, I . . ."

"I know you're cold. Just hold on a minute more." His eyes were fastened on the far bank.

She could see the horsemen clustered there. She didn't know which one was Pablo, but one man held her skirt over his head and danced about. She could just make out the laughs and hoots. "Where are Will and Birdie and Sam?"

"Upriver, just across. Sam's got the rifle as well as his six-shooter."

Abbie gasped. "I left mine in my skirt."

Cole nodded grimly. "I thought of that when we were half-way out. Right about when you tried to drown me."

She flushed. "I'm sorry. I didn't mean to fight like that."

"For once I wished you were more like the late Mrs. Farrel. You nearly had me beat. I was this close to knockin' you silly just so's I could get a hold and keep it."

Abbie gave him an impish smile. "You've got a hold now."

He let out a slow breath and shook his head. "You sure pick your times, Mrs. Jasper."

She felt giddy. "What's the matter, Cole? Don't you feel romantic, up to our necks in freezing river water, fighting for our lives?"

"I've a suspicion that's when it hits you most."

She reached a hand through the water to his chest. "Cole . . ."

"Not now, Abbie."

"I just want to thank you."

"For?"

"Not drowning me."

"We ain't outta this yet."

"*Aiyee!*" The cry came from the far bank and gunshots erupted.

Abbie jumped, but the shots were not toward them. The others must have been spotted. She heard the bang of the Winchester and saw the men scramble from their horses and fall belly down to take cover.

"That's our signal." Cole yanked her up the bank toward dry land. "While they're occupied we'll get loose of this river."

She followed, scarcely able to press her legs through the water. They were farther from the side than she'd thought. The shelf went a good way, and they plodded waist-deep, stooping, expecting any moment to find bullets aimed at them. But Sam and Will were keeping the men busy.

So far Birdie's prediction held true. Pablo kept his men to their side. It would be fatal for them to cross now, with Sam armed and ready to pick them off if they tried. Even outnumbered, the river made a formidable defense. She silently thanked Birdie's good sense.

Abbie climbed onto dry land and fell to her knees in the bushes. The wet underthings clung to her, but she had no time to think of impropriety. A gunshot whistled through the reeds, and she ducked automatically. Cole flattened himself beside her. They'd been seen.

Her breath came in short gasps as Cole rolled to his side against her. He pressed his fingers into her hair and held her face. His eyes were deeply green as a mountain meadow. "I gotta get to my gun. I want you to stay here."

"No."

"Two of us movin' through is a better target than one."

Her fear rose. "Stay here with me. Please."

"I can't. Sam can't do this alone. It ain't even his fight."

"If we just stop shooting, maybe they'll go."

Cole dropped his head. "They won't go, Abbie. They'll wait until dark, and they'll cross."

"But Birdie said . . ."

"Birdie don't know everything, and I don't have time to argue."

Shame rushed to her cheeks, but before she could turn away, he kissed her. His mustache was damp, his chin scratchy, but his lips were ardent as they'd not been before. It caught away her breath, but when she opened her eyes, he was already moving away from her.

She didn't call him back. Cole was doing what he must, what his honor demanded, even though it was not truly his fight, either. Taking Birdie along had been her doing and Will's, though it had bought Cole's freedom.

A bullet thumped the bank beneath his crawling figure,

and he flattened, then crept on. She wished she could go, as well. At least she could help reload. Cole's concern had been for them to move together. If she went separately . . .

A bullet whizzed past. She wasn't any safer staying where she was. She crawled through the growth. Her wet underthings were already muddy and spoiled. She snagged the lace of her camisole and tore it free, then crept forward. Either they didn't see or didn't bother with her.

Abbie kept on. One shot sprayed dirt in her face, but though she flinched she didn't slow, so intent was she on reaching her destination. She followed the edge of the river-bank, staying as close to the ground as possible. Her knees were raw, her arms shaking and weak, but she pressed through the bushes, grimly determined.

Rounding a bend, she could see Will huddled behind a bush with blood on his sleeve. Sam was out of sight, and Cole, too, had disappeared. Birdie lay flat with her chin on her arms. Only the crease between her brows betrayed her concern. Will startled, then recognized her and relaxed.

Abbie crept to where he crouched. "Are you hurt badly?"

"Just a graze."

"Where's Cole?"

"He and Sam moved down that way for better cover." He motioned with his head.

Abbie looked where he directed. She could see Cole's back bare to the wind. His shirt lay before her on the bank, just be-yond the lapping water. "Where are the horses?"

"Sam hobbled them some three hundred yards yonder, down that gully."

She eyed the shirt again. "Cover me."

"What are you . . ."

She didn't wait to argue but sprang, crouching low toward the shore. Gunshots stung the sand at her feet as she snatched the shirt and ran. Will scarcely got off two answering shots before she was back. She saw Cole turn at the ruckus, his scowl in place. She crawled to his thicket and handed over the shirt.

He frowned. "Do you ever do what you're told?"

"Just put on the shirt and don't bother thanking me. You'll catch your death without it." From the corner of her eye she caught Sam's grin. "I'm going to the horses to retrieve clothing for Birdie and me. Have you cartridges enough?"

Cole shrugged into the shirt and buttoned the yoke. "I've a mind to hobble you with the horses."

Abbie glared. "You're not the only one with wits, Cole. I can handle myself."

"Tell that to the man usin' your six-shooter."

She punched his shoulder, then drew back when he winced painfully. She'd forgotten the old bullet wound. "I'm sorry."

Cole grunted and rubbed the damaged joint. "It's bad enough I have to drag you kickin' and screamin' through a floodin' Rio Grande. Now you . . ." A bullet splintered the thin trunk of the bush beside them, and Cole caught her down. "A'right, go. Fetch what you need an' keep your head down."

Abbie scrambled clear. She took a zigzagging path away from the river and arrived at the horses, winded and with her feet cut and bruised. She had to search through the packs as the things had been redistributed for the swim. She found her one spare pair of slippers, but her boots were either washed away or on the far shore with Pablo and his men.

She pulled on her forest green serge dress, did up the buttons, and began to tremble. She'd been creeping about in bloomers and camisole before God and everyone without a thought to her near naked condition. What would Monte say? The thought stabbed her. It wasn't Monte who mattered now, it was Cole.

Well, he'd hardly noticed. At least he hadn't shown it. He'd had survival on his mind. But she had better get Birdie covered up before Will learned her anatomy by heart. Abbie dove into her pack and found the brown linen dress. It should be just drab enough to dull Birdie's beauty.

Abbie balled it under her arm and started back. It had been awfully quiet while she stood with the horses. Both sides seemed to have ceased firing. She stooped low and made her way back to Will and Birdie.

Birdie sat now with her knees wrapped in her slender arms. She hung her head back and let the sun dry her long shining hair. She seemed not the least unnerved to be sitting half clothed under Will's bashful gaze.

Abbie tossed the dress to her. "Here. Put that on."

Birdie's lips turned up at the corners. It was like a cat gloating over a dead bird. She stood slowly and stretched. Immediately there were shouts across the water.

Abbie yanked her down. "What are you trying to do?"

"I was only obliging you."

"You can dress yourself just as well sitting down. Now see to it."

Birdie held the dress to her chest and looked about to retort when there came a single gunshot. Abbie watched a rider raise a white flag on a pole and walk his horse into the water. She felt Cole creep up behind her.

She turned. "What is it, do you think?"

"Parley."

"They'll ask for Birdie."

"I reckon so."

"What'll we do?" Abbie glanced to see Birdie slipping the dress over her head. She wasn't fond of the girl by any stretch, but she'd given her word. And beyond that, she had to champion the girl's determination to get free.

Cole's focus was on the rider, now advanced to swimming depth and entering the current. He frowned. "His horse is swimmin' deep. It's got a poor breadbasket to handle the water."

"Breadbasket?" Abbie tried to catch his eye.

"Its chest cavity."

"How can you . . ."

Suddenly the horse went down. One moment it was there, the next, horse and rider had sunk beneath the surface. Cole sprang forward to the water's edge. Abbie's breath caught short. Surely he wouldn't go in after the man. He would be an easy target for the dozen remaining guns.

Abbie clenched her hands at her sides as Cole stood and searched the flow. The white flag surfaced on its pole, spun, and shot away down the river's center. Cole stood in plain view of the opposite bank, but no one fired. They all stared at the water. It rushed on, gray and dull, with no sign of the man whose life had been engulfed in its depths.

At that moment the clouds opened and rain fell in thin sheets. Abbie got to her feet and walked to Cole's side. He stood unmoving. She touched his arm, but his eyes remained on the water, his face inscrutable.

His voice sounded dry. "He should've known that was no water horse. It maybe could've swum the river without him, but never with a rider."

"Come back, Cole. They can see you."

He looked out across the river. The dozen men milled uncomfortably. One stood staring into the river even as Cole had. Abbie had never laid eyes on him, but she knew it was Pablo. He was staring death in the face. Slowly he raised his head. She almost felt his gaze meet Cole's.

They stood frozen. Neither moved for his gun, yet neither released the other. A dark man with a broad-brimmed straw hat stepped close to Pablo. He spoke, but still Pablo did not move.

Abbie felt Cole's tension seeping from his pores. His fingers dangled near the gun, immobile like the rest of him. Did he know she was there? Did it matter? She waited, scarcely breathing. What power held them?

Oh, Lord, you are master. Govern Cole now. Give him wisdom and strength. Make him strong enough to let go.

Slowly Cole raised his hand and took the hat from his head. As slowly, he lowered it to his chest and held it there in respect for the man the river had claimed. Across the water she saw Pablo's stance change. Would he go for his gun?

Lightning slashed. Pablo took one step back. He brushed away the man beside him with a gesture. Then, with a last glance across the water, he turned his back and waved his arm at his men.

No sound of argument reached her as she watched, silent in the rain. The men across the bank gathered up their things and mounted. Still Cole waited, and Abbie waited beside him, uncertain what to make of it.

"Are they leaving?" Her voice sounded small.

"I reckon so."

"Why? They were willing to kill and be killed. Why would one man's drowning change that?"

"Superstition, likely. If Pablo thinks that was the river's warning, he won't press his luck. My guess is Pablo figures he beat death once today. Better not risk it again."

"But . . ."

Cole turned. "Do you have to argue God's will? Sheez, woman. Weren't you prayin' alongside me just now?"

"How did you know?"

"You had that pinched up, pensive look you get when you're beggin' the Almighty."

"You never looked at me once."

"Don't think because my focus is elsewhere I cain't see you."

"I don't believe it."

"Oh yeah? Then how about the little blue ribbon you had

woven through the waist and neckline of your . . . whatever it is you swam in."

Abbie felt her jaw drop.

Cole caught her arm and started up the bank. "And whereas under better circumstances I might appreciate it, I'd just as soon Sam and Will not get another eyeful."

Abbie's sudden humiliation left her speechless. Then her temper came to her rescue, but before she could vent it, Will clambered up with Sam on his heels.

Sam sent his gaze across the water. "You reckon that's it?"

"I reckon we owe a word of thanks to Birdie here." Cole tipped his hat to where she sat in the sand in Abbie's brown dress. "Crossin' the river was a wily move, young lady."

"*Gracias, señor.*" Even the drab fabric couldn't dull the flush of pleasure that filled her face. Abbie felt a jealous pang.

Cole took a look at Will. "How's the arm?"

"It's nothin'."

"Better let Abbie doctor it anyhow. No sense it gettin' septic." Cole rubbed his shoulder. "And she has a way with wounds." He gave her a teasing wink.

Abbie raised her chin, scarcely noticing the rain. He'd deserved the sock she gave him. And after his embarrassing comments, she had half a mind to do it again.

Twenty-Six

Cole felt almost giddy riding along the river. They'd challenged death, and the Lord had been with them. He wasn't used to thinking that way, but he'd put his trust where it counted when the chips were down.

Likely none of them would be riding now if they hadn't crossed, and Cole might not have crossed if he hadn't sought wisdom from above. Years ago he'd have called that nonsense. Now it seemed right wise. Still, it had been touch and go for a while.

He and Pablo could have shot it out. The distance across the river was enough to spoil a man's aim, but not enough to keep the bullets from striking. Cole had felt the challenge. Pablo could have taken him in speed, but he was a hothead. The man would have fired wild.

Cole shook his head. He hadn't been of a mind to kill. Surely not in front of Abbie. But he wasn't one to back down. Why it came to him to lay it down, he wasn't sure. Maybe Abbie's prayers. He'd more felt than seen her as he'd claimed to.

He'd struggled, his pride not wanting to give in, to be the one to let go first. Then he'd thought of the man rolling under the river. The one carrying the peace terms. It seemed only right. Doffing his hat to a plug-ugly who'd likely see Brother Lewis's infamous flames was no contradiction. It wasn't for him to judge.

Cole glanced at Sam riding beside him. What had brought his brother around? It had pained Cole to think they'd be at odds for good. Sam meant too much to him for that. But for the life of him he couldn't see how to make it right, except to show he was willing to die for him.

Maybe Sam knew that. Maybe it helped. Likely Cole would never know for sure. That's how it was with them. They didn't talk about the deep things. Those got sealed off, unspoken. But it kept them close, knowing the shared things were there.

Nor had Sam said where he was heading. Maybe he had no plans. Maybe Sam was drifting, just as he himself had when Abbie cut him loose. Maybe Sam would come back to the ranch with them. Cole could sure use him.

But that was up to Sam. Right now Cole was just grateful his brother had seen fit to stand by him. He couldn't have handled the crossing alone. There was a limit to any man's strength, and without Sam he wouldn't have attempted it.

Cole's shoulder was paining him something fierce. Crossing the Rio Grande three times was enough to tax a sound man, much less one with a recent injury. He just hoped he hadn't done any real damage.

He glanced back at Abbie and Birdie riding just behind, and Will bringing up the rear. Will's arm was bandaged, but as he'd said, the wound was little more than a sting. The kid had held his own. He could keep his head up. Cole caught Will's grin and returned it.

It put him in mind of the first time he'd spit in death's eye. Only in his case it hadn't been from a bullet. It was the stallion known as Devil. None of Cliff's men would face the beast, but Cole at fifteen thought he was invincible.

He'd gotten so far as hooking his lariat on the demon's neck when it came straight for him. Another horse would have charged and veered, or reared up to use its hooves. This one came straight on with murder in its eyes. At the last second

Cole had spun, grabbed the mane, and sprung astride.

He'd only kept his seat for a breath before landing so hard the world went dark. He heard later that two of the guys had pulled him free before Diablo's hooves could finish him off. He had three broken ribs, but he was alive.

Cole reached up and rubbed his shoulder. Yes, indeed, he was alive.

Abbie watched Cole's and Sam's backs as they rode. They couldn't travel far after the exertion at the river, but Cole didn't seem to think they'd be followed. She wasn't so sure, but she was too tired to argue. Besides, Abbie had a worse concern—that they would have to cross back.

She pushed the thought from her mind. There were places the river was fordable. Surely they'd take advantage of that. Surely . . . Sam glanced back briefly but looked past her. He'd come along with them, though he hadn't spoken of his plans.

At least he and Cole seemed at peace. Maybe they'd shared words, though she hadn't seen when. Maybe they needed none. She slid from Zephyr's back the moment Cole called a halt. The rain, too, had stopped and the earth gave off a ground mist in the last of the sun's rays. Will led the horses to drink at the river, and Sam collected brush for a fire.

It would be nice to have a hot meal and a fire's warmth. Abbie gave the supper her best effort, though the supplies they carried were plain enough. She managed a cobbler made with a small bag of dried peaches and what flour and sugar hadn't been wet by the river.

The steamed jerky and boiled potatoes filled their bellies while the cobbler perked up their weary spirits. Birdie seemed the least affected by the day's events and sat humming by the fire. As Abbie washed the last of the dishes, her arms ached from her bout with the river.

Her neck was stiff, too, no doubt from Cole yanking her

along. Well, he'd had no choice, especially the way she'd fought him. What was she thinking? She wasn't thinking at all. It was pure reflex, and one that nearly killed them. But they'd made it.

Abbie shook her head and wiped the skillet dry. She set it on the canvas and pressed her hands to her lower back. How she had strained that, she couldn't say. She felt another hand there and turned, startled.

Cole took her arm and led her from the camp. Abbie felt the fire's heat fade as she crossed the stubbly plain beneath the open sky. Cole walked without speaking and stopped at a driftwood tree trunk lying prone and bleached by wind and sun. A prior flood must have wrenched it from the bank and left it stranded there. The moon shone on its silvery length.

"Set there a minute."

She sat down, looking at him curiously. What was he doing? Cole took the harmonica from his pocket and patted it against his thigh. He looked up to the sky, then cupped the metal with his hands and put it to his mouth. The soft wailing notes formed a slow waltz as the harmony chased the melody up and down his hands.

Abbie wrapped her knees in her arms and listened. A smile tugged her lips and filled her heart when he drew out the last note and pocketed the harmonica. She raised her hands to clap, but he caught them in his and pulled her to her feet.

"Now you hold that tune in your head." He hooked his arm around her waist and caught her hand up, palm to palm with his.

"What are you . . ."

"I'm dancin' with my wife."

In the darkness, Abbie heard the smile in his words as he swept her into the slow waltz that lingered in her mind. Cole always was a good dancer. He had both a natural rhythm and personal style, and he danced as though he enjoyed it. She looked up to find his smile, but his expression was deeper, wilder.

"See, on the dance floor, you gotta watch yerself. You hold a girl too close or too long and folks start to talkin'. But out here, there's none but the stars to notice." Cole drew her against him, and Abbie moved where he led as though they were one.

Her heart sped as he increased his steps, sweeping her in widening circles. The cold night air caught her breath as it quickened and shortened. The edges of his mouth deepened beneath the ends of his mustache.

A warmth and tingling shot through her limbs. She felt her pulse throbbing to his rhythm, and the tune he softly hummed. Years of soothing a herd with his voice gave him a confidence and ability she couldn't resist.

Abbie slid her fingers from his shoulder to his collarbone. "I never knew you were so . . . romantic. You weren't like this before."

"As I recall, you didn't want to be courted. You cain't have it both ways, Abbie, but I was kinda hopin' you wouldn't mind now." He brushed her cheek with his beard-roughened jaw.

Cole was right. She hadn't wanted his courting all those years ago. She'd pretended he was merely keeping company, visiting, and he'd kept it that way . . . until he asked to marry her. He had made it easy to say no. But now she'd said yes. Her pulse throbbed almost painfully.

She loved him—his strength, his goodness, this side of him that was tender and deep, even playful. But she was not prepared to be swept off her feet. Could she risk committing all she had to loving him?

Abbie had seen today how closely he walked to death, how carelessly he challenged fate. Even now his eyes had a reck-lessness, a cocky daring. Was this some victory ritual such as she'd seen Gray Wolf and his braves hold when they'd slaughtered Buck Hollister and lived to tell of it?

She pulled away, shaken. "Thank you for the dance, Cole. But the others must be wondering."

He stood still, his eyes glittering in the dark. Abbie didn't realize she held her breath until he released her by looking away. He made a small laughing sound, bowed jauntily, then hooked her waist in his arm and led her back to the fire.

As they entered its warmth, his hand slipped away, and she had a moment's misgiving, as though she'd been offered a prize and had turned it down. She glanced up, but he wore the noncommittal face she'd seen when they started out. There was only a hint of regret in his eyes, and then it was gone. Abbie wished her own could vanish as easily.

Lord, you ain't making this easy. Maybe I ain't got the right to complain. I ain't served you as long as Brother Lewis. Maybe you only look after the details for them as serve you well, or maybe I'm missing something I should see. But either way, I could use some advice right about now on how to love the woman you've given me.

Cole turned in his blankets to see Abbie lying close by. Her face was soft in sleep, but it had been sharp enough when she dismissed him. Hadn't he shown her yet what she meant to him? She was as skittish as a maiden and twice as wary. He'd never seen her look at Mr. Farrel that way.

Even angry with Farrel, or hurt as she'd been plenty of times, her face had held a yearning, a desire to please. Cole kicked himself for the envy he felt, knowing it was surely not God's intention. If Brother Lewis were near, he'd have a word or two to say on that subject.

Cole shook his head. He'd thought to woo her, to bring her along gently. He'd thought maybe now she'd allow him to do the things he'd always wanted, to court her rightly. Maybe she thought he'd had more on his mind than a dance. Maybe he had.

But what he really wanted was to gentle her. To take away the fear and share the joy of being alive and together and safe. He almost felt charmed. That he walked free was remarkable. That they'd escaped Pablo was amazing. That Abbie had married him was nothing short of a miracle. He shouldn't spoil it with doubts.

But he wished God would show him what to do. Maybe Cole just didn't know how to listen. He'd thought the urging to cross the Rio Grande had been divine, and it seemed to turn out that way. He'd felt the inclination to let go the fight at the opposite bank, and Pablo had gone along. But he sure felt cut adrift when it came to Abbie.

Maybe God didn't cotton to romance. But that was foolish. He'd started it all Himself with them two in the garden. Cole pushed up from the saddle he used as a pillow. He'd counted on a sound sleep this night after the sleepless ones previous. Maybe he was still too worked up with it all.

He climbed out of the covers and started to stand, but instead, he went to his knees. It felt strange, even a little foolish, but he folded his hands as he'd seen Brother Lewis do. The ground was dry and hard, having absorbed all the moisture and secreted it away. Cole bowed his head.

Lord, I reckon Brother Lewis would say surrender this care to you. So here goes. I want to love my wife as I should, and if it ain't too much trouble, I'd like her to love me, too. But as the preacher said, what I want ain't always your plan. So I'll just leave it up to you to make things happen as you will.

Cole opened his eyes and saw Abbie watching. He hadn't prayed aloud, but he felt as though he'd been caught doing something foolish. He kept his thoughts from his face as he unfolded his hands and rocked back on his heels, squatting cowboy fashion. She rose up on one elbow. The question was in her eyes, but she didn't ask.

His own whisper came hoarsely. "Go back to sleep, Abbie.

I'm just gonna have a look around." Cole stood and strode away before she could argue. God sure had a way of humbling a man.

Abbie watched Cole until his silhouette merged with the darkness. He'd been on his knees, hands clasped in prayer. At first she'd thought she was dreaming. She couldn't have imagined a less likely sight. But then she'd realized it was a waking sight. It was real.

Abbie knew Monte had served the Lord, but she'd never seen him pray, not on his knees, not . . . humbly . . . simply . . . seeking God. Yet seeing Cole thus hadn't diminished him. Instead, she felt . . . honored. Had he indeed come to trust God? Could she doubt it any longer?

She recalled the warmth with which he and Brother Lewis had parted. She recalled Brother Lewis's testament to Cole's conversion. Had that been God's purpose in all of this? Had she been only secondary to what God had in store for Cole Jasper?

Abbie felt a trembling inside and recognized it as shame. She'd given Cole so little credit. She'd dared to think he had no trust in the Lord. She'd felt smugly secure in her own faith and inwardly disparaged his lack.

She sat up and brushed the hair from her face. She couldn't see him out in the night, but she slipped from the covers and pulled on her coat. Will and Birdie and Sam slept soundly, no doubt exhausted from the day. Abbie was certain any sound she made would waken Sam, but she crept silently as Blake had taught her.

She made out Cole's frame, hands hooked at the waist, legs apart and slightly bowed. He didn't seem arrogant now, or insolent or even teasing. His back was straight, but his head hung forward. She approached, and he raised his face and spoke low.

"I've lived all my life by my own compass. I think now God wants to give me a new map, but I ain't sure how to read it."

Abbie reached out and clasped his hands but didn't speak.

"I ain't sure why, but . . ." Cole swallowed and looked aside, then fixed her again in his gaze. "I'd like to ask His blessin' on us. Just seems the thing to do."

Her chin trembled as she nodded.

"Lord, you created us, and you got a plan for us. All we want is to serve you as you see fit. Please bless our efforts, as it ain't likely we'll get it right on our own, first off anyhow."

A tear crested her eyelid and slipped down her cheek.

Cole caught it with his thumb. "Doggone, Abbie."

She pressed his hand against her cheek. "I've wronged you, Cole. Can you forgive me?"

"Ain't nothin to . . ."

"Please."

He drew her slowly into his arms. "I forgive you, Abbie. And . . ." He dropped his forehead to her hair. "I love you somethin' awful."

She closed her arms around his waist and rested her cheek on his chest. "I love you, too, Cole. I believe there's a chance we'll be happy."

"One heck of a chance if I have any say in it." He gave her his crooked grin.

She smiled back. It was a start. And maybe the best start they could hope for.

Twenty-Seven

Standing beside her in the yard of the Lucky Star, Cole wrapped his arm around Abbie's slender waist. He felt an awesome rightness in the gesture. She was his to protect, to love and cherish, and right now, his to comfort. Though Sam had told them about the fire Crete Marlowe set, it was still hard to look at the marred face of the house.

He was glad he'd asked Will and Sam to hold back a bit with Birdie while he and Abbie rode ahead to have a look. Cole could only imagine what Abbie was feeling. That house held a lot of memories, both good and painful. It could have been worse. The structure was sound, though the portico and the front rooms were blackened and the windows boarded.

He stroked his thumb down and up her back. "We'll fix it back up, Abbie. I got some money put by."

She pulled her gaze from the house to him. "How?"

"Bustin' broncs paid good. I squirreled away whatever Ma didn't need. And then Mr. Farrel was generous. He paid a good sight more than I could spend." Abbie still looked at him askance.

"Well, I've . . . passed some time with Lady Luck at the poker table. It ain't a fortune, but it'll get us by."

"Mama!"

Abbie spun at the cry, and Cole watched the small, dark-haired boy spring through the door and down the steps. Abbie

279

rushed to meet him. That was all right. Cole could share. Jenny followed more slowly and stood with that big-eyed look both wary and pleading. What surprised him was that she had it turned on him instead of Abbie.

Jenny caught her hands behind her back, which made her skirts stick out in front. It was a defensive pose that tugged his heart. "Did you really marry Aunt Abbie like your wire said?"

"I did. Twice."

She puzzled that a moment. "Why twice?"

"Your Aunt Abbie wanted a church weddin', which Father O'Brien performed when we came through." He didn't need to explain the doctrinal dictates Abbie had cited, nor the fact that her vows had been much more forthcoming the second time.

Jenny looked over her shoulder at Elliot, still wrapped tightly in his mama's arms with her tears falling in his hair.

Cole waited for Jenny to turn back, then squatted down. "Come 'ere."

She came. "Are you . . . mad at what I said?"

"What you said?"

"In my note."

He reached out and cupped her thin elbows in his hands. "No, I ain't."

She bit her lip. "Then you don't mind if I pretend you're my pa?"

"I don't mind."

She came closer until she was right between his knees. "May I call you Pa?"

Cole looked into the dark depths of her eyes, eyes that had no right to be so yearning. "Unless your Aunt Abbie says otherwise, I cain't think what I'd like better."

Jenny pressed in and wrapped his neck in her arms. He held her snug against him. It nearly made him soft, the way she burrowed into his heart. But then, he'd been a hard-riding cowboy a long time. He reckoned a little tenderness might just be in order.

Abbie squeezed Elliot as though making sure he was truly there, real and solid in her arms. The burned house was nothing if her children were safe.

"You were gone too long, Mama. You won't leave again, will you?"

She felt his need and answered it with her own. "No, I won't. If I have to leave I'll tie you to my back and take you right along."

"Me too?" Jenny left Cole's embrace, and he stood up.

Abbie reached and pulled her close. "You too. Absolutely." She looked up at Cole. She hoped he knew she meant him, too, hoped he knew how she loved him. The intensity still surprised her. She hadn't looked for it, hadn't expected it, hadn't believed she could love again.

It wasn't the same star-swept love she'd had for Monte. It was a love born of risking their lives for each other and of Cole's faithfulness. He hadn't given up on her, even when she'd sent him away. Had Monte known when he put her in Cole's charge? Had it been his final blessing to them both?

And now Cole's faithfulness belonged to God, as well. He had told Father O'Brien he'd been baptized by Brother Lewis in the Rio Grande. She could scarcely picture it. But her heart swelled as she stood and took Cole's hands. "I can't think what could be better than a hot bath, a good meal, and a soft bed."

He gave her a crooked smile. "I can. But I cain't say it in front of the young'uns."

Abbie's heart jumped and she felt fire in her cheeks. As long as she lived, she'd never get over loving Cole Jasper.

He bent and kissed her cheek with a low chuckle. "What's the matter, Abbie? You're blushin' like a bride."

Acknowledgments

Special thanks and blessings to my new sisters in the Lord, Patty Deakin and Betty Busekrus, for your support and encouragement, and Betty, for your unfailing eagerness. Thanks to Dorothy Ranaghan for kind words, to Al Heitzmann for your warm notes and helpful comments, and to Mary Jane Heitzmann for your unflagging promotion. And always, thanks to my family for your love and belief, to Barb Lilland, my editor, who makes it better, and to all those at Bethany who make a dream reality.

All thanksgiving to the Lord our God who dwells with and within us and makes all things possible.